T0381101

Witness to Addiction

MY SON'S JOURNEY and HOW EACH PERSON
CAN FIGHT AMERICA'S OPIOID EPIDEMIC

MICHELE GERBER, PH.D.

WESTBOW
PRESS®
A DIVISION OF THOMAS NELSON
& ZONDERVAN

This book is a work of non-fiction. Unless otherwise noted, the author and the publisher make no explicit guarantees as to the accuracy of the information contained in this book and in some cases, names of people and places have been altered to protect their privacy.

WestBow Press books may be ordered through booksellers or by contacting:

WestBow Press
A Division of Thomas Nelson & Zondervan
1663 Liberty Drive
Bloomington, IN 47403
www.westbowpress.com
844-714-3454

Scripture quotations are taken from the Holy Bible, New International Version®, NIV®. Copyright © 1973, 1978, 1984 by Biblica, Inc.™ Used by permission of Zondervan. All rights reserved worldwide.

ISBN: 979-8-3850-0122-4 (sc)
ISBN: 979-8-3850-0123-1 (hc)
ISBN: 979-8-3850-0124-8 (e)

Library of Congress Control Number: 2023911291

Print information available on the last page.

WestBow Press rev. date: 9/25/2023

I have been given
One moment from heaven
As I am walking
Surrounded by night...
I remember all the best days.
Snow falling around me
Like angels in flight...
I'm on my way home

Enya
On My Way Home
Emi Music Publishing, Ltd.

CONTENTS

CONTENTS

ONE

SHOCK

Anything that is to give light must endure burning

There comes a time every year, usually in September, when a shadow passes over the sun and you know it is no longer summer. By October 6, 2014, that time had come and gone. The poplar trees along the banks of the Columbia River in south central Washington State were brilliant yellow and the nearby Virginia creeper leaves were bright red. The pungent autumn smell of burning leaves was not in the air, as almost no leaves had yet fallen from the trees. Instead, the air along the river shore smelled faintly of decay from exposed muck, as the river was very low, and from dead salmon that had come up from the Pacific Ocean to spawn and die. The magnificent river was still and glinted like a mirror. The Columbia River is almost always blue, but the water next to a small island slightly offshore looked brownish that day. The mouth of the muddy Yakima River was just upstream, dumping water that looked like chocolate milk into the shallow Columbia. Were it not for the colored leaves and the scent of decomposition, you could easily have thought summer had returned, for the thermometer reached a record high of ninety-three degrees – nearly twenty degrees above normal. The temperature, like many things that day, was deceptive.

Early in the afternoon, my son Jon hurriedly paddled his canoe to a small island, strode on his long, lanky legs across its width, and sat down in a patch of quack grass. Cattails and teazle grew behind him at the water's edge. Milkweed, wild rose and willow bushes, and two red maples surrounded him. They looked burnished and not quite

1

vibrant – a bit ragged if you looked closely – near to the end of their brief season on earth. Jon unwrapped a 357 Winchester lever-action rifle he carried with him inside a sleeping bag and loaded in one cartridge. It was a jacketed hollow-point, the type that expands as it enters its target. He reached forward and around with his long arms, placed the rifle's barrel just in front of his heart, and pulled the trigger. A large elm tree right in front of him was the last thing he saw on this earth.

The shot obliterated his heart so completely he hardly bled, the coroner told me later that evening. I knew, although no one told me, that Jon shed tears and was terrified before he pulled the trigger. Some things a mother just knows. In his journals I read later, he had written graphically of how it would be to pull the trigger of a gun on oneself: "Terrified. Probably shaking uncontrollably. Knowing this is the end. Last seconds on earth. Ready to meet your maker and face his judgment – Right – Now." Although I had not yet found these words, Jon had told me a few years earlier that he had wept the first time he shot heroin into his body. He described inserting the needle, pulling it back a little to make sure it was in a vein, and watching "a little red mushroom cloud" of blood flow back into it. He had told me so many things that were deep and personal and humbling about himself and his addiction, that I thought I knew him very well. But I never saw the shot coming, never dreamed he was even thinking about it; never, I realized, knew my son as well as I thought I did. As author Norman Maclean famously said, "It is those we live with and love, and should know, who elude us."[1]

The day had begun normally for me, and that ordinariness is one of the most shocking things about it. It did not seem to be a day for bells that could not be unrung, choices that could not be undone, or doors that would close forever. I went to my volunteer shift at the local hospital, guiding family members through the maze of pre-operative visitation rooms, doctor consultation rooms, lunchrooms, and discharge instruction rooms they had to navigate while their loved ones underwent surgery. I had chosen this volunteer assignment because I wanted something completely different after my recent retirement from my research and writing career. I also felt drawn to people in distress, because my years as the parent of an addicted person had brought me to and through many horrific times. I had developed some compassion I wanted to share. That morning, I held the hand of a woman a bit younger than I who was literally ravaged by cancer. I had seen her come through our operating suite several times already, and she looked worse every time. I grasped her hand with one of mine as I wrote her husband's contact information in my roster. I wanted to tell her I could see her suffering, and I was heartbroken. I hoped my touch would convey my feelings to her. I greeted a nine-year-old girl with cervical cancer, reading with horror in her chart that special instruments – exceptionally small – were on hand for her examination and surgery. Actually, I felt fairly good about my own life that morning, despite the unresolved problems with Jon. Some positive things were happening with other members of our family, and I was beginning to learn some of the peace that came with "releasing him" to choices and behaviors I could not control.

After my shift, I ate lunch in my car while I did a few errands, as I hadn't yet been able to shake the habit of hurrying that came from many years as a working mother. Then I went to my exercise club to swim laps. Swimming always relaxed me, and it was there I customarily prayed and gave my daily thanks as the rhythmic laps unfolded. This day, the laps seemed uncharacteristically tedious, which was odd, but I had no sense of foreboding. When I left the club, I saw I had missed calls on my phone from Jon's girlfriend Lara and from my daughter Dori. I grimaced a little at the one from Lara, because I assumed Jon was using her phone because he had once again run out of money. Jon had come to me so many times in utter destitution that I was worn down, exhausted with things I could not fix, and not anxious to return a call that would plunge me back into the vortex. I drove home.

Our phones—the house landline and my cell phone—rang three times in quick succession as soon as I arrived. The numbers showed it was Lara's mother Alyssa. I let the phones go to voicemail, but called back after the third message. Alyssa told me Jon had asked Lara to go back into an exclusive relationship with him, after she had begun to date others when he wasn't able to stop his drug use. She had refused his request, Alyssa said, and he had gone off threatening to kill himself. "If it was my son, I'd want to know," she said. I was still raw from my last encounter with Jon. After his years of drug use, relapses, rescues, fresh starts, and broken promises, I just didn't want any more drama. "Compassion fatigue," a term used by nurses and those who work with the chronically ill, didn't begin to describe the depth of my depletion. Why couldn't he just grow up, stop wearing his hat backwards, and running out of gas like teenager, I thought. Still...I walked down to my bedroom and then into the yard to pet the dogs and circled back into the kitchen. I told my husband Evan I was going to drive to the river's park where Lara had last seen Jon and where she and Alyssa now waited.

By this time, it was late afternoon and I drove straight into rush hour traffic. It took at least forty slow minutes to get to the park, and along the way, I contacted others from the recovery/sober living community who had been reaching out to Jon earlier in the summer. Through the grapevine, and without my permission, some of these people contacted my daughter Dori – Jon's sister – and she was soon on her way. When I arrived, police cars and a police boat were there, along with a small crowd of onlookers who was starting to gather. I went to the police, told them who I was, and asked for a status. They had been called by Lara's mother, and their boat had gotten stuck in the mud of the shallow water. They had sent for a smaller boat that could get to the island, and they were waiting for it to arrive. Their radios crackled every few minutes as they milled about. The small boat arrived, ventured the short distance to the island, and then returned. Evening was coming and they needed searchlights. I did not know they had already called a Code Sixty, found Jon deceased, and needed the searchlights to take official photographs of his body.

I talked to Alyssa as Lara sobbed and buried her face in her mother's side. I learned that after a long and mournful conversation with Lara, Jon had told her he had nothing to live for and thrown his computer and phone over the side of his canoe into the river as he paddled away. When she screamed that he had a son, Eddie, who needed him very much, Jon only said, "I never get to see him anyway, and I already called him and told him I love him." His last words as he paddled away, had been: "Tell my Mom I love her."

I felt a cold shudder and could not believe what I was seeing and hearing. I went to the policeman who seemed to be in charge and said, "Let me go out with your guys on the next boat so I can talk to my son – I can talk to him about anything." He called me "ma'am" and told me, "We can't do that, we have our procedures." Dori arrived and kept vigil with us as dusk came on. The rest of Lara's family appeared as the autumn light gave out. About 6:30, the head policeman called for Jon's family to gather around him at the end of the dock. We did. "We found him," he told us, "and he is deceased."

Dori wailed and spun around, as did Lara. Both were caught by family and friends, while I just stared at the policeman in disbelief. "What? How?" I asked fairly calmly. I did not know then that quiet focus indicates total shock, as much as does shrieking and crying. I was in complete shock, a protective shield against the searing pain to come. I would remain in this state throughout the evening and the next several days. "Single gunshot wound," he said. "Where?" I asked. "The heart," he said. "How long ago?" I asked. "About three to four hours ago now, near as we can tell," he said. By then, a fire truck had arrived, and with it, the fire district's chaplain. I calmly told her my son's full name and address. She asked which funeral home we wanted to contact, and I told her the one our family always uses. She said since the death appeared to be a clear case of suicide, the body and possessions should be released that very night. Could we wait a bit longer for that decision?

By then, others had called my husband Evan and he was on his way. A hearse was also on the way. The police paced about. "You never know about these suicides, do you?" one said to the other. Darkness was gathering, and soon, I was told, the police boat would be bringing my son's body back to shore. My mind was spinning. Did I want to see it? Did I want to take his immediate possessions – the canoe, the rifle, his car? It was not real – could not be real, this scene I was living through. It simply could *not* be my life, my nightmare – it had to be someone else's. The boat carrying Jon was making its way toward shore. I wanted Dori *gone* when it reached shore, but Evan arrived just then, and Dori stepped toward him for a hug. "Just get her away from here quickly," I whispered to him urgently. He hugged her briefly and then sent her on her way with a friend who did everything right that night. The coroner and a policewoman approached us. It was fully dark so I could not see the leaves and grass stains on them. We told them to dispose of the rifle, as we never wanted to see it. We also did not want to see Jon, because what was left of him was not him. They could tell the hearse to go. We would be in touch with the funeral home in the morning. We also would be back to the river shore in the morning to take his canoe and car. Could they please lock his car for the night and make sure it was not ticketed or towed? I stayed until the hearse pulled away. I glanced back at the dark river, and, against the advice of everyone there, I drove myself home. By then, the Demon also had departed the scene. His work there was done. He thought he had won.

That night, of course I did not sleep. However, I did not cry either. In fact, I did not cry for many days due to prolonged shock – a phase I now know as the first stage of grief. That night, when it seemed morning would never come, my mind raced all throughout. We had not been a dysfunctional family. We worked hard, had a comfortable middle-class life, played with our children, taught them, and loved them to the ends of the earth. I had never known an addicted person in my life until Jon became one. I had no preparation, no plan, no manual, as I never had during all the years I tried to navigate the troubled and twisted thicket of his addiction. Reasoning tells us that when a person violates God's laws of health, we can expect sickness and suffering. Our bodies require healthful living habits to function properly. Jon had been sick with addiction for a long time, and I had worried for a long time, but still I never had an inkling – not the faintest thought – that he would take his own life. Part of my shock was because he had kept so much hidden from me.

One thing that puzzled me the most was that my unwavering mother's sixth sense had failed both me and Jon. Since I became a mother, an inexplicable instinct has alerted me at times when any of my children has been in peril. At times when they experienced concussions, broken bones, car accidents and other traumas, I always knew something was wrong. I would become intensely uncomfortable and fidgety, especially if I couldn't get to them or a phone. This phenomenon had not happened that day with Jon. Later, as good friends discussed it with me, they had two theories that seemed to make sense. One theory is that the real Jon – my Jon – was not at the river on October 6. The poor man on the island that day was just a tattered remnant of the person he had been, already hollowed out, already gone, no spark or spirit left to send me a message. The other theory is that what happened on that small island on October 6 was not a bad thing – it was deliverance. It had set him free and given him the peace and wholeness he longed for so desperately but had lost in this life. Jon knew no other way to kill his addiction than the way he chose on that island. His pride and determination demanded that he slay it and triumph over it, and, in a way, he did. I was challenged by these incredible friends: If, as his mother, I truly loved him, I had to be happy that he was no longer cold or hungry or broke or sick or afraid, as he was so often during his time on earth. Their challenge bent my head. Yes, I loved him that much and more, but I could not be happy.

Jon left us a perplexing legacy. He was brilliantly intelligent, wickedly funny, creative, witty, sensitive, generous, extremely loving and tender, loyal, helpful, physically strong and capable, mechanically skilled, interested in the world and the universe, insightful, and welcoming. He was also deceptive, undependable, erratic, maddening, sometimes a thief and a bully, and an accomplished liar. He did not always fulfill basic obligations. His addiction made him an enigma. Those of us who loved him stood on shifting sand, never knowing which Jon we were going to encounter or whether we would see him at all.

Jon's early teenage curiosity about drugs became a fascination that grew to an unhealthy habit that metastasized into an obsession and eventually brought on a ravenous and fatal illness. Drugs, which he thought would expand his consciousness and his world, instead constricted his life and trapped him. He took drugs, and then they took him. By the time drugs were not pleasurable or desirable to Jon anymore, his brain was so used to them, so dependent, so mis-wired, that he had to keep taking them. Jon was extremely sick when he died. Over the next years, I would read a great deal about new knowledge being discovered in brain science. Jon's body and brain had been damaged by addiction in ways that today are physically measurable and traceable in addicted people. Neurons, conditioned by drugs, leapt across synapses in his brain in new patterns that became so entrenched and habituated that deep cravings for more drugs would never leave him. He became a tormented and tortured man. Essentially, he lost his freedom of choice, and no longer owned himself.

Jon never bargained for drugs to win nor believed they could claim him so thoroughly. Living as a carefree, fun-loving bachelor in a raucous, gorgeous ski town after high school, he often told us he would settle down at some point, get married, and get a "real" job. He estimated these things would happen by the time he was thirty-five – a horizon that then seemed to him very far away. Meanwhile, however, he said he wanted to have as many adventures as possible, including some experimentation with drugs and alcohol. Nearly three years before his death, when his drug use had morphed into addiction and Jon had completed a successful stint in inpatient adult treatment, I talked to him about my fears after a close young friend died of an overdose. "I am quite a resilient strong person," I wrote to him. "I'm willing to work hard at any task in life from motherhood to school to yardwork to jobs. But there is one thing I am not able to do – stand at the grave of one of my children. No – I cannot do it. I CANNOT bury you so don't even skirt around the edges of things that can kill you. It would DESTROY me. Believe that – and fight hard!!! But also let me know if you're losing the fight and just go back into treatment – that would not be end of the world."

He responded that he would be fine – he was in control. "Mom I can't take the image of you reflecting on [our friend's] death and thinking of me. PLEASE don't do that. It may all seem reckless...to you but there are strictly adhered to precautions. And backups for the redundancies. It may be hard to believe but I was always very careful. I value my life Mom. Besides, I am, as you read this, getting that behind me. And leaving it there. I hate the thought of you worrying. It kills me. I always tried to spare you that...I love you...I'm still comin' along.

Giving another shot at this. I promise you I will be ok. No matter what it ends up taking. I won't refuse help. I don't want to be an addict. I have it. I'll be ok."

However, he wasn't OK and "it" wasn't OK. "It" (his addiction) clawed at him as a savage beast. It stung him viciously. There are no precautions and redundancies in drug use. Jon was carried away on a flood tide of evil he always thought he could control, but which he found to be wild, unrestrainable, and overwhelming. He talked about the malevolence of drugs many times, but did not realize the strength of the riptide that would take him under. Foolish choices made in immaturity combined with the chance factors of susceptible genes and body type to produce in him a fatal compulsion to pursue poison. His death was profane, as was the addiction that caused it.

For many years prior to Jon's death, our family, Lara, and other close friends tried to warn him. We pleaded, threatened, helped, withdrew help, lectured, brought in professionals, reasoned, prayed, and sometimes just begged him to stop. We did everything under the sun, and in doing so, lived a journey with him that was at once remarkable, terrifying, wondrous, confounding, and essentially beyond belief. None of us understood addiction nor walked in his shoes when he went into dark parking lots or sought out people with slumped shoulders and evasive eyes. "Why?" we would ask. "Why not come back to us – to life and health and dependable schedules and a daylight life?" He had once lived inside my body and my heart had beat for his. However, the fact that I had *had* him, did not mean I could have him. I was never in control, even when I thought I was. Even as I stood in his path waving my arms and jumping up and down frantically, I could not stop him as he ran past the red flags. Jon had an outsized illness, and, in grotesque bites, it ate him alive. Every one of us who loved him would have given all we had if it could have been different. The hardest truth for a parent, I learned, is that love is not enough. Love can't fix a fatal disease, reverse the laws of biology and nature, or stop a raging infection in its tracks. If it could, Jon would still be here, for we loved him that much.

The shot Jon fired on October 6 carved gaping, gothic holes in me that will never heal. Just as drugs owned Jon before the shot, and his life was not his to rule and direct, so grief has owned me since the shot. Grief does not care or teach or heal – it only hurts. And it does not go away. The passage of years means nothing to a bereaved mother. My grief sneaks up on me and takes over on its own timetable and at its own will – nauseating me, buckling my knees, undermining my will, and choking off any transient pleasures. Grief demands fierce allegiance. It is absolute. "I possess you," it says, "and I will tell you whether you are permitted any sunshine or even simple contentment today."

For me, a great light has gone out, and I will never be the same. I will see Jon in every trip on the Columbia River he loved, every hike, every loud motor, every tall and skinny young man seen from behind, every crab and fish and crawdad that resembles those he caught so easily, every deep voice that calls out, "Hey Mom" on a ski slope, every handsome waiter, every smooth bartender, every father hoisting a young boy over his shoulders, every goofy movie, and every new photo or visit with Eddie. Will the privilege of knowing such a complicated man be able to sustain me in this bottomless grief? I don't know. My loneliness for him is at the heart of this grief. To say I will miss him until the end of my days is an understatement so profound it is almost not worth saying.

Would I do it all again? Would I have my thirty-six years as Jon's mother, confidant, and friend, even knowing the terrible denouement I would face? Absolutely, in a heartbeat – yes, without hesitation. I wouldn't have missed it for the world, although of course I would want a different outcome. What Jon did not give me in longevity is nothing compared to what he did give me. If I could have taken his pain upon myself, I would have done that, too. In becoming a mother, I chose to become a "hostage to fortune," to use a common phrase that describes the plight of all parents, who love so much their destiny is no longer their own but is tied to the fate of their children. When children hurt, the parents hurt. The modern disavowal of co-dependency means nothing to parents. We know parenthood means pain, whether the normal pain of separation in adulthood or something far worse. We love with no guarantees. All children are on loan, and loans have to be repaid.

Now, after nine years of grieving the loss of Jon, my pain is not less but different. It comes in waves and spikes, ambushing me at times when I dare to think I have achieved some semblance of balance, pushing me to anguish so profound I almost cannot breathe. Like most survivors of trauma, I have to be a whole new self, because being my former self does not work. My heart is unquiet, but in my head I know I have much for which to praise God, and giving thanks is the surest way to move forward. Above all, I am thankful Jon lived long enough to find the saving power of Jesus Christ and declare his faith in 2013. For this reason, I know he is safe today, and free of the failure, shame, and black depression of his crippling disease. His spirit, dwelling in Heaven, soars over us and I will see him again. For all the things Jon tried to do right in this world, the love he surely had for his family, his mighty attempts to beat his disease, his faith in the light of God, his goofy grin, his corny jokes, and his single-minded devotion to his son Eddie, I also give thanks. For my family — Dori, her brothers and sister, Eddie and Evan — I bow down before the Lord of the universe in profound gratitude. They all suffered with me through Jon's ordeal, and they sustain me now.

The total despair and defeat my son must have felt at the end of his life haunts me. How could this social, gregarious man, who had thrived in so many places, wither from lack of social contact and love right here in our midst? How had he parted company with reality and become so undone? When I lost Jon, I still had much to learn about brain science, stigma, addiction, mental disorders, and the terrible denial and silence that surrounds them. Addiction killed my son, but so did ignorance, prejudice, and shame. I knew something of the disgrace he felt for not being able to conquer his disease, because he had flatly told me about it. But why did we all have to reinforce that shame? Why did we make him feel weak, unworthy, and stripped of dignity because he could not defeat the cravings of his disease? Why did we finally tell him to "grow up" and "go figure it out"? We could not enable, for that path surely leads to death, but there are things we could have done differently to let him know he was a good man whom we honored and valued, sick as he was. Therein lies torment — my endless fight with my own demons as his mother.

In the last few months of his life, Jon wrote a passage that later gave me some small measure of understanding about his state of mind as darkness enveloped him. "Evil," he wrote in a private journal, "has a nasty habit of attaching itself and demanding more pain, more harm, while its influence over us steadily spreads like vines through our bodies. It is capable of gaining absolute power over individuals. It finds absolute joy in people's absolute misery. It's a bottomless void, a black hole that only grows hungrier the more we give in to it. It will own you. It will feed on you. As you grow weaker it will destroy everything you love and make you watch. You'll feel shame, guilt and fear pretty much constantly. It will make you watch as it slowly rots away who you were supposed to be, and the ones you love the most will grow to resent you and be ashamed of you. This is not a game. Evil is not your friend, it will show you the same cruelty it shows any of its victims. There is a LOT more misery where you're headed. How do you not know this... by now?"

That first night that Jon died, I had not seen this passage. I understood almost nothing, except that my beloved son was gone from me. He had left us all for a place we could not follow. I was reminded of a strand of a poem: "I heard...[God's] call; I turned my back and left it all."[2] Sleepless, churning, wounded beyond all comprehension, I was consumed with knowing, tracing back, finding out where and when our lives had come unraveled. When did we pass through the looking glass, where black was white and white was black, and nothing made any sense? When had Jon slipped into the dark space of addiction, as distinct from just drug use? And when had he reached the dead end of the imperatives of biology, where cell and brain damage and addiction were so deep and long that reboot was not possible? When did the wheels really leave the ground – his tether to sanity and self-preservation? How did he come to believe that the answer lay on an island with a rifle in front of an elm tree?

My heart was just as blown away and destroyed as his, yet mine still beat and I had to function. I had to continue to live without Jon and with the knowledge of what he had done. I wasn't given a choice, or a chance, or a warning. Nothing was given, but everything was taken. Before I rose that first morning after he left us, I resolved I had to *know him*, to the extent that I could. My remembrance would be fierce. I had to re-trace the places he had moved to and from in his desperate attempts to outrun his disease. I had to read his journals; study his photos, tickets, and receipts; talk to his friends, his last landlord, some of his employers; and sit with his belongings. Even then, on that first awful night, I knew I would try to write his story – to be his "story holder," to honor him, although never to honor some of his choices. Having started Jon's life's journey with him, I would finish it. I would *bear witness* to the horror and the joys we had lived. Long ago, I had been given a place on the fifty-yard line of his addiction, and now I would ponder and preserve what I had seen, learned, felt, and experienced. I had to write our story for it to make sense. It would be my work of redemption. It would be my way through the awful silences I dreaded – the emptiness of not hearing Jon and having him. If the researching and writing were just for me, just an obvious attempt to hold him close for longer than I was allowed, so be it. If they also could help to lessen the stigma of addiction and suicide, bring about the recognition of addiction as a medical brain disease, praise Jesus Christ – the great God of the universe, and have lessons for others, then so much the better.

TWO

THE WAY WE WERE

It is Christmas 1979, and my son Jon is twenty-two months old. A cheerful, active boy, he is changing rapidly from a sweet and placid baby to a determined, impulsive, and strong explorer. He is so smart and eager to learn and remembers so much from each of his experiences, that I hate to curtail his freedom to explore. However, he requires constant vigilance since he yet has no sense of danger. He begins his day by standing at the foot of his crib and insistently calling out for me. When he finishes his meals, he abruptly and decisively yells, "Done," and attempts to dive over the side of his highchair. He has a vocabulary of about fifty words, a fact remarkable for his age. He is, I tell my parents, "such a gem that I wish I were more free to enjoy him."

However, I'm not more free because we have just moved to Denver, Colorado, our second cross-country move in four years. My then-husband Elliott is busy in his new job and our other son Jeff is an active handful who has just turned three and a half years old. Our big house, with a long and lovely patio facing west toward the front range of the Rocky Mountains, is ample and charming. However, it is a maintenance disaster. Vacant for a few months before we arrived, it has no window coverings, a flat and leaky roof, ugly wall coverings, a furnace that never seems to keep us above chilly, and no sprinkler system in the yard. Its tall windows were coated with tough grime inside and out when we moved in, and I have scrubbed them and started sewing curtains to cover them from the darkness that falls so early. I work on these tasks mostly between eight and eleven p.m., when the boys have gone to bed. Other challenges include finding a pediatrician and dentist, making friends with other young families, and getting ready for Christmas in a strange place.

Still, we are glad to be in Denver. Indeed, some of the sweetest times of my life will be during our five years in this house. My little boys and I laugh a lot and devise mini-adventures by going to local parks, fast food restaurants, and walking around watching huge bulldozers and front-loaders build out the neighborhood. The boys are intrigued endlessly by these machines, as well as by sidewalk bugs, fireflies at night, and water painting designs that evaporate on the driveway. I'm charmed by my sons, fascinated at their expressive delight. I feel I am doing what I am meant to do, and they are teaching me the things I need to know about being their mother. I am blessed and I know it. I begin calling us the Three Musketeers.

In Denver, life speeds up. Our family starts traveling to regional sights and attractions every weekend. We pack up granola bars, diapers, juice boxes and clean clothes, and catch festivals in picturesque nearby towns such as Georgetown and Morrison, as well as the Buffalo Bill Grave and Museum, Lakeside Amusement Park, and the Denver Zoo. The air is clear and dry, the mountain vistas stupendous. We find a family-style restaurant in the foothills overlooking Denver and make it our special place every Saturday or Sunday night as we drive back from an adventure. We are all tired and happy when we get there, and enjoy the fact that foods are served in large bowls and platters and passed around the table as we would at home. We usually arrive home with both boys asleep in the back seat. I am content as we ride through the quiet darkness, even as I know the chores of the household await. I know I will be working on them until midnight.

Christmas morning Jeff and Jon, clad in snuggly, one-piece, fleece sleepers with padded feet, race downstairs and towards the Christmas tree. They find some large plastic trucks, a stuffed bear, books by the venerable Dr. Suess, and other gifts. They play much of the day, interrupted only by Jon's afternoon nap. We call our families. We miss them but we feel very blessed. As parents, Elliott and I thoroughly believe our destinies are ours to shape. We have beautiful children, we take good care of them, and all should be well. I cannot know the burdens that await.

On a cold day during Christmas week, I write down my feelings in

Jon's baby book. "Jon is incredible," I begin. "He fills me with so much joy...He will never lack self-confidence, because I will be telling him and showing him so much that he is <u>loved</u> and special and wonderful... is he too good to be true?...Jon is so expressive – he smiles and reacts to each situation with his <u>whole</u> body...He's reckless and determined and endlessly mischievous...He is so precious, so golden, so beautiful, so perfect. My boy – my blessing – my heart." I mean simply that he has ensnared a huge chunk of my being. I have no idea of the thuds, stretches, contractions, plummets and near stoppages my heart will undergo later with him.

In Denver, I experience a phenomenon I have never seen before. Often after a snowstorm, the sun will come out the next day and warm everything to nearly sixty degrees. I have never lived anywhere where winter gave me breaks. In all the places I have lived, winter set in, grim and determined, in November and never let up until April. In Denver, even in mid-winter, there are days the boys can play in the yard in our oversize sandbox filled with white crystalline sand, wearing only light jackets. I notice that I can see the weather coming a full day ahead, and it is always changing. It can be cold and cloudy at our house, but if I see a bright sky above the Front Range to the west, I know we will have sun tomorrow. The opposite also is true. Snow can come in with a fury and pile up, causing us to play indoors. Within the next few days an intense sun sends the snow rushing down the gutters next to the sidewalk. When the melting starts, the boys and I go out in boots and rain gear and chase the water toward the storm drains, splashing, watching the sidewalks clear and then dry. We rush inside to get pails and brushes or colored chalk and make extravagant designs on the sidewalk. Then we throw handfuls of snow onto our artwork and watch our patterns change to strange, elongated shapes before disappearing.

By spring, my boys and I are integrated into a network of stay-at-home, suburban mothers. In a neighborhood babysitting cooperative, we trade hours as we watch each other's children in our homes and yards. Our family joins a nearby church whose minister is kind, scholarly, and loving. We resume our weekend forays to explore Colorado, visiting Breckinridge, Estes Park, the two-mile high city of Leadville, and the

10,000-foot grassland of South Park where vistas seem to stretch beyond the possible. We also travel south to the western theme park of Buckskin Joe's,[1] which has staged gunfights and other entertainment, nineteenth-century frontier-themed buildings, and a donkey roaming around as mayor of the town. The boys love it. During my years in graduate school before having Jeff and Jon, I could never imagine myself as a stay-at-home mother. Yet, I am engaged and content in my current life in ways I never dreamed.

I live in organized chaos. There are no video cassette recorders (VCRs) yet, so I schedule around the daily mid-morning Sesame Street[3] television show. The boys love this show, as well as the few Peanuts[4] specials and other child-appropriate shows they are allowed to watch. As Easter approaches, Jon claims to be the Easter Bunny and generously hands out make-believe goodies, hoping by power of suggestion to make the real things appear. I write to my parents about a typical day: "Two hours ago, there was a deafening din in here as the dishwasher, clothes washer and dryer all were humming and four children ran around playing. I was babysitting through my mothers' co-op for two little girls aged two and four. They were sweet and the boys actually shared their toys well, but still there was chaos. Everyone took turns playing in the water, coloring, painting, etc., and in between there were games of tag, racing trucks on the brick hallway, and having snacks. Right now, Jon is napping, Jeff playing in the backyard, the girls have gone home, and I have tonight's biscuits in the oven and eggs boiling so Jeff and Jon and I can color Easter eggs after dinner...Sometimes I am frazzled but other times I thrive on all the activity."

I then become philosophical, continuing: "Sometimes I am frustrated because the house is never all clean at once, with the laundry and mending done, boys all clean, and me free to read or do my nails. However, other times I look around at the busy mess and think life will never be so good again, and then I stop whatever I am doing and get down on the floor with the boys and play with them and tell them how beautiful they are to me. Sometimes I think I am just fighting the

---

[1] Buckskin Joe's closed in 2010. It was bought by Bill Koch of Florida.

17

messes and the work; but then I realize I am really fighting against time itself, which is laying the nastiest plans of all. How can it be that the things you love the most are programmed to leave you?"

During our years in Denver, the boys and I sometimes visit my parents in Arizona. Jon and Jeff swim in pools, feed ducks at a pond, visit a neighbor's rabbit, color with Grandpa, and we go dancing at a silly country/western place called The Barn.[2] We really just bounce up and down and swing in circles. The boys paint Grandpa's driveway with water, and torment him with endless games of Chutes and Ladders.[5] On one visit, a picture of the boys on an outing with Grandpa appears in the local newspaper. Other times, my parents visit us, with Grandpa getting a workout coloring, doing puzzles, and building with Legos[6] and Lincoln Logs.[7] At home, Elliott and I paint rooms and hang wallpaper. These projects are do-it-yourself, as our budget demands. We are busy with a contentment that fills me. The young Denver Broncos quarterback John Elway is the hero of both Jeff and Jon, so we get them bright orange Broncos shirts bearing Elway's number seven.

The year 1981 arrives clear, cold, and beautiful. Jon makes his first drawings. His strokes are bold, using vibrant colors. No shapes are discernible. He turns three in February. Although he never asserted himself in the "terrible two" stage, he now affirms himself by refusing to pick up toys and getting into things belonging to Elliott and me that he has never touched before. I can't gauge the meaning of this behavior. Years later, I will read that Bill W., the founder of Alcoholics Anonymous (AA), states: "Defiance is an outstanding characteristic of [many] alcoholics."[8]

That summer, Jeff and Jon declare it their mission to kill every ant in Colorado. "Bug-hunting" is one of their biggest thrills. They also hunt for "fire-breathing dragon flies." Again, we swim daily in the neighborhood pool, make sandcastles in the backyard, and paint the driveway and patio with water. In August, Elliot and I celebrate our tenth wedding anniversary. That fall, Jon enters pre-school two mornings a week. His drawings are still just scribbles with strong,

---

[2] The Barn restaurant that we visited is no longer in business.

bold colors. However, when asked to place facial features on animals or shapes, he draws smiles, a healthy sign. The pre-school teachers comment that his self-concept is very good, he is cooperative, willing to share, inquisitive, extremely social, and he especially enjoys craft time.

The following year, Jon's second in pre-school, he begins to form actual figures in his drawings. All the creatures he draws are smiling, and his picture of his family shows the four of us standing close together, grinning, near a house. His teachers comment that he is capable and well adjusted. However, he "sometimes likes to get his classmates' attention by making little noises and funny faces." We are expecting a new baby on Christmas Day, but we still attend neighborhood and school parties, wrap gifts, and write letters to Santa. The boys help me bake cookies, standing on chairs at the counters, the little aprons I have made for them covered in flour. Christmas comes and goes with no baby, as does New Year's 1983, and the first week of January. Our entire church is praying for me to go into labor. Finally, on a frigid night in the second week of January, Dorianne Pamela is born. My blessings are outsized, and my whole life seems charmed. 1983 will be the sweetest year of my life.

Jeff and Jon are fascinated that Dorrie is real – she actually moves and cries and is a living creature. After a couple months, as she starts to smile and notice faces, both boys delight in trying to entertain her. They both hover at her infant seat or stroller making funny faces, redoubling their efforts when she begins to laugh. They give her silly nicknames such as Doodle Bug, Lady Bug, Love Bug and, as she begins to reach for them, they call her The Grabber.

We manage a home party with neighborhood friends for Jon's fifth birthday and a patio party for Jeff's seventh birthday in April. We follow the boys' accustomed activities, as well as Jeff's new soccer team events throughout the spring. By this time, Dorrie is a most portable baby, not fussy, and comfortable almost anywhere. She sleeps whenever and wherever she needs to, in her car seat, stroller, infant seat, crib or body carrier. I begin calling us the Four Musketeers. Although I am intensely busy, I experience a level of deep contentment and happiness with my three children I have never known. I stop sometimes and just wonder at my gifts, my knees almost buckling with gratitude. I love Colorado so much I tell Elliott I want to buy cemetery plots there and never leave.

In late spring, Jon graduates from pre-school, wearing a flowing white gown with an oversized black bowtie and cap. His preschool teachers conclude their report to us by saying, "He greets activities with enthusiasm and takes pride in his accomplishments. Jon loves to converse, and he is caught talking at times when he should be listening. He is eager to learn." In the fall of 1983, he begins kindergarten. He receives satisfactory marks, but his teachers report he needs improvement in listening and following directions, having good work habits, self-control, and being cooperative and organized. He writes that he likes himself because he is nice to others. At Christmas, Jeff and Jon wear their first clip-on neckties with button-down dress shirts to church. My throat catches when I snatch a fleeting glimpse of the tall, slender men they will become just before they change back into stretchy play clothes.

In the spring, Elliott accepts a job in Ohio. He consults me, and I very reluctantly agree to go. The job offers more financial security, but I am deep-down heartbroken to be leaving Colorado. However, I rationalize that I will be much closer to my sister Pam, her husband Fitz, their daughters, and all the people with whom I grew up in the eastern United States. I tell Elliott this move, with all its family disruption, definitely must be our last.

In Columbus, we rent a house where we will stay until our house sells in Denver. Jon enters first grade, and his fall reports echo previous ones, saying he is satisfactory in most areas but talks too much while working, is slow to complete assignments, does not use time wisely, and is deficient in working independently and caring for materials. He learns to write simple sentences and his drawings, still portraying smiling faces and rainbows, now show more artistry and talent than most children his age. A local bank holds a children's coloring contest and Jon is among the winners.

By January 1985, we have sold the house in Denver and bought a house in a north Columbus suburb with a big, screened porch facing a yard that backs up to undeveloped forest. With trepidation at all the disturbance in their lives, we enroll the boys in their new school at mid-term, so they can make friends in the neighborhood before summer comes. By spring, we are settled in the new house, and Jeff and Jon love the yard and the woods. I marvel at how quickly they become experts at catching frogs, and before long, we have a terrarium filled with all sizes of these creatures. The boys play endlessly in the woods behind our house and soon are joined by other boys of similar ages in the neighborhood. Quickly, solid little friendships are blossoming.

We discover the high-quality Columbus Zoo and the Center of Science and Industry (COSI), an interactive museum with multiple child-friendly exhibits and live shows. As is our custom, we travel around the region on weekend outings. Jon does well in the second half of first grade in the new school, where he earns several certificates of achievement for story writing. His stories are imaginative and fanciful, filled with twists and turns of plot. They always contain a boy who figures his way out of a dilemma using his wits or his strength, and always have a happy ending. However, the talent we notice most in Jon is his drawing. He sketches dinosaurs that look absolutely authentic, along with whimsical creatures with two or more heads, arms, legs, fins and claws. None of the stories are hurtful. All have suspense, but positive endings. As has become customary, his teacher notes that he participates enthusiastically in class discussions, but does not work well independently, use time wisely, or have good study skills.

That summer, the boys learn to fish in nearby Wyandot Lake. They also play dress-up in the house, putting mops and robes on their heads, fashioning eye patches, and putting fake beards on Dorrie. In August, while Elliott is away, Dorrie accidentally locks herself in her room, and Jon figures out a way to open the lock with a hairpin and releases her to my huge relief. For this achievement, I nominate him for a Care-A-Lot Bear[9] award through *Woman's Day*[10] magazine. He receives the award and is featured in the local suburban newspaper.

Jon begins second grade in September 1985, and joins his first soccer team. He maintains his imaginative story writing, and his obvious talent in art continues to amaze us. He is evaluated at school for an enrichment program for gifted students, but conference reports again show a need for improvement in completing assignments on time, practicing good study habits, paying attention, and making use of independent time. His teacher writes that he is "sensitive and caring, excels at problem-solving strategies and has distinct scientific abilities." However, she is "concerned that he daydreams a great deal." In a school assignment about future careers, Jon writes he wants to be an artist because he could work whenever he wanted and would feel good doing this work. He would not have a boss (because he says he would hate having a supervisor!), would not have to join a union or association of workers, and could not be put out of work by new inventions.

In spring 1986, one of Jon's chalk drawings is selected for display in the central school district office, and with excitement, we learn both he and Jeff have taken first place in their respective age groups in regional art contests sponsored by the Columbus School of Art and Design. Their artwork is displayed in the state capitol building. We go to visit the displays and, as Jeff stands below his, pointing upward, I notice the long slender arc of his arm and it stabs me. He looks so grown up, developing so much in the body style of my father and his. The fleeting path of his childhood catches my breath.

Jon's second grade school year continues, with teacher reports now familiar. His academic work is fine, his stories are creative, but he needs improvement in observing rules, caring for materials, working independently, using time wisely, and practicing good study skills.[11] When he likes an assignment, he will execute it with excellence, adding great detail to stories and drawings. If he is not interested, he may avoid the task altogether. At our conference, his teacher calls him a "random child," but no one suggests he may have attention deficit disorder (ADD). We don't think of it either, as we don't realize ADD can exist apart from the excessive physical movements of attention deficit hyperactivity disorder (ADHD). Our failure to recognize his condition will be one of the worst mistakes of our lives. Jon writes a letter to his teacher telling her he likes her and thanks her for teaching him, and his letter appears in the local newspaper. As the school year ends, Jon is given the Best Scientific Inventor award in his class, and the school chooses a batik sunburst that he has made to hang in the Greater Columbus Arts Festival.

The house and yard are busy and happy as Jon begins third grade in Fall 1986, and joins Cub Scouts. I become a den mother. Jon prefers to be with friends and almost never chooses quiet, solitary play, drawing or reading. When I ask him about his preference for constant company, he explains, "That's how I get happy." We hear the familiar reports from Jon's teachers that he needs to improve in organizational skills, listening, and caring for materials. However, his fall report on several types of animals is long, detailed, and well done, and his stories continue to be exceptionally creative for an eight-year-old. He writes in one story that he loved living in Colorado, "because the air smelled like roses all around. Not a blade of grass turned brown. You could see the Rocky Mountains from miles away." At Christmas, both Jeff and Jon are shepherds in a church pageant, and Dorrie poses in a flowing red dress with a huge white bow next to her brothers and the baby Jesus. At Dorrie's birthday party in January 1987, the boys put on a magic show to the delight of her small friends.

In the meanwhile, during 1986, I realize it has been ten years since I have held a full-time, professional job. I am worried because the value of an academic degree goes down if it is not used. I worked so hard for it, and it was so central to my life before I had children. We get a home computer so I can teach myself to use it. We set it up in a tiny room just off the garage next to the washing machine, and I buy a manual and set out to resurrect my resume. I send out many applications to local colleges, museums, foundations, and newspapers. I find I am known as a "re-entry woman," which makes me feel as if I am being fitted for the nose cone of a rocket. Most of my applications aren't even answered, but in the fall, I receive two part-time offers. I am so excited I accept them both. One assignment is to teach a class at night at a local college. The other job is to research and collect materials for a new exhibit in post-World War II history for a major museum. Both jobs will start in early 1987. I figure that, with some daycare for Dorrie and some afterschool care for the boys, I can work around my new job commitments and still be home part of the time for the children. I am excited and scared, but I think I need to take the plunge.

THREE

TROUBLE FINDS US

The year 1987 brings major changes. I begin my jobs, and although the pace is hectic and exhausting, the children seem flexible, and we work out our times apart and together. In the spring, Elliott comes home with the news that we will move again, this time to Richland, Washington. I think stability for the children would be served better by staying in Ohio, and the boys announce they do not want to move and leave their friends. Elliott urges me to fly to Richland and see the area for myself. Bewildered, I agree to go and find a small town in a desert landscape 3,000 miles from the places I was raised and have familiar ties. The economy there is in a decided slump, and I see plywood boarded over business windows. Elliott's company arranges two job interviews for me, but both of the interviewers tell me they only accepted the interviews as a courtesy and have absolutely no work for me. I miss my children and am never so glad as when it is time to fly away.

I leave on a tiny airplane of twelve seats bound for Seattle and find myself sitting next to a man about my age who is talkative and friendly, but not flirtatious. As we fly over the crystal blue band of the Columbia River and the green circles signaling irrigated agriculture below, and then pass above the Cascade Mountains, he enthusiastically points out sights below. Looking down at the Stuart Range of the Cascades, he tells me he and his best friend and their wives spent a beautiful week hiking and camping there the previous summer. Landing in Seattle, I thank him and tell him I'm glad he has found a home he loves, but I will never be back. Shortly afterward, Elliott accepts the job in Richland. I almost cannot breathe.

In the last week of May, we tell the children we will be making yet another long-distance move. Jon rebels, acting out in school, and is given a two-week, in-school suspension. I tell his teacher that the news of the move coincides exactly with the period when he began to misbehave. "When Jon is upset or is facing uncertainty," I state, "he generally 'acts out' his fears." I ask that he be allowed to get up and walk up and down the hall, as long as he does not disturb others, when he is feeling upset. At the end of third grade, teachers' reports again show Jon needs to improve in caring for materials, working independently, listening, and completing assignments on time.

The summer is very difficult, as tension over the approaching move rubs us raw. In August, I realize I cannot bear to see another moving van drive up and pull my life apart. I decide to drive to Denver with Dorrie to visit my best Colorado friend Sarah just before the moving truck arrives. In Denver, I fall into Sarah's arms, crying and shaking, babbling about my uprooted life. She comforts me with her gentle wisdom and one of her favorite Bible verses: "Trust in the LORD with all your heart and lean not on your own understanding; in all your ways submit to him, and he will make your paths straight."[12] I visit my former minister — the gentle, humble, learned man who baptized all of my children. Without prompting, he counsels me with the exact same verse! "I don't know what awaits you in Richland, Washington," he tells me, "but the Lord, who has been good to you, will be with you and continue to watch over you." Tearfully, reluctantly, hugging him and Sarah, I depart for Richland with Dorrie. The only Biblical reference that seems relevant to me is exile in the desert.

While I do not like Richland, I notice the sunsets are beautiful. We are staying temporarily in an apartment complex, and we place the boys in school immediately since it is already the third week of September, 1987. Three weeks later, we rent a large, rambling house on a golf course across town and move the boys to yet another school near the house. Jon is in fourth grade, and his new school is the fifth one he has attended in his short life. He is also living in his sixth house. He writes fanciful stories and illustrates them with life-like animals and whimsical creatures. In general, his stories are creative and positive, but his conference reports follow the accustomed pattern: Jon is very likeable, but does not stay on task, he has many late assignments, and is disorganized compared to other fourth grade boys. He cannot find his belongings and doesn't place them where they should be so the class has to wait while he searches, or else the class goes ahead and he misses activities. Still, he is so obviously brilliant he is referred to the school district's Gifted and Talented Education (GATE) class for fifth grade. In truth, his intelligence is so high it literally is off the charts.

Throughout this school year, Elliott and I try to mend our relationship that has been damaged by many moves and discovered incompatibilities. We join a small, sweet, local church and participate in its activities. Still, as a couple we are strained and distant. I read the local and regional newspapers, trying to discern the key issues of the region so I can research them, learn more, and perhaps use my new knowledge to find a job. I feel the value of my hard-won education is slipping away from me like sand through an hourglass.

When a marriage falls apart, many ugly and hurtful things are said and done that do not warrant repeating. Such is the case with us. We are very different people. The specific incidents and episodes do not matter, really, but they are searing. After seventeen years of marriage, including ten months in Richland, Elliott and I separate in the summer of 1988. Hearing the news of an impending divorce, my father immediately flies to Richland to query me and make sure I understand the gravity of my decision. He explains the seriousness of divorce, both emotionally and financially. Then he fastens his clear blue eyes directly on mine and takes a deep breath. He tells me that boys the ages of mine (twelve and ten) *must* and need to spend time – perhaps the majority of time – with their father. They want to learn how to be men, and, if they stay with me, they will be afraid of missing out on crucial male information and training. He tells me that when the time comes that Jeff and Jon ask to move in with their father, I must let them go with good grace. I must not cling and refuse, because they will resent me. I must see them as much as possible and be cheerful and not tell them how much their absence hurts me. It turns out to be the most important advice I ever receive in my life.

The first thing I buy after separating from Elliott is new sleeping bags for the children. I am determined our adventures and fun won't end because of our new life circumstances. Within two weeks, we attend a church barn dance at a farm and sleep overnight in the hay. By summer's end, Elliott has filed for joint custody and invited Jeff to live at his apartment. Jeff wants to try it, and in October I agree to it, but with many evenings and weekends to be spent with me.

In the fall of 1988, Jon enters the GATE program, which is held at yet another school that is new to him. He is in fifth grade, and this school is the sixth one he has attended. Jeff enters middle school, another change for him. Dorrie enters kindergarten, and I am pursuing an independent research project I hope will lead to a job. By this time, I have obtained a few far-flung consulting projects that send me around the state. It's a tenuous existence, with very low pay, and I must rely on babysitters when driving home from distant assignments in the evening. There are no cell phones at this time, and I sometimes find myself at phone booths outside gas stations, crying and trying to explain to sitters or neighbors that I need another sixty or ninety minutes before I can get home.

In October, I move out of our big, rented house into a much smaller one, and fill small but snug bedrooms with favorite possessions of the children. That winter, a social worker visits both Elliott and me to advise the court on custody arrangements. Rather quickly, she decides that Jeff can live with Elliott, and Dorrie can live with me, but Jon is a puzzle. The social worker reports it is clear we both love him and can provide adequately for him, and he loves both of us and his brother and sister. Unable to decide, the courts make a temporary ruling wherein Jon can live two weeks at a time with each of us, then switch to the other, then switch back. He is just turning eleven years old, and he is loved so much he is torn apart. Jon tells me he doesn't think we should "split up the kids," but there seems no other way for us to proceed. Elliott travels a lot for his work, so Jeff comes to stay with us often.

The GATE program is marvelous. The teacher provides creative modules in skeletons and anatomy, electricity, pioneer experiences in a wagon train along the Oregon Trail, modern house and cabin construction, science fiction, rockets, the river, and other rich topics that engage Jon's imaginative mind. The class goes on field trips, hears from, and works with, a wide variety of guest presenters and experts, and does many hands-on activities. The teacher also brings in a police officer to present anti-drug education. The officer tells the students that sinister strangers exist and may approach them with offers of substances that sound like fun. He emphasizes the dangers of these substances. Today, research shows that some messages meant to discourage drug use may unwittingly encourage it, because the messages arouse curiosity about drugs. This outcome occurs in Jon. Later, he will tell me the officer's statement about sinister characters offering strange substances sounded exciting to him. He says he hoped someone mysterious would approach him, and he intended to try the wares. Still later, he will tell me it is not malicious strangers who introduce you to drugs – it is your friends.

In the second half of the school year, he writes a long, detailed story mocking the famous Muppets[13] characters. He re-names them the Fluppets and portrays them as drug users and dealers. In the story, the Fluppets consume cocaine and marijuana, wield huge hypodermic needles, get drunk on wine and take over a suburban street that Jon calls Potato Lane. They operate a chop shop that parts out stolen cars, and Jon helps to bust them in a massacre that involves vivid descriptions of weapons. A children's television character who embodies innocence also appears in the story as a drug dealer and is shot by Jon. He writes another story about hunters who shoot "druggies," and Jon portrays himself as a "drug cop." He fills these stories with irony and mockery, at one point saying that he misses a shot because, "I didn't use my time wisely." He is telling us clearly that he isn't a child anymore. Is this just fanciful daring or is his mind starting to focus on darker subtexts? To the surprise of no one, his work is rated as extremely creative, illustrated with well-drawn characters, but often late, messy, and produced without staying on task and using time carefully. At one point in his fifth-grade year, Jon must write me a letter explaining that he and a partner were not following directions in a science experiment and caused a ball of steel wool to turn red hot and burn a mark in the laboratory desk and floor.

In the fifth grade GATE class, Jon soon becomes best friends with a boy named Matt, who, like Jon, is intelligent and inventive. Matt is also extremely talented in music, and his mother is a concert pianist. The boys become inseparable, playing in the hills behind our houses, often spending the night at each other's house, and making up cartoons and movie scripts. Video cameras and camcorders are just becoming available, and soon the boys are making amateur movies. They create props and costumes out of electronic parts, clothing scrounged from thrift stores, artwork, cardboard, food, etc. Sometimes they take clothing from our closets and "modify it" without telling us, looking sheepish when found out. Their movies are full of action and sound effects, as the boys jump off decks and garage roofs at our houses, explode balloons filled with ketchup or watery cherry jelly hidden in their shirts, mimic Monty Python, dance or pantomime wildly, and devise other antics for the film plots. They also take apart radios, electronic toys, and other devices to create sound effects and parts that can move in their sets. One afternoon, a neighbor calls Matt's mother asking her if she is aware that fiery bursts are occurring in her garage. She hurries out to stop the boys from filming an explosion scene not far from the family boat's gasoline tank! The "Jon and Matt Movies" became famous throughout Richland as the zaniest, most creative things their parents, teachers, and schoolmates have ever seen. Other people we don't even know in school and church ask to see the Jon and Matt Movies. Many years later, Matt will remark that Jon "always needed so much input." Even after a hilarious, creative night, Jon was ready to plan another madcap film, while Matt sometimes just wanted to rest and slowly pick out some notes on one of his instruments.

In the meantime, during Jon's fifth grade year, I begin seeing a single father my age named Evan. He is raising his two children alone, a boy named Brett who is three years younger than Jon and a girl named June who is one year younger than Dorrie. I'm not looking to find a special man, but I meet Evan at church and gradually we start going on outings together with our children. His family orientation charms me, and, as lonely single parents, we make pizza and other simple dinners together with our children, take our children on hikes, help at each other's children's birthday parties, and drive to our children's dance recitals and soccer games together. We spend time in his boat, exploring the azure Columbia River, sometimes drifting lazily and sometimes speeding along, watching the endlessly varied patches of rocks, pebbles, plants, and fish life we can see through the clear water. Evan has a log cabin a few hours away, and we take our children fishing there, build campfires and snowmen, have snowball fights, and play endless rounds of Monopoly[14], Sorry[15], Go Fish[16] and other games. Evan's best friend Marty and his wife and children – two girls near the ages of our children – often join us. The children sleep in sleeping bags throughout the cabin, often talking and laughing all night. Romance gradually blossoms and Evan and I marry in the summer of 1989. Marty gives the toast at our wedding reception.

Dorrie, Jon and I move into Evan's large house near a park along the Columbia River. The river, fifth largest in the nation, becomes our anchor. It offers fun, exercise, clear water, beautiful sunsets, solace and quietude, a clean smell that fills our noses, settings for beach campfires, and spots to view wildlife. In the mornings, we wake to the calls of shore birds and the throaty hum of boat motors. We build an addition onto the house so each of our children can have a room and not feel crowded. Jon has a room of his own, but continues his split-time life between Elliott and me. Elliott's persistent travel for his work means that Jeff is often with our new blended family. We love having him and feel that, despite adjustment problems typical in the aftermath of all divorces, we are building a happy, supportive home. Evan and I delight in all of our children, taking as many of them as will come, and as often as possible, to the cabin. We also take them to catch crabs in the ocean, ski in Idaho and Washington, carve pumpkins, cook and watch movies, and many other fun activities. Our lives revolve around them whenever we're not at work. Jon and Brett, both gifted, play together, taking apart toys and radios to make new devices because both are so curious about the components and mechanisms inside. These boys both will grow to be mechanical and electronic geniuses. Brett will say many years later that when we blended our families, he at first did not like stepping down from being the oldest child to a middle child. However, he will add, "Having a stepbrother as cool as Jon made it all worthwhile."

The GATE program continues through sixth grade, so for only the second time in his life Jon remains in the same school for two consecutive years. The program is engaging, creative, and well-suited to him. Jon and Matt remain best friends, and Matt often accompanies us to the log cabin and on trips to the Oregon coast.

Over the winter, Jon lets us know his life of bouncing back and forth between his father's house and mine every two weeks is stressful. His teachers confirm he seems more disorganized than ever, needing improvement in being timely, following directions, staying on task, and using time constructively. He often starts assignments at one home or the other, leaves them behind when he transits, and never turns them in. The consensus opinion is that shuttling between the two households is not a good situation for a boy who has always struggled with disorganization. Jon indicates he would like to try living with Elliott and Jeff. Wounded to my core, I remember my father's words and I consent. I try to be graceful and cheerful on the Saturday he leaves, but my heart contorts in pain. After he goes, I am inconsolable. Many times, I walk along the Columbia River shore crying or talking to myself, sometimes just trying to breathe. After he moves out, he still joins us for many trips to the cabin, visits our house to hide Easter baskets for Dorrie and June, and he loves to come and play with our new black Labrador puppy.

I now know the move to Elliott's house was stressful for Jon, even though he chose it. He was the child in the middle, torn, missing me, and hating the divorce and all the changes in his life. He became angry, no doubt contributing to his turn to drugs to soothe and tranquilize his turmoil. Later he would recall, "I loved my Mom but being a young boy I naturally wanted to live with the guys...I know that hurt my Mom. Probably deeply."

Jon enters seventh grade and middle school in the fall of 1990, and becomes a teenager on Valentine's Day, 1991. By this time, my research project has led to a book and a full-time job. Our lives seem to be settling into reasonable routines wherein Elliott and I both see the children a lot and they know we are both close by and both love them. Jon continues to spend considerable time with us, cheerfully dressing up for Halloween with the "little kids" in our house, helping to decorate the Christmas tree, and teaching Brett to catch garter snakes at the park by the river. One spring Saturday, I go into our yard to see Jeff, Jon, and Brett hastily covering a pail under our deck. When I ask to see the contents, they show me nine little snakes. I screech and insist they take them back to the park, as I am sure at least one will get loose in our yard. They grin and take them back. Letting the snakes go is almost as much fun as catching them, they say. Jon and Matt make more of their amateur films, refining their theatrics, music, and artwork. Jon's grades are fair, but he continues to have the same organizational and study problems that have been habitual. At Elliott's house, Jon's room is messy and chaotic.

In September 1991, Jon enters eighth grade at the same time the Seattle grunge band Nirvana releases its album *Nevermind.*[17] By January 1992, this album will be number one on the national charts, propelling the grunge movement, Nirvana, and its lead singer and guitarist Kurt Cobain to fame and widespread emulation. Grunge music features dissonance, half-spoken lyrics, murmurings about inchoate hurt and anger, and meaninglessness. The grunge movement boasts that it is unkempt, alternative, and based on DIY– do-it-yourself or do your own thing. It speaks to a vague malaise never quite explained. Grunge music has been called "the sound of homes breaking" and "the poetry of depression."[18]

Jon begins the school year as much the same boy we have known – social, creative, friendly, sometimes childlike, disorganized, but not hostile or distant. He and Matt build a model of a historic building, produce a well-researched report, and show the model in a school History Day competition. They stand by their display in matching shirts, looking wholesome. It will be the last really good piece of schoolwork we see from Jon in his teen years. He is enthusiastic at Christmas and participates in family activities, including energetic snowball fights. However, sometime over the winter, he tries marijuana and begins to smoke conventional cigarettes. We have no idea. Maybe he is breaking barriers in self-confidence or fear, maybe trying to calm and center himself, maybe fantasizing about adventure, or maybe just experimenting. Jon later recalls that "I was a naturally rebellious kid – smoking cigarettes at a young age and running amok whenever I got the chance. I was very attracted to 'bad kids' in school." Defiantly, he decides it is cooler to be reckless and venture outside of accepted boundaries rather than be meek, compliant and good. The social hierarchies of middle school assert themselves, and soon he is in a clique with a particular style. It certainly is not comprised of kids interested in academic or sports achievements, volunteer work or clean-cut appearances. Fortunately, his friendship with Matt remains strong.

By Jon's fourteenth birthday in February 1992, his eyes are spacey and his hair is longish and flat, lopped over to one side of his head in an uneven part. He loves the grunge sound and ethic of checking out and not caring about much, and follows Kurt Cobain's lyrics and interviews closely. We don't worry too much because it seems like just a phase. He still participates in family squirt gun fights, birthday parties, and goes to Jeff's cross-country running meets with us. In May, he attends our annual group trip to the Oregon coast, endlessly fascinated with the starfish, tiny crabs, and other creatures he pulls out of tide pools amid the rocks. Throughout the summer, we tow the children behind our boat on huge tubes. At Labor Day, we all gather at our cabin with Marty and his family and Matt. The children float down the Wenatchee River on rubber rafts, and the boys camp out in tents on the property. We cook huge dinners and play games. Finally, looking at Marty one day I have a startling realization – he was the man who sat next to me on the airplane leaving Richland in 1987, when I said I would never return. He and his wife had camped in the Stuart Range of the Cascade Mountains with Evan and his first wife the year before Evan's marriage ended. Amazed, I wonder at the gifts I have found in this new place I fought so hard against. I wonder about fate, God making straight my path, and where I and my children are meant to be.

In Jon's ninth grade year, we notice he is distancing himself from us quite distinctly. He doesn't help Dorrie to dress for Halloween or attend Jeff's cross-country meets. In November, we arrange to sit for a professional photograph of Evan and I with our blended family of five children. Jeff dresses up in a sport jacket and tie and arrives looking debonair, but Jon is not with him. We call everyone we can think of, but Jon cannot be found. After waiting as long as we can, we have the portrait made without him. Perhaps, we think, he is just acting out the normal determination of a fourteen-year-old to separate from parents. Later, we will learn he had gotten high and was afraid to let us see him in that condition, so he hid under the bed of a friend. As his adolescent love affair with drugs blossoms, Jon is blissful.

At Christmas, Jon's hair and eyes are flat. At his fifteenth birthday dinner in early 1993, he is fidgety and anxious. When he opens his main gift, an envelope containing seventy-five dollars, he sighs deeply and says, "This is great, because Seth was going to kill me if I didn't pay him." We don't know any of his friends named Seth. A few months later, Seth, two years older than Jon, will be found hanging in his room. A petty drug dealer who also was badly addicted, Seth had taken his own life.

The summer that follows brings troublesome signs we again minimize. Looking back, it seems astounding we were so naïve. Drug use just never occurred to us. We don't know what we don't know. One evening, Jon and a friend of his named Jerrod come over to have tacos on the deck with me. The other children are off with friends and Evan is on a business trip. I love my time with Jon and Jerrod, hearing their deepening voices that hint of manhood, seeing faint shades of beard growth beginning on their faces. They are fifteen years old – almost men, but mostly boys, laughing at goofy jokes and eating ravenously. I wish I could have more evenings like this one. I have agreed to drive them to a dock a few miles away along the Columbia, so they can fish until darkness and then walk back to Jerrod's house. I leave them at the dock and start to drive home when I see black thunderclouds gathering quickly. I turn the car around and go back to get them, but they refuse to leave. The water looks ominous, and I point to the thunderheads. They say they don't care. Reluctantly, I leave them, thinking the worst thing that will happen is they will get wet. Their plan to use drugs never occurs to me. Fifteen years later, Jerrod will be dead of an overdose.

In tenth grade, Jon is spending even more time away from the family. We don't know it, but he is driving friends' cars without a license and riding with other unlicensed friends. One night, he and a friend are driving on a country road when she swerves to avoid a rabbit. Jon is thrown into the dashboard and cracks his shoulder bone, but never tells us. He wraps it himself with Ace™ bandages and wears baggy shirts until it heals, without ever seeing a doctor. Twenty-one years later, this girl will be dead of an overdose.

One fall weekend, we allow all the children to attend a large festival at a local church. Jeff and Jon can go without adults, and Brett, Dorrie, and June each have been invited to attend with friends and their parents. Evan and I grab the rare opportunity to take out our boat and float just offshore to relax and listen to bird sounds. The Columbia is slow and languid, a lovely sapphire blue on this perfect early autumn afternoon. Soon after we get settled in the boat, however, I begin to feel a strange sense of unease. Quickly, the sensation grows to agitation and then almost panic. Something is wrong and I feel I must get back to shore. There are no cell phones. As soon as I get home, I rush to our answering machine and find that Jon is in the hospital with a concussion. It turns out he had left the church festival and gone to a park along the river to do "power hits" with a group of kids. He chewed up some speed tablets and then toked as much marijuana as he could and held it in his lungs. The idea was to "blow the mind" with a wild rush or pass out. He had passed out and fallen to the pavement, hitting his head. At the hospital, he tells us he has tried marijuana for the first time that day, and it affected him strongly because he wasn't used to it. He promises never to smoke it again. We are suspicious, but still naïve, and glad he is awake and healing.

Jon spends Christmas with us and seems to enjoy dinners, gifts, and sledding. However, his hair and eyes are flat and he looks pale. His artwork has changed dramatically. He draws human-shaped creatures with many eyes — eyes in their arms, torsos, and legs. The eyes stare boldly outward, looking blank. Are they seeing, challenging, or revealing? Do they represent creatures whose brains are so full that they see more than we see? Does Jon think they offer protection, or wisdom? Often, skeletal bones show on these creatures. A stretch of arm or chest will have no flesh on it with carefully, anatomically correct bones and ligaments drawn underneath. Some of the figures have just half of their faces. Does Jon feel like half a person? Does he wish that he was, so he would have just half as many thoughts and ideas to juggle? Other drawings are replete with creatures either pornographic or with horns, cavernous mouths, and claw-like noses. Some characters look foolish and weird, with buildings growing out of their heads and arms. He makes a detailed pencil sketch of a phantasmagoric tree with elaborate vines curling backward from it. A craggy man's head grows out of the other side of the tree trunk with a large fork twisting from the vines into the man's ear. Jon also draws cartoon stories, stretching on for pages, with dialog sometimes silly and satirical, and sometimes violent. The symbol for anarchy often appears in the margins, on the T-shirts of characters, or tucked surreptitiously into various parts of the sketches. We still don't get it.

He listens frequently, and talks about, the band, Jane's Addiction.[19] It is prominent in the alternative genre and features songs about alienation, absent fathers, cheating, violence, wanting to disappear, and children with "pin" eyes. We don't know it then, but pin or pinned eyes refer to the narrowing of pupils to pin-size when a person takes opiate drugs. He also likes the music of The Doors,[20] a rock band from the 1960s whose lead singer, Jim Morrison, died of an overdose seven years before Jon was born. The Doors, sometimes thought to be named for the book *Doors of Perception*[21] by early psychedelic drug experimenter Aldous Huxley, re-surges in popularity with a certain set of teenagers in the 1990s. The Doors sing about many obvious allegorical references to drugs, oblivion, and meaninglessness. Why, we wonder, do the kids like this music? To us, the lesson of Jim Morrison is clear. He wasted his talent and life pursuing a dangerous illusion. Why would anyone admire that? The Demon is whispering, but we do not hear him.

We allow the growing evidence of Jon's drug use to slip by us just as people can allow hopes to overwhelm facts as they watch a person slipping into dementia. As dementia creeps into a life, gradually friends and family notice some forgetfulness, confusion, inattentiveness, or perhaps extra grouchiness. They tell themselves these signs are typical of all aging people. Then one day they find dollar bills stuffed inside a cereal box, and their hearts thud. They know – this is dementia. So it is with Jon in his tenth grade year in school. He seems okay to us, until he clearly isn't. Our suspicions are confirmed that winter when we learn corroborating information from another family. We take him for a drug assessment. The counselor rates him as having low risk of dependency, but a fairly high rate of drug use, and recommends he attend four AA meetings per week. Jon promises not to use any more marijuana. However, by spring we all realize he is using drugs and must enter inpatient treatment. Elliott and I confront Jon in Elliott's living room. He is only sixteen, so we can compel him into treatment. He slouches, denies, and argues, but only weakly. The stubborn resistance we expect is missing. Later, he tells us the only reason he assented is that he was on a "trip" on the hallucinogen LSD (known as "acid") [22] and was watching "lizards run up and down the curtains" while Elliott and I talked to him.

Back at work the next day, I close my office door and make the final arrangements with the treatment center. I am so flooded with relief I can barely stand. I cry for several minutes before emerging from the office. Now everything will be all right, I am convinced. We have identified the problem, and now we will fix it. We will have our brilliant boy back. We love him so much it has to work, and I know it will. I look for good things to come. I am so ignorant, so naïve, so unprepared. I am exactly like the parents described by William Cope Moyers, a man in recovery and a passionate treatment advocate. He writes of parents whose "love, hope, fear and ignorance about the symptoms and progression of chemical dependency blind them to the truth...When young people look healthy and relatively happy on the outside, how could they possibly be suffering from a chronic, progressive, inevitably fatal disease?" [23]

FOUR

SEARCHING FOR SOLID GROUND

The Silver Star Recovery Center is located on a beautiful property that used to be a ranch and orchard in central Washington State. Elliott and I arrive with Jon in April, as blossoms begin to flower on the remaining fruit trees. The time seems propitious for new beginnings. Life will almost never seem so simple again.

We leave Jon in the adolescent boys' unit and return the following weekend for an afternoon visit, bringing Jeff and Dorrie. We all play ping-pong and make small talk. One week later, Evan and I travel early in the morning to the rugged canyon wall that rises above Silver Star. We hike on the canyon's rim long before visiting Jon. The ashy, sandy volcanic soils support few trees, but sagebrush, ryegrass, wheatgrass, saltgrass, bunchgrass, cheatgrass, Russian thistle, and prickly pear abound. Tiny wildflowers are beginning to bloom among the rocky outcroppings of hard black basalt. I first saw the regional landscape of eastern Washington as harsh and forbidding, but now I feel close to it. It is lovely in its sere, arid character. Walking along, looking down on the immaculately manicured Silver Star property with its white buildings and dark shingled roofs, we find solace. This place looks solid, competent. Here, we believe, Jon will find himself again and turn away from his foolish, dangerous flirtation with drugs.

In the 1960s and 1970s, Evan and I had seen some of our classmates crash their lives with drugs, ruining their brains, personalities, and prospects. The slang term for them at the time was "crispy critters" because they acted as if they had "fried" some of the synapses in their brains and could no longer think clearly. Surely, we believe, the lessons of Janis Joplin, Jimi Hendrix, Gram Parsons of The Byrds, Keith Moon of The Who, Sid Vicious of The Sex Pistols, Morrison, and many other famous musicians who died from drugs were self-evident. Even Morrison and Kurt Cobain of Nirvana, another addicted person, spoke out against the destructive path of using drugs. Jon's curiosity about drugs was just that, we think, and soon will be behind us. There is much about our boy we do not know. We don't know he has been sexually active, been present at a robbery (although he did not participate), and has taken LSD and whatever types of speed he could, whether they were medications given to friends for legitimate purposes or other uppers obtained from petty dealers in the park near his high school. As yet, he has not been exposed to cocaine.

When Jon has been in treatment about two weeks, Cobain is found dead in his Seattle home. Cobain's suicide note is widely purported to have said he could no longer find pleasure in life, family, and music. Silver Star's counselors, who have more mileage on them than the teens in their care, try to explain the inability to experience pleasure in music and life as the result of drug use. Today, the descriptive term is anhedonia, a brain condition in addicted people that results after drugs have altered the brain's pleasure set point so normally pleasurable events and sensations no longer register. Anhedonia occurs because drugs have flooded the brain's reward center with dopamine and other chemicals to such an extent that only super-charged sensations (such as those produced by taking drugs) can be felt. It is unlikely the counselors use the term anhedonia, but, through bitter experience and observation, they recognize the plight. However, the adolescents do not. Their drug use has not yet altered their brains to anywhere near that level. Years later, Jon will tell me he knows exactly why Cobain killed himself.

Toward the end of Jon's four-week stay at Silver Star, Elliott and I attend a three-day family session to listen and learn about drugs, the founding of AA and the Twelve-Step philosophy.[24] We have individual and group truth sessions with our drug-using adolescents and other parents. We are not ready to use the word "addict" – it doesn't seem Jon's situation has progressed that far. The one thing I grasp immediately is that I don't know how to understand drug use or even how to approach it. One of my customary tendencies is to intellectualize – to learn terminology and facts. But here I have an innate sense this approach will do no good. An emotional approach probably won't work either, as not one fiber of me can fathom wanting to check out or feel things that are pure fantasy. I'm a very grounded person, often very literal. How will I comprehend this boy whom I love so much, so I can see why he went down this path, and how to guide and persuade him from doing it again?

At one of the early information sessions for parents, counselors tell us the success rate (defined as abstinence from drug use) for adolescents after their first inpatient treatment is between ten and eighteen percent. Apparently, many teenage drug users see their parents' admonitions to stop as just a way to prevent them from having fun. The parents' words are no match for the way drugs make them feel. The young users are not ready to call themselves addicts and admit they are powerless over their addiction(s). This situation certainly does not fit their self-concepts. William Moyers described his first stint in drug treatment exactly this way: "Everyone was telling me that I had a disease that was permanent, progressive and deadly...I nodded my head, pretending to understand what words like 'unmanageable' and 'powerless' and 'denial' meant."[25]

Despite the sobering data on teen success levels, I am sure Jon will be among the small fraction of those who triumph. He is bright, well loved, physically agile and strong, creative, and social. He won't give in to oblivion – there is too much life to be lived. Unbeknownst to us, the Demon cruises through the adolescent wing of the treatment center, casing his prospects. He doesn't need to waste too much effort here right now. Quite literally, he has time to kill. The youngsters who truly can't resist him will show themselves soon enough, and then he can feast.

One of the first lectures we attend at Silver Star is by a young woman counselor whose husband is recovering from a cocaine addiction. She recounts his many lies and ruses to fool her and keep his habit, and her eventual decision to remove him from their home. She still loved him, but his behavior gave her no choice. She often felt like wavering and letting him come home when he knocked on the door cold, hungry, and strung out. However, she stayed strong, and she states that her refusal to acquiesce finally led him into recovery. After he had been in recovery for six months, she let him come home. They were now joyous together and had another child. She blushes and crunches up her shoulders as she tells us this happy ending. The message is clear: A loving spouse or parent must be strong and not allow drug use, and that strength very often leads the addicted person to reform. Many other stories told by staff members convey the same message. Most are alcoholics and people recovering from addiction themselves, and have been on the receiving end of tough love.

We sit with the parents of a young boy in Jon's treatment group as the mother expresses her feelings. She is very angry, and her story pours out. She and her husband spend most of their time working hard to support their children. Their two oldest boys are alcoholics with many failures in life. Their third boy, the one in treatment with Jon, had started stealing and using drugs when they called the police and had him arrested and then diverted to treatment. As she speaks, her rage turns to howls. She rocks back and forth. She cries in a way that is messy and embarrassing, but riveting. "I hate them," she says. "They have ruined our lives and our happiness. I don't even want to go home. I don't want anything to do with my life anymore." We are galvanized. We cannot imagine being in her position, not wanting or expecting restoration. We cannot visualize being desperate or brave enough to call the police on our own son. We don't and can't understand her despair, yet I feel a chill. Watching her, something in me knows the water in which we find ourselves is much deeper than I realized.

However, there are many signs of hope, as well. Jon's treatment journals reveal he is still a boy who wants to please, remembers who he is in our family, and wants to be a part of us. He begins his stay at Silver Star resenting being away from his girlfriend at home, but feeling relief that, away from us, he at least can chain smoke in peace. However, he listens to other teens in his group whose parents reject them, and he writes about, "how...lucky I am for getting help now and having a guaranteed place to call home and loving parents who, through all the [horror] I'm putting them through, still take care of me and make me feel comfortable at home." After a week, still in withdrawal from his drug use, he writes, "My thoughts are getting clearer and I want to get sober...If I had weed right now I'd get stoned but I hope I don't feel that way when I get out but I've got three weeks to work on that." He shares in his groups and participates in and receives analyses and feedback from the groups. The sessions, he writes, "brought out sheer honesty not only in me but in the whole group...[they] demand rigorous honesty and give the group a chance to really get to know the person."

Jon chafes at the rules at Silver Star, but submitting to discipline has been an issue his whole life. He believes in, he says, "educated freedom." Midway through his time in the center, we visit for Easter and bring him several small gifts he likes. He writes that his attitude is improving: "Since I've been sober I laugh much more and for little things." After a boy in the row behind him in assembly has a seizure, Jon writes he felt, "a serious shock...when I got outside I was shaking...[and] felt sick to my stomach and very light headed...my heart sank and my eyes watered up." The next day, counselors discover the boy had seized because he was part of a small group who broke into the center's clinic and stole medication for ADHD that was essentially speed. Three boys are discharged from the center due to their involvement, and Jon writes he is, "glad I wasn't a part of it...I'm not sure what I would have done if I had known or was offered speed. However, I don't think I would be here now if I had known. Ignorance is bliss."

At the end of the three-day family session with Elliott and I, Jon writes he had been "nervous about...confessing things" to us, but we talked openly and deeply during the sessions. "My parents and I are on a much better level of communication," he writes. "I got to sort out some things...This whole thing has helped my parents understand some of my behaviors...I'm glad we had family sessions. I'm also glad it's over." On his last day at Silver Star, he is positive but nervous. He journals that "I've never wanted sobriety more...I wish time would slow down here. I only have one full day left before I'm thrown back out into the constant test of the real world...I've never been happier or felt better being sober. I know I can make this work but once I get out it won't be easy." If only we had known that four weeks is not nearly enough time to address a serious addiction.

Things seem hopeful when Jon gets home. He and his father negotiate a compromise whereby Jon is allowed to smoke in Elliott's home. He and Elliott sometimes smoke together. Jon attends AA meetings, and shyly brings me small gifts as a way of making amends as Step Nine advises. During the summer, Jon and Matt take our old red canoe and paddle around the Columbia and Yakima rivers near our home. The Yakima is more docile, but the Columbia never fails to delight. With its blue, clear, and clean-smelling water, and stunning cliffs, it is always the favorite destination.

On Labor Day weekend, Jon and Matt join us for a large gathering of friends and family at our cabin and camp out in tents. We all play practical jokes on each other and hover around a large campfire at night, talking endlessly. In the fall of 1994, Jon attends some of Jeff's cross-country meets and continues to write and draw very creatively. His stories are fantastical, long, and full of twists and turns. Sometimes they contain gunfights or fistfights, but mostly they satirize his surroundings, including processed foods, jocks at school, the pursuit of wealth, people who peel out in their cars to look powerful, and school authorities. He also satirizes himself, including for his forgetfulness and disorganization. He thanks me for good and sensible advice and jokes that "someday I'm gonna use it." He draws me a "coupon," good for a free babysitting session with Dorrie and June, and tells me it comes with official rules. It is void, he says, "if lost, stolen, bent, folded, eaten or used for more than twenty-four hours."

However, in the late fall, about five months after leaving Silver Star, Jon begins using drugs again. His use escalates far more than we realize and by spring 1995, it is clear to us something is very wrong. One night when Dorrie is sleeping over at Elliott's house, Jon does not come home. She and Elliott stay up waiting and watching, Dorrie in tears. On another occasion, Elliott is out of town and Jon has a party at his house. By this time, with Jon and Jeff in eleventh and twelfth grades, Elliott often gives them permission to stay home alone when he travels. Being teenage boys, they take his offer and do not come to stay with me. On one such night, Jeff is in his room trying to study and ignore the noise and mess of Jon's party. Soon Jeff hears his father's Jeep roar out of the driveway. Several minutes later, he hears sirens in the neighborhood. Two of Jon's friends have crashed the Jeep into a tree in a front yard a few blocks away, totally wrecking the vehicle. In June, we place Jon in Porter Terrace Treatment Center near Portland, Oregon. He adamantly does not want to be there.

I write to him every few days, encouraging him to be honest, be healthy, value himself, and come back to the family who loves him so much. My parents and Pam send cards of encouragement, and Dorrie writes to him poignantly saying, "I can't even begin to tell you how much I love you. I would do anything in the whole wide world that you need or that you want...I don't know what to do because there still is a big problem...if you're unhappy we will help you...don't worry everything is going to be OK." Nevertheless, she tells him she won't lie and cover up for him anymore. He has been sneaking wine bottles from our house and blowing marijuana smoke through the outflow ducts in our home heating system. She has seen it and tried to "help" him by confusing and diverting us so we wouldn't have clear evidence. I drive to the treatment center to talk with him one Saturday, following a nearly 200-mile stretch of the Columbia. The river, true blue this day, looks wide and bountiful, well-equipped to support both Washington and Oregon as it marks their state borders. The cliffs along the river are striking, verdant, and huge. Jon and I take a supervised hike and I give him some small gifts. The visit goes well until it becomes plain he wants me to sign him out and take him home. Because he is just seventeen, we still have parental control. When I say I will not release him, he becomes sullen and sarcastic. I leave - sad and worried.

Years later, I will learn from his journals at Porter Terrace that his favorite drug is marijuana, which he uses every day after school and in the evening. His second favorite class of drugs is uppers – methamphetamines (meth) and crank, which he uses about once a month. He has also used more acid and had some "fantastic trips," and by this time has tried cocaine. He takes five to ten hits of acid about once a month. He sometimes mixes these chemicals with alcohol and smokes marijuana to come down off speed. He writes that meth makes him, "exceptionally happy and made me love everyone and bond with total strangers" and speed helps him concentrate and work. He says he has not tried to control his drug use, but enjoys it, and thinks about drugs often when he is in school. Unbeknownst to us, he has nicknames – Junkie Jon, Pothead, and Tweaker. When asked by the counselors to name things he has done on drugs that were dangerous, frightening, unfair, regrettable, or expensive, his list is long. He has had unprotected sex with multiple partners, fallen fifteen feet out of a tree, stood in a campfire, and once used so much meth that "my heart rate got way up there...and I had a bit of a heart attack and thought I was going to die for sure." He also has shoplifted, ransacked a house, sold drugs, stolen from friends, stood up his girlfriend, embarrassed several people, lied, disrespected his family, beat up someone, and lost or foolishly wasted "a lot of money." Later, he will describe his high school drug use as, "very experimental...I was a party type. I did every different type of drug there is but I never found one I truly liked. I did coke a lot and I did meth a lot...I mean I did horrible amounts of meth. I liked it OK but after a while it stopped working. Besides the side effects were horrendous...I was able to walk away with reasonable discomfort."

While in Porter Terrace, he estimates his chemical use in high school has cost him 2,000 to 4,000 dollars, and cost his parents two stints in treatment centers. In addition, while on acid, he has taken chances by driving all night without a license, skiing too fast, and swimming far out in cold ocean water. He has lost at least three good friendships due to drugs, including that of Matt – his best friend. Why did he use drugs? Mostly because it was super fun, he writes, but also to fix his lack of motivation and his ADD.[3] He has never told us he believes he has ADD. I do not see this journal until after his death. The gulf is cavernous between what we thought we knew – the life we thought we were living – and the reality of our boy and our life. The Demon, sauntering by, takes note.

Back home after his time in Porter Terrace at the end of his junior

---

[3] Today it is well-documented that ADD and ADHD are potential precursors of addiction and/or alcoholism. The underlying desire to calm one's brain can lead to self-medication, especially with the "downer" (non-stimulant) drugs that Jon prefers.

year of high school, Jon is cooperative. He seems so much like himself. He teases and arm wrestles with Dorrie, chases and splashes her good-naturedly at the river, attends a weekend at the cabin, and keeps his hair fairly clean cut. He has developed a poor reputation with the teachers in his high school, and no "clique" fits him as he begins his senior year. He tries to avoid the stoners, but doesn't like other groups, so he drops out in November. I am devastated, as education always has had a high value to me – a privilege, a path to an income, vastly mentally stimulating, treasured. The high school's policy is not to re-admit students who have dropped out. However, I visit his school and plead with authorities. They make an exception and take him back. At Christmas, he is very loving, but he drops out of school again in January. That same month, a neighbor of Elliott's sees Jon entering a basement window of his house, thinks she is witnessing burglary, and calls the police. The police find a rather extensive marijuana growing operation in the basement, unknown to Elliott. They confront Jon. He is one month shy of his eighteenth birthday, so he is still considered a juvenile. His charges are dropped and he is diverted to community service.

Shortly afterward, he drives to the local community college, where he takes a state exam and receives his General Equivalency Diploma, four months ahead of the time his high school classmates graduate. He is friendly at home, attending birthday parties for the other children and Jeff, and doing yard work for us. In May, Jon and a friend are arrested for tagging the high school with graffiti. The damages amount to 600 dollars, so we make him work off his portion by getting a job delivering pizzas. In the summer, we enroll him in a class at the community college, but he hardly works at it and fails the class.

We are desperate to find something that motivates Jon, and I ask him bluntly for suggestions. He says he would like to learn about cars and possibly rebuild a motor. I consider an idea and consult Evan. We decide to stop trying to round off the square peg (i.e., Jon) to fit in the circular hole that suits us, and simply remind him the world is cruel to those without education credentials or usable skills. I buy him a used Volkswagen, and he happily and carefully begins dismantling its engine on the floor of his father's garage. He buys the Chilton

Repair Manual[26] for Volkswagen Beetles and works deliberately and tirelessly. We rarely have seen a project take such hold of him. He lays out each part meticulously and maps it on the garage floor. He studies it, reads, thinks, and soon figures out for himself the workings of the internal combustion engine. He is indeed gifted. Then he cleans each part, replaces any that are bent, thinned, or worn, and re-assembles the engine. He drives the car for several months until eventually it is smashed in a minor accident on an icy hill. He loves the car, builds wooden models of it, and sketches it endlessly.

During the fall of 1996, Jon enrolls in another class at the community college, but withdraws from it. He signs up for a full course load in the winter of 1997, but only attends and completes his art class. In the spring, he enrolls in two classes, but withdraws from one and fails the other because he almost never attends. He enrolls in one class the following fall, but never attends. Other than trashing school, his behavior is quite good overall. He works steadily at the pizza delivery job and sometimes takes shifts working behind the counter. He becomes a valuable jack-of-all-trades to the store's management, as he also fixes equipment and pitches in for any chore that is needed. He participates in family events and spends considerable time with Dorrie when she severely injures her arm. He is clean-cut and cooperative. We know he drinks alcohol and smokes cigarettes moderately. We also suspect he smokes some marijuana, but not to excess. However, we realize school does not interest him at all, and it seems foolish to waste more time and money enrolling him. We sit down with him to brainstorm plans that will interest him, make money, and bring some growth. As a result, he applies to be a ski lift operator at the Sun Valley Resort in Idaho, and is soon accepted. He leaves for Sun Valley, about eight hours from our home, in early November 1997.

FIVE

SUN VALLEY

Sun Valley is flat-out gorgeous. Founded in 1935, when multi-millionaire Averell Harriman purchased 4,300 acres just outside of Ketchum, Idaho, Sun Valley became the first destination ski resort in the United States. Conveniently, Harriman's Union Pacific Railroad brought visitors to the groomed slopes and rustic, yet opulent lodge that he built. From its opening in 1936, Sun Valley Resort attracted many of the "beautiful people," including wealthy travelers from the east coast and Hollywood stars, including Marilyn Monroe and Gary Cooper. Soon, golf courses were added, along with the world-class fly-fishing opportunities that already existed in the Wood River, Silver Creek, and many other nearby streams. In 1939, famed author Ernest Hemingway finished his novel *For Whom the Bell Tolls* in the Sun Valley Lodge. After World War II, Hemingway spent a great deal more time in Sun Valley, and in 1961, he killed himself by gunshot in a house he had bought there. By that time, Hemingway was an advanced alcoholic. He is buried in the Ketchum cemetery.

Sun Valley boasts 285 days of sunshine per year, and averages only seventeen inches of rain, but 121 inches of snow. At 5,850 feet of elevation, this more-than-mile-high town has low humidity and clear air that smells of fresh forests. Bald Mountain, known as Baldy by the locals, towers just above the town at 9,180 feet, and smaller Dollar Mountain, at 6,638 feet, is nearby to the east. The two massive mountains soar over Ketchum and the Sun Valley resort, casting angular shadows that contrast the blue sky, white snow, and deep green forests in dazzling patterns. As Jon arrives in late fall 1997, the area bustles with the activity and excitement of the coming ski season. Snow has started to fall as he checks into one of the resort's employee dormitories that will be his home for the winter. He is tall, physically fit, coordinated and capable on a snowboard, gregarious and stimulated by his adventure. He is remarkably handsome in a craggy, flannel-shirt-by-the-wood-burning-stove kind of way, and he fits in and makes friends immediately. Neither he nor we have any idea he has just walked into the maelstrom of the worst addiction epidemic in modern history, just as it is gaining momentum.

Jon is assigned to operate the lift at the bottom of Seattle Ridge, a collection of bowls and slopes very near the top of Baldy. His lift sits at nearly 7,700 feet, and is a modern, high-speed quad (where each chair seats four people). He travels by lower chair lifts to his position each morning, taking along his snowboard so he can ride it down the mountain at the end of the day. He adorns his dorm room with posters of the ski area, cartoon characters, and blue jean companies.

My birthday arrives very soon afterwards, and Jon sends me a warm and funny card, writing that he is, "having a great time up here...I've been getting to know people and everything's looking good...Anyway, thank you for all your help and support. I truly couldn't and probably wouldn't have had this opportunity without you...Thanx for believing in me...Don't worry, I'm doing GREAT." On Christmas Eve, his phone call clearly indicates he is homesick. He is nineteen years old and has never spent a Christmas away from at least one of his parents, and he is wistful. However, as we talk, the shouts of young voices build in the background and I can hear people calling, "Jon, c'mon!" His spirits revive quickly, and he says, "Hey, I've got to go. We're all going out together."

In February, at the time of Jon's twentieth birthday, Evan and I visit and ski with him. The healthy outdoor work combined with glamour in a woodsy, casual way, and the opportunity to prove himself to others, seems perfect for Jon. He tells us he loves his life in Sun Valley. We learn of a thriving community that exists among the young employees of the various businesses in town. They are all quite poor compared to the rich clientele they serve, and they have developed a whole society based on barter. They trade amongst each other the services of the businesses where they work. If a person drives a taxi, he will give free rides to his friends in exchange for free food if the friends work at a restaurant. The most prized jobs that command the most favors are those manning the big ski lifts at River Run Plaza and Warm Springs Day Lodge. They serve as entry points to the whole mountain. Once past these points, a person has access to all of Baldy. Employees at these stations can let their friends pass through the turnstiles to ski or snowboard for free, thus earning a plethora of favors and paybacks.

In the evenings, the young employees rule the streets of Ketchum. Bars along Main Street and Washington Street between Second and Seventh Avenues are loud and crowded with young adults playing cards, talking, laughing, shouting, playing pool, and literally spilling into the streets. Among them there is the Demon, invisible, watching, taking notes. We know Jon drinks alcohol, probably nightly, but he seems so healthy, cheerful, and purposeful that we do not worry. He is showing up for work each morning, earning money, budgeting, apparently pleasing his employer, making friends, and already has a girlfriend. She is Krissy Lyons, a Seattle girl who is taking a break from her studies at the University of Washington. She has a wholesome smile, a good job in a Ketchum restaurant, and talks with obvious love and animation about her family. She is petite and blonde, having the physical characteristics that are Jon's lifelong preference. Both Jon and Krissy are star-struck by the celebrities they have seen and contacted in Sun Valley. Jon has placed Arnold Schwarzenegger and his wife Maria Shriver on his chairlift, given an impromptu snowboard lesson to Emilio Estevez, and Krissy has served Tom Hanks and his family at her restaurant. Both have been on the same dance floor as Demi Moore. It seems to us Jon is flourishing, becoming responsible, and leaving behind the alienation of the grunge/alternative persona.

The snow season is short in Sun Valley, lasting only about five months. When the winter ends, Jon and Krissy decide to come to Richland and move in together. They rent a small apartment, and both sign up for summer classes at the local community college. Jon gets a part-time job, and is smiling, clean-cut, and plays good-naturedly with Dorrie. At nearly the same time, Dorrie decides to change the spelling of her nickname to Dori, reasoning that her given name only has one letter "r" in it and Dori sounds cuter. Jon teases her, saying he is going to call her "Dor-eye." They attend a book signing I have in a local bookstore, clowning among the bookshelves and mugging for my camera. Dori will recall later this episode as one of the last times she will feel completely at ease with Jon, free to laugh joyfully. On Mother's Day, he gives me a beautiful, openly affectionate card, again thanking me for believing in him and signing it, "With Love from your Son and Friend."

In the summer of 1998, Jon enrolls in two classes at the community college, but completes only one. For the fall quarter, he enrolls in three classes, but completes only Sociology. Krissy is much more serious about her studies. She uses our home computer for much of her work, and many evenings we glimpse her in our home office, her small back bent forward and shoulders hunched slightly over her assignments. In mid-fall, Jon and Krissy decide to move to the Seattle area so she can re-enter the University of Washington. They move into her mother's spacious home in a northwest suburb of Seattle. Jon immediately gets a job in a sporting goods store mounting and adjusting bindings on skis and snowboards. The store is abuzz with ski and boarding talk, and filled with brochures from ski areas all over the west. The store owners are given new equipment and passes to try out the latest products, and sometimes they let employees try the new gear. Jon and Krissy often drive in the late afternoon to a ski area where they ride their snowboards for a discount rate from four to nine p.m. on lighted slopes. He looks clean-cut and cheerful. He comes home at Christmas, bending his lanky frame to the lowest branches of the Christmas tree to hang paper ornaments he made as a child. We meet at our cabin to ski together on a few winter weekends.

By spring 1999, Krissy's mother is anxious for them to move out. Jon and Krissy rent a small apartment in Seattle, along North University Avenue (famously known as "The Ave") in a region known as the "U District," near the University of Washington. Rents are high throughout the area, and the place they find perches precariously on the border between a neighborhood that might be called "funky" or collegiate, and one that is downright frightening. It sits just where the tattoo and T-shirt shops, Asian restaurants, espresso and bicycle stores, and sidewalk art displays of the U District give way to all-night convenience and liquor stores and street people. Krissy's father is not a bit happy with their place and calls me. I don't know the city as well as he, but I am concerned, and we both warn Krissy and Jon to be careful, stay in at night, and lock their door. Krissy registers for a full schedule of day classes. Jon gets a job driving a van, delivering supplies for a catering company, and setting up events. He is excited to cater a reception on the lawn of the spacious, waterfront property of Bill Gates, billionaire founder of the Microsoft Corporation.

One day, Jon and another friend from Richland go into downtown Seattle to attend a concert given by Matt, his former best friend from his school years. Matt is on his way to becoming a professional musician, has his own band, and is living in Seattle. Soon, he and Jon renew the friendship that had been severed in high school by Jon's drug use. Jon writes that the two old friends have "even come up with a few ideas for more of those silly movies. Things are wonderful."

In July, Jon, Krissy, Jeff, and Dori travel to meet Evan and I on an island off the Washington State coast where we rent an oceanfront cottage each summer. We catch Dungeness crab and other seafood and have big feasts on our sunny porch. Jon looks healthy and laughs and clowns with abandon. In August, I take Jeff, Jon, and Dori to visit my sister Pam and her family in their home in Atlanta, Georgia. As we arrive, I see Pam and her husband Fitz visibly gasp when they see Jeff and Jon. Here are full-grown, tall men with deep voices – not the boys they saw twelve years ago. Pam and Fitz are wonderfully hospitable and take us sightseeing throughout the region. We go to Centennial Park, where the 1996 Summer Olympics were held, and tour the Coca-Cola Factory and CNN Broadcasting Studios, where Jeff, Jon, and Dori join the audience and appear in a live television show. Pam and Fitz seem captivated by my boys-become-men, and Fitz disarms the burglar alarm in their home each evening so Jon can slip out to smoke cigarettes without setting off a siren.

In the fall of 1999, Jon gets a new job in Seattle driving a van and picking up donations for a charity. He also enrolls in a class at Shoreline Community College in a north Seattle suburb. In October, Krissy moves out and we are not sure of all the reasons. Besides her father's strong objections to the neighborhood, we surmise she wants to pursue her schoolwork intensively, probably with a partner or roommate who studies in the evening as she does. I later learn from her that Jon had been going out at night to talk and "hang out" with street people, ostensibly as research for his class. He has spent time with prostitutes and homeless people, as well as pimps and drug dealers patrolling their turfs. She objected, but he would not stop. She suspected drug use, and they argued. Later, Jon states Krissy left because, "she got sick of my lack of ambition." After she is gone, Jon cannot afford the rent on his own, so he asks me to come over at the end of the month to help him find a new place to live. I go to Seattle for the Halloween weekend, driving our large station wagon to help with moving. I stay at Jeff's apartment. On Sunday morning, I go to a coffee shop and buy the newspaper to look for affordable apartments or rooms to rent. I have a clunky, early model cell phone about as big as a shoebox, tethered to the floor of my car. I go outside several times to start the car and call Jon, but get no answer. Around noon, I drive to his apartment and am hit by one of the many shocks I will receive over the years as the mother of this impetuous, incautious, charming, air-headed, and ultimately tragic young man.

Evidence of a huge party spills out of the door, including more empty beer cans and liquor bottles than I probably saw in all my years in college put together. The stench of stale beer, cigarette smoke, and unwashed bodies assails me. Jon turns his eyes away from me, ashamed. Watching a parade of very hung-over people move off, I gradually realize he has new roommates who are planning to stay. They are street people – two very rough, rude, and tattered young men. I pull Jon aside. "What are you thinking!!??" I ask him. He admits he has let them move in to "help with rent," but the meaning is clear. They are either paying him in drugs or bringing in their share of the rent from dealing drugs. I give him a doleful "Mother look," and he dutifully gets in my car. We drive around to a few possible rental places, but all are either taken, located in ghettoes, or no one answers our inquiries. By early evening, I see the search is hopeless and I stop to riffle through the yellow pages of a phonebook in my car. I locate a complex of storage units just before it closes and pay for a unit. "You're coming home with me," I tell Jon in a tone he understands to mean he should not argue. We go back to his apartment and begin loading his belongings. I ask the roommates to help, but they just walk away. After several trips to the storage unit, it is midnight, and we have stashed all his things that won't fit in the unit into my station wagon. We grab some fast-food sandwiches and begin the nearly four-hour drive back to Richland. I will worry about retrieving his possessions later. For now, I have my boy and we will figure out a different future.

Back at home, Elliott, Evan, Jon, and I conclude the best immediate alternative is for Jon to return to Sun Valley. It seems like such a healthy choice, and his first year there was successful for him in so many ways. Hiring at the ski resort is over, but he knows many other service jobs likely are available in the town. Not being an employee of the resort, he won't be able to live in a dormitory. However, he is confident he knows enough guys who have returned to seasonal work in the town so that he can find room with some of them. As the days grow short and dark in mid-November, almost exactly two years after he first ventured to Sun Valley, Jon returns there. Almost immediately, his suppositions prove correct, and he has a job driving a taxi and a place to live with four other young men. We relax, not realizing what is to come. "We never know what lessons are in store for us," says Sue Klebold, whose son Dylan and another boy killed thirteen people and themselves at Columbine High School in Littleton, Colorado, in 1999. She continues presciently: "Especially when our prayers are answered and events seem to turn out the way we want."[27]

SIX

THE WRONG PLACE AT THE WRONG TIME

Addiction is the Biblical plague of our time, killing one American every five minutes. Drug deaths are now the leading cause of deaths in Americans between the ages of eighteen and forty-eight. In 2021, 294 people a day died from drug overdoses in the United States.[28] This death toll equates to more than a September 11, 2001, event every ten and one-quarter days! Other addicted people died of complications of drug use such as abscesses, infections, pancreatitis, liver disease, and suicide. In fact, according to the Centers for Disease Control (CDC), the number of drug-induced deaths may be underestimated because death certificates often list only the immediate cause of death, such as pneumonia, when the underlying cause may be drug abuse.[29]

Much has been said and written in recent years about the push made by pharmaceutical companies, physician and nursing associations, hospitals, and clinics to prescribe abundant pain-killing drugs in the late 1990s and early 2000s, bringing heartache, tragedy, and bewildered sorrow to communities large and small, affluent and poor. In the mid-1990s, opiate-derived drugs named hydrocodone, oxycodone, OxyContin,[30] Vicodin, Percocet and, to a lesser extent, Lortab literally flooded the market in pill form as medical providers sought to take pain out of the treatment experience. Hydrocodone is a direct opiate derivative synthesized from codeine, an alkaloid found in the poppy plant. (The poppy plant is the source of opium.) Oxycodone is another direct opiate derived from thebaine, an additional alkaloid found in the poppy plant. (Thebaine is used most often to tranquilize elephants and other very large animals.) Molecularly, oxycodone is similar to heroin, and heroin is a cooked and refined version of opium. In late 1995, OxyContin was licensed as a timed release (i.e., continual release) version of oxycodone. Hence the name Oxy-Contin. However, addicted people soon found ways to crush the pills to snort the drug or liquefy (i.e., dissolve) and inject the contents to create an immediate rush of euphoria. OxyContin pills became known as "peelers," because one could hold a pill in one's mouth to dissolve (peel off) the coating, and then crush it between the teeth and swallow it for a sublime high. Using this method to get high was known as getting "peeled back." When the pills weren't being called peelers, they were known on the street as "the devil's balls."

Vicodin and Lortab are combinations of hydrocodone and acetaminophen, an ordinary fever-reducer and mild pain reliever used in many over-the-counter medications. Percocet combines oxycodone with acetaminophen. Combining an opiate with acetaminophen in a pill makes it harder to liquefy and inject. All of these drugs are highly addictive, as is their basic source – opium. However, OxyContin pills, pure as they were, proved to be extraordinarily popular and addictive. As the company slogan of manufacturer Purdue Pharma said, OxyContin was "the one to start with and the one to stay with." Trenchantly, *New York Times* reporter Barry Meier stated, "In terms of narcotic firepower, OxyContin was a nuclear weapon."[31]

During the late 1990s and early 2000s, everything changed in terms of opiate pain prescriptions. In 1996, cancer doctors were the largest prescribers of OxyContin, but in 2000, family doctors were the largest single group of prescribers.[32] Physicians and nurses with prescribing credentials began routinely handing out these opiate-derived medications for a variety of sports injuries including strains, sprains, and broken bones; fibromyalgia; arthritis; post-surgical pain in even minimally invasive surgeries such as laparoscopies; and sometimes for dental work, headaches and vague, minor pain complaints. Enough pills to last for weeks were often prescribed, "just in case" the pain returned. It was not unusual for patients to leave a physician visit with sixty-to-one hundred pills, when only six-to-ten might be needed.[33]

Furthering the push toward more pain medications, in 1995, the

American Pain Society introduced a campaign entitled, "Pain is the Fifth Vital Sign," advocating that medical personnel assess and treat pain with the same importance as other vital signs. In 1998, the Joint Commission on Accreditation of Healthcare Organizations, which certifies health care organizations and hospitals in the United States, as well as the Veterans' Health Administration, adopted pain as, "the fifth vital sign." Hospitals then could be rated on how well they assessed and treated pain.

Many well-known companies participated in the lucrative market that blossomed with Purdue's success with OxyContin. A Johnson & Johnson™ subsidiary named Janssen Pharmaceuticals™ marketed Duragesic, a long-acting skin patch containing the powerful synthetic opioid called fentanyl, and opiate tablets called Nucynta. Another Johnson & Johnson subsidiary called Ortho-McNeil Pharmaceutical™ sold Tylox, a painkiller containing oxycodone and acetaminophen. Johnson & Johnson even bought Tasmanian Alkaloids (now Extractas Bioscience), a large poppy farm in Australia and formed Noramco™ to import and process opium alkaloids into drug materials for other manufacturers.[34] A DuPont™ subsidiary known as Endo International™ marketed Percocet and a closely related drug Percodan, while an Abbott Laboratories' subsidiary Knoll Laboratory™ made Vicodin. Mallinkrodt Pharmaceuticals™ manufactured generic oxycodone pills in such copious amounts that it out-sold Purdue during 2008. Cephalon™ marketed an opiate lozenge called Actiq (street nickname perc-a-pop), and an effervescent dissolving tablet named Fentora. Perhaps most potent of all in terms of each dose, Insys Therapeutics™ marketed a sublingual fentanyl spray called Subsys.

After the U.S. Food & Drug Administration (FDA) approved OxyContin in late December 1995, its manufacturer Purdue Pharma sponsored more than 20,000 pain-related programs promoting its product. Purdue said OxyContin produced addiction in less than one percent of people who took it and that pain canceled out any euphoria from the drug.[35] As Barry Meier chronicled Purdue's rise from obscurity because of OxyContin sales, "vast opportunities beckoned. Medical and public awareness of untreated pain had been kindled, the perception of narcotics risk had been minimized, and regulatory initiatives had been slowed...Quickly, sales of the new painkiller boomed, bringing record profits to Purdue and setting the small drug maker on the path to realizing its dream of becoming a pharmaceutical powerhouse."[36] By 1999, a full seventy-five percent of Purdue's sales force was working to promote OxyContin. Bonuses for individual salespersons sometimes exceeded $100,000 per year.[4][37] Overall, the bonuses Purdue paid to sales representatives increased forty-fold between 1996 and 2001. According to Sam Quinones, *Los Angeles Times* reporter who wrote *Dreamland*, a definitive book on this addiction epidemic, Purdue paid its sales representatives the highest bonuses "ever recorded in the industry."[38]

In the meantime, some people liked the opiate pills not just for their pain-relieving properties, but for their generalized mellow-to-euphoric effects, and continued taking the full amount prescribed. By the time their liberal prescriptions ran out, these people were semi- or completely addicted and sought more. They returned to their doctors with murky or unspecified complaints, and, if successful in obtaining more pills, became thoroughly addicted. Other people stopped taking their prescribed pills after a few days and simply stored the remainder in their medicine cabinets, often for years. This practice gave rise to a phenomenon known in the addiction community as "mirror-diving," wherein people sorted through the medicine cabinets of their friends, parents, grandparents, and other acquaintances, and stole the pain pills under the pretext of needing to use the bathroom. Usually, because the unused medicines had been forgotten by the persons for whom they were prescribed, they were never missed.

When Jon arrives back in Sun Valley in late November 1999, he walks straight into the teeth of conditions that will presage the worst addiction epidemic in American history. We have no idea of the gathering storm. The town is awash in pain pills. He finds a thriving market among the young people, amply supplied by the local physicians treating the many sports injuries incurred by the impetuous, if only partially skilled, winter workers in the area. Pain pills become an

---

[4] $100,000 in 1999 is equivalent to $170,000 in 2022.

integral part of the barter economy among the young employee crowd. It is precisely the time, according to Sam Quinones, that "A revolution in medical thoughts and practice was underway...[and] a culture of aggressive opiate use"[39] emerged. Barry Meier states it was at this same time that "The boundary lines between 'severe' pain and 'moderate' pain, 'chronic' pain and 'acute' pain, blurred and became lost. A drug once reserved as a last line of treatment for the most severe pain cases was promoted as a treatment to be used on medicine's front lines for a wide range of general and transient pain problems...setting the stage for the disaster that followed."[40]

A few years later, a 2004 federal government survey finds the average age of a pain pill abuser is twenty-two. Jon will soon to be twenty-two when he arrives back in Sun Valley in the fall of 1999. He probably has never stopped smoking marijuana, but not to excess since high school. He has a high tolerance for alcohol and jokes he can drink until companions get sick or pass out under the table. Sometimes, he says, he would drink a fifth of whiskey and, "I could still function and remember the night...I'd be fine. And I almost never experienced a hangover." Many years later, we will learn that an important portent of alcoholism and addiction is the physical ability to drink or use drugs to a copious extent. Jon later writes, "I knew how to drink before my second time in Sun Valley, but that was where I perfected the art. We partied all night. Every night. Girls. So many girls. Our place was the party spot every night after the bars closed."

In addition to having high tolerances, many people who become alcoholics have lower levels of endorphins (the endogenous chemicals responsible for most of our pleasurable feelings), even before they become addicted. For these people, their genetic predispositions mean drinking alcohol dramatically raises their endorphin levels, whereas drinking raises the endorphin levels of other people only slightly. Still other studies show people who develop addictions to alcohol or drugs often have fewer dopamine D_2 receptors in their brains, causing them to need more stimulation to feel gratified. They are more prone to impulsivity and compulsivity. In addition, several genes are known to be associated with addiction. The unfortunate people, Jon among them, whose endorphins respond strongly, or who have a shortage of dopamine D_2 receptors, or those who are born with a certain genetic heritage, literally fall in love with alcohol (and/or drugs).[41] Although I am unaware of the extraordinary risks posed as my son's body betrays him, the Demon, who spends a good deal of time in Sun Valley, knows these things very well.

Soon, Jon is in the midst of a group of young people who dare each other to new heights and feats on their snowboards, often boarding off trail or outside the boundaries of the ski area. They climb off the regular ski runs to find pockets of deep powder snow and build jumps and ramps. They fling themselves off these makeshift, often uneven, inclines to get air and attempt flips and elaborate turns. Even worse conditions arise when they return to a jump after a day or more when night freezing has been followed by sun and then more freezing, and the jump has hardened to the consistency of concrete. Later, Jon describes the innocence they felt: Normal teenagers and young people just past their teens, he writes, "are natural thrill-seekers....They are constantly busy pushing norms and breaking rules...sometimes laws...They are known to risk life and limb in a death defying stunt for bravado and bragging rights, daring each other into danger, [but] it's ok tho...[they] are indestructible...They have to push boundaries and overstep lines... all humans at that stage have the...[impetuous] years of adjusting...to a world so vast and unending, so alive and beating, so complex, confusing and exciting...[Later in life] the wildness goes away on its own and people adjust into adulthood."

Within a few weeks in Sun Valley, Jon sprains his shoulder and is prescribed Vicodin at a local clinic. He likes it. Further in the season, he breaks two ribs and receives Percocet. He later recalls this time period as, "when my love affair with opiate pain pills began. I remember breaking some ribs and not being that bummed out about being off the mountain for a month because I was too excited about getting some drugs from the doctor. That's about the time I learned to manipulate doctors. I loved pills in Sun Valley as well as alcohol and all the coke we were doing." Dr. Judith Grisel, a behavioral neuroscientist in recovery from addiction, says quite simply that "the tale of opiate users is one of such love and such great suffering as to make *Romeo and Juliet* seem like a middle-school melodrama. This class of drugs delivers heartbreak like no other, initially providing a sense of security and well-being."[42] For Jon, the suffering and heartbreak will come later.

That winter, Jon sends photos of himself posing with a group of laughing young people clowning in front of gorgeous winter scenery, and other photos of himself flying backwards through the air on his snowboard. Through barters in town, he tries OxyContin in 2000. It produces warmth, relaxation, and melts away every care and tension. By that time, sales of this drug by Purdue Pharma have reached one billion dollars per year, with eighty percent of the company's annual revenue coming from it.

At the end of the winter season, he decides to stay in Sun Valley for the summer. By now, he is working as a barista in an espresso shop. "Everything's good here in Idaho," he writes to me. "I have been thinking about you...and loved that last batch of stuff you sent me... Give my love to Evan and Dori. I miss ya." He travels home for Jeff's graduation from the University of Washington in June, and poses with big grins with our family. Jeff will be going to work in a bank, and Jon teases him about his "preppy," buttoned-down lifestyle.

In July, Dori and one of her friends and I drive to Sun Valley to visit Jon. We find him living in a tent in a campsite a few miles outside of town. The trunk of his car is filled with books by American masters including Hemingway, John Steinbeck, F. Scott Fitzgerald, and Upton Sinclair. He has always wanted to live "off the grid" and insists he likes this natural life, but I suspect he lives in a tent because he can't afford to live indoors without his roommates who have returned to their homes for the summer. We stay at a condominium owned by friends of mine, and he lodges with us there, relishing the hot shower, my home cooking, and a fluffy bed. He performs calisthenics on the floor and amuses us by chuckling that he must keep up his muscle tone "for the ladies — haha." He and I sit up having a great discussion about the books he is reading, as I had loved many of them in college and graduate school. Conversations like this one with Jon are delightful, as his intellect is sharp, and he interjects insights that always surprise me. The next day, he makes substantial tips at work and buys a cell phone. He comes back to the condo and activates it, standing on the deck with his long arm stretched out to test the signal in various directions. He looks healthy, and his grin is wide and mischievous. I don't want to leave. A month later, he loses the phone when it falls overboard during a canoe trip on Redfish Lake with friends. I suspect substantial beer drinking and pill consumption contribute to the cell phone's fate in the lake.

Jon comes home for an end-of-summer visit to wakeboard in the Columbia River with all of us. He is strong, capable, and loves to show off, competing with Jeff and Dori as he masters swoops and sharp cuts close to the foamy water. He takes a photo of Jeff climbing back into the boat after his turn on the wakeboard, dripping wet and smiling, the sun glinting on the ultramarine Columbia. Jon loves that photo and keeps it with him the rest of his life. Back in Sun Valley, it's getting cold and he doesn't have the money to rent a place to live. I still think Sun Valley is a good, healthy place for him, so in September, I send him funds to get into an apartment with three other guys. "Hello from heaven!" he writes in October. "I just got settled into my apartment and couldn't possibly be having a better time...I wanted to thank you again for your help and support...I love you." Soon he works himself up to a waiter/server job in an upscale restaurant and can't get time off to come home for Christmas. By this time, he has a new girlfriend. She is Diane Jackson, a petite blonde from Wisconsin. They have their special times together, but generally spend lots of time with a group of young people. A friend from Richland who visits Sun Valley early in the winter observes Jon inside a raucous tavern, playing cards at a table, cigarette hanging out of his mouth, confident and very much at home in his environment.

At Jon's February birthday in 2001, we visit Sun Valley. One day on the mountain, he wants to show us his skill in getting air. On his snowboard, he sails off a trail, flies over our heads, and lands perfectly in front of us while maintaining his balance. At the same time, a family with a young child has stopped right next to us and views his landing as dangerous. The mother in this family calls out to a ski patroller who is nearby, and the patrol professional moves toward Jon to cite him for unsafe behavior. Jon points his snowboard straight into the trees and takes off downhill at astonishing speed, the patroller right behind him. Jon's bright yellow ski jacket flashes once and then disappears. Evan and I look at each other with resignation. "This is going to be embarrassing for Jon," Evan tells me, "so when we get to the bottom and he is caught let's stand back and not make it worse for him." I agree. After skiing to the bottom of the mountain, however, we don't find the scene that we expected. Instead, we find the ski patroller looking around with frustration, having lost Jon. His downhill skills and coordination were no match for Jon. We should not smile, but we do.

The next day, Jon takes Evan up the mountain to a special place where he and his friends have built a jump. Eager to impress Evan, Jon climbs to the slope above the jump and sails off on his snowboard, flying over Evan's head. However, the worst possible freeze-thaw-freeze conditions have ensued in the previous two days. Jon lands on hard-packed ice, breaking a rib. Painfully and carefully, he and Evan make their way down to a lodge to meet me. Evan wants to take Jon to the hospital, but Jon won't hear of it. He approaches a young employee whom he knows, they exchange brief conversation, and she reaches into her purse and hands Jon some pills, which he immediately swallows. By the time I arrive, he is mellow and not feeling any pain. Broken ribs can't be set, he says, so he won't bother with treatment. He says he will simply "take it easy" for a few weeks.

Later in the visit, we meet some of Jon's friends and remark on the exhilaration of skiing down beautiful Baldy with powder snow flying up around our legs. "Yeah, and it's even better with a line of cocaine up your nose," quips the friend. I shoot Jon a look of alarm, but he grins and spreads his hands flat, palms down, moving them back and forth as if to say, "pay no attention." Apparently, all the clues we need are right there for us, but we do not recognize them. We don't know about the prevalence of the pills and other drugs in town, or the extent of Jon's involvement. Of course, we don't know that in 2016, a Columbia University study will find that, among young adults aged eighteen to twenty-five, the odds of developing a prescription opioid disorder rose thirty-seven percent among those who were non-medical users between 2002-2014.[43] Many years after leaving Sun Valley, Jon confesses that one night there he took sixty Vicodin, and, "felt nothing but great...I didn't even get a stomach ache." When I tell my own doctor about this event, he is astonished Jon did not collapse or precipitate liver failure due to the large amount of acetaminophen in the pills.

We also do not know Jon and his friends organize "drug runs" to larger cities to buy marijuana in bulk and wield their own brand of justice in the world of buying and selling. "Good pot," as he later writes, cost between 300-400 dollars per ounce in Sun Valley. "It was hard to come by and always in high demand." On one occasion, one of his roommates named Jerrod was traveling to Seattle when Jon and other friends raised money to send with him to buy four ounces at a bargain price. Jon was planning to divide and sell his share in Sun Valley. However, on the way back to Sun Valley, Jerrod became snow-bound in Boise and spent the night with an acquaintance there. When he arrived back in Sun Valley, some of the marijuana was missing. Angry, Jon gathered up the friends who had contributed to the pot fund and drove to Boise. Continuing the story, he writes that when they reached the house where Jerrod had spent the night, "Without any hesitation or discussion we hopped out of the small car and straight up the front steps...I pounded on the door. Right as he [the occupant] began opening the door I pushed my way past him followed by my friends. 'You stole from the wrong people,' I told him. I could see in his eyes that he was truly scared." Some of the friends wanted to beat the man, but Jon, the biggest one present, would not allow it. They decided that each of the Sun Valley friends would take a possession of his choice from the frightened man. Jon took a guitar and amp, Jerrod took a snowboard, another of the guys took an eight-track mixing board, and the fourth friend, "just kept staring at this comically oversized beanbag chair. An hour later we were climbing the frozen twisting pass in the dark packed into a two-door compact with all of this gear and the four of us. The trunk hatch was open as far as it could go and out of the back of this car stuck a ridiculously oversized beanbag chair." Reading the story at a drug treatment center with Jon years later, I wonder at many things – my own naiveté, the seriousness of Jon's conduct, and the huge discrepancy between his actions and his realization of their import.

Jon travels back to Richland in June 2001, to attend Dori's high school graduation. He and Jeff surround her with huge smiles, each with an arm around her. I recruit Jon and Evan as card dealers at the all-night party parents organize to keep the graduates from more dangerous activities on their big, exciting night. Jon loves this assignment. Wearing a Hawaiian shirt and assuming a semi-serious look, he manages his card table by welcoming everyone and letting each graduate win at least once. He relishes all the food and seems as happy and excited as he was at birthday parties when he was very young. The hit songs of 1983, the birth year of most of the graduates, blare from the disc player – *Every Breath You Take*[44] by the Police, *Billie Jean*[45] by Michael Jackson, and *Flashdance*[46] by Irene Cara.

Jon extends his visit and drives to Seattle with me to visit Jeff for two days. We walk around Gasworks Park and Seward Park and visit the newly opened Experience Music Project. This interactive museum of popular culture has many exhibits featuring iconic Seattle musicians, including Jimi Hendrix and Kurt Cobain. Jon and Jeff reminisce about the grunge movement and other follies of their high school years. We go to dinner at a beautiful restaurant on Puget Sound. On this June night, darkness doesn't come until nearly ten p.m. We pose for pictures on the deck with the Seattle cityscape and a dark blue and pink streaked sky behind us. My sons are so impossibly handsome. I am so blessed. My heart is so full.

In late August, Dori and I drive to Sun Valley to visit Jon and Diane. Definitely a couple, they seem quite happy together. Both work as servers in different restaurants. The Ketchum air smells so fresh and wonderful I keep running to open windows and doors wherever we go, just to inhale it. In late fall, Jon tells us he and Diane have broken up, he has quit his job, and he will be coming home for good. We haven't yet discussed his future plans when he shows up at our front door to surprise me on my birthday. His left arm isn't in the sleeve of his jacket, and when I glance at it, his look turns sheepish. He has broken a bone in his hand in a fight with a guy who was trying to date Diane. The relationship is tenuous at this point – they might be getting back together. He doesn't know.

Later, he will confess he came home because, "everything had gotten too wild" with the pills, alcohol, and cocaine in Sun Valley. "I did ridiculous amounts of that," stuff, he says. "I was over the edge... [but] the coke was not hard to quit." He spends much of December with us, smiling broadly in every Christmas photo. However, he recalled later that "Nothing seemed very fun. My family was happy to have me around and we did festive holiday things but still, I couldn't seem to enjoy anything. I thought it was over a girl I left in Sun Valley, but looking back I see that it was probably withdrawal from all the drugs and alcohol I left behind. At the time I didn't know the symptoms." At the same time, none of us know the Drug Abuse Warning Network, which tabulates hospital emergency room reports of drug overdose cases, has noted that incidents involving painkillers containing oxycodone have jumped 350 percent between 1994 and 2001.[47] Prescriptions for Oxycontin have risen from approximately 300,000 in 1996, to six million in 2001.

During the December holidays, Jon makes several phone calls to Diane and decides to go back to Sun Valley. He plans to leave after our family spends two days following Christmas at our cabin, skiing, snowboarding, and snowshoeing. Jon and Dori ride with Jeff in his compact car, which is not equipped to negotiate the steep driveway of our cabin. They park up on a county road and trek down to the cabin carrying their duffel bags. After dinner, we watch silly movies and go to bed.

The next morning, we all tramp up the cabin hill to begin our ski day. First with disbelief, and then with horror, we look at Jeff's small red car, its windows smashed in, its dashboard electronics ripped out, and skis and other gear strewn out in the snow. The car has been robbed, with the snowboards and accessories taken, but the skis left nearby. Our hearts beat fast as we call the county sheriff. When he arrives, he tells us that since only cool items like snowboards and the dashboard music system have been taken, the crime probably has been done by young people. There is almost no chance of the belongings being found and returned, he says. Our two days of planned activities are ruined, so we pack up all our gear, food, and dogs and head home. It only makes sense for Jon to return right away to Sun Valley and secure a new job and housing. He leaves us two days earlier than planned, surprising Diane who greets him joyously. That night, a baby is conceived. Later, when I learn of this occurrence, I think of the old saying: "A coincidence is God's way of remaining anonymous."

Within a few days, we receive word Jon has been hired by the Sun Valley Resort to staff a snack bar/restaurant at the base of Baldy, and has secured a room in an employee dormitory. The resort has been receiving complaints about the raucous behavior of young employees in the bars and other gathering places in town. Anxious to please the well-to-do guests and the increasing crowd of affluent retirees building homes in the area, the resort is placing restraints on noisy and drunken behavior where it can. It has a strict policy against drinking parties in the employee dormitories. During January 2002, I receive a late-night phone call from Jon. He and Diane are in a motel in Pocatello, in eastern Idaho. He has been fired from his job and summarily evicted from the employee dormitory for hosting a loud party in his room. They are on their way to Diane's parents' home in Wisconsin. They don't know their plans – they just needed to leave Sun Valley very quickly. They travel on, two days later reaching the small town near Madison where Diane was raised, and settling in to contemplate future choices. Very quickly, they both get serving jobs at a mid-priced restaurant. Although I know nothing about his habit, Jon has become accustomed to a ready supply of pain pills in Sun Valley.

Jon age 6, hands on railing, with Jeff

Jon age 8, Cub Scout

Jon age 9, far right, with Mom, Jeff and Dorrie

Jon age 11, school football

Jon far left, age 13, with mother, Jeff and Dorrie

Jon age 18, pretend arm wrestling with Dorrie

Jon, age 19, working at SunValley ski lift

Jon, age 20, clowning with Dori

Jon, age 21, getting air in Sun Valley

Jon age 21, in Sun Valley

Jon, far right, age 22, with Jeff and Dori

Jon, center, age 23, clowning with Jeff, Dori, Brett and June

Jon, age 23, climbing mountain with snowboard in SunValley

Jon, far right, age 23, with Mom and Jeff

Jon, left, age 23, with Jeff and Dori

Jon, left, age 23, with Mom and Jeff

SEVEN

FATHERHOOD

S omehow in Madison, Jon manages to connect quickly with people who can supply him with his needs and desires for opiate pills. Drug-seeking people find each other, whether it's a sixth sense, a subtle perception, or a meta-sensory nexus that is inexplicable to the non-addicted. Was Jon addicted at this time? Probably yes, but not strongly. He most likely would have been able to give up the pain pills, albeit not without some discomfort. However, he had no motivation to stop. The pills made time pass quickly on the job, he told me later. They made him cheerful and seemed to be harmless. He thought he could stop any time he wanted.

After three months in Madison, Jon and Diane decide to return to the Northwest. Seeing a chance to get all our children together, Evan and I plan a fun Mother's Day weekend in Seattle. We rent a suite with kitchen in a high-rise overlooking Lake Union, and everyone manages to come except Brett. The city puts on a most beautiful display of sun and spring weather for us. Evan and I shop the famous Pike Street Market for fresh Dungeness crab, shrimp, scallops, and other seafood. We bring these treasures, along with salad greens and warm sourdough bread, back to our suite and begin preparing a feast. The young people joke and toast each other and watch seaplanes land just below us in Lake Union. Jeff and Jon turn Dori upside down on the floor while she kicks and protests loudly and playfully. Fulfilled and humbled by our blessings, Evan and I watch and listen, taking in every silly joke to repeat to ourselves later as we relive the banter. The evening seems glorious. We do not know that a United States Drug Enforcement Agency (DEA) study has just found that OxyContin was either definitely or very likely involved in nearly half of drug overdose deaths examined in the past year.[48]

Jon and Diane are staying at Jeff's condominium. Later that night, Jeff overhears a whispered discussion. Diane tells Jon she is pregnant. They quickly decide settling in Richland will bring many advantages of stability and help with the baby. The next day, at a festive lunch in a waterfront downtown restaurant, they say nothing about their news. As we part ways, I remind them once again that they need to replace their dangerous, nearly bald tires. Back in Richland a few days later, they ask me to meet them. They have some good news, they tell me. I arrive to find them sitting in the sun on the hood of their little car, smiling, one of Jon's long legs dangling down. I'm positive they have gotten new tires and say so. Mischievously, Jon's grin just gets wider. "You're going to be a grandmother!" he says. I literally leap for joy, rushing at them with a huge hug and congratulations. The news isn't just good, it is over-the-top fabulous!

Immediately, we begin discussing plans. They want to rent a small house with a yard, and Jon will need a steady job. A new restaurant, the Spillway Bistro, will be opening soon, the most expensive and lavish in Richland. Jon is hired right away, with his experience in an upscale restaurant in Sun Valley, his perfect diction, and his handsome charm. He helps open the restaurant. Its location along a sunny curve of the Columbia River is enchanting, and he works the tables inside under the high beamed ceiling and outside under colorful umbrellas. He does well, often holding the sales records for nights, weeks, and even months. He speaks knowledgeably about the wines, engages customers in friendly banter, and knows when and how to end a conversation. In July, Jon and Diane visit Evan and me in the cottage that we rent for a week every summer on an island off the Washington coast. Jon relishes the adventure of pulling up crab traps, reaching in to grasp the angry, flailing crustaceans, and measuring them to make sure they are sufficiently large to keep. He takes slow, gentle walks with Diane along the shoreline, and in the evening, sits silhouetted against the setting sun in chairs facing Evan at water's edge. He confesses to Evan he doesn't feel prepared for fatherhood. He is twenty-four and has no real idea how to care for a baby or deal with the finality of the loss of his carefree youth. Evan tells him no one really feels prepared, but the baby will teach him everything he needs to know. In August, Jon and Diane rent a four-room bungalow. Even though it is late in the season, Jon plants vegetables and flowers and carefully tends the dry and dead spots in the lawn.

In the last week of September, their son Edward Jon is born. During labor, Jon goes outside for several cigarette breaks. He tells me later pain pills are in his pocket, and he swallows some. Still very apprehensive about becoming a father, he is calmed by the pills. However, joy, wonder, and abounding love take over when Eddie is born. Jon says later, "The minute he [Eddie] opened his eyes I knew I had a whole new purpose in life, maybe for the first time."

Jon and Diane experience parenthood in typical fashion. They are sleep-deprived and awkward, but happy. Jon is surprised at the enormous, literally indescribable rush of love he feels for his baby. The tiny creature, helpless yet expressive, warm, responsive to touch, completely lacking in pretense, and early to smile and make eye contact, absolutely captivates Jon. He loves this boy with his whole soul, he tells me. He holds and gazes at him endlessly. He writes later, "I worked hard and supported us. Everything had come together. I hardly drank...I was happy, content. I can honestly say, boy I've had some good times in my life, really good. But those days laying on the floor with my baby boy lazily changing diapers and coming home to my own family – those were the happiest days of my life."

However, because Jon is a night worker with shifts usually from four-to-eleven p.m. or later on weekends, much of the child care falls to Diane during the evenings when it is virtually impossible to be out and about with a baby. She has no women friends in Richland, and winter is coming on. By Christmas, obvious tensions have grown between them. By this time, Purdue Pharma is selling nearly 30 million dollars worth of OxyContin every week![49]

Pressures and divisions in a relationship are hard to dissect. No one can judge except the two people involved, and, after things fray apart, their recollections are tainted with sadness and blame. We will never know all the variables and problems that drive Jon and Diane apart. Jon, a very social creature, sometimes goes out for drinks after work with co-workers. How often? I don't know. How much does he drink, and is drinking his primary motivation? How many pain pills and other party drugs are shared at some of these gatherings? How late does he come home and how long does he sleep in the mornings after? Does he participate in baby care after waking up or only doze on the sofa with the baby? In late spring, Diane decides to go home to Wisconsin with Eddie, and Jon encourages the visit. He gives her spending money for the trip, and we tell her to enjoy herself and recharge her spirits, as many new mothers need and take such respite. The last night before she leaves, the young family comes to our house for dinner. Eddie, nearly nine months old, is trying to take his first jolting, headlong steps while hanging onto furniture. Jon kneels on the carpeted floor with him, reaching out his long arms, smiling, urging him to "walk to Daddy." We watch, sensing that the barrenness Jon will feel during the coming separation is just dawning on him.

Soon after Diane arrives in Wisconsin, she rents an apartment and secures a job. In July, Jon travels there to see her and Eddie. The visit is cordial and somewhat welcoming, but strained. Jon tries to convince her to come back to Richland, but she says she needs more time. In August, she informs him she is not coming back. Jon would write later of his reaction: "I'd lost my whole world. The grief was so overwhelming that I didn't know how I'd go on. I wasn't living for anything. My happy little family had left me all alone. I lost my sense of purpose and I was literally crushed and heartbroken. I resumed my old doctor shopping." He also finds an old friend who had been crippled in a motorcycle collision and "he kept the pain pills comin'. I was lost, lost." The Demon is now more than a shadowy apparition in Jon's life – he casts more than a casual scaly eye towards my son. The friend from the motorcycle accident would be dead of his own addiction several years later.

Jon files legal pleadings for custody of Eddie, and Diane files for a change of venue to place the court supervising their parenting plans in Wisconsin. To our surprise, the local judge grants the change of venue, and all decisions regarding Eddie move nearly 2,000 miles away. Jon's car hurtles into our driveway. He looks stricken, ill, and dazed as he sits down on our front porch, head bowed in one hand, cigarette in the other hand. I rub the top and back of his shoulders. He is sobbing and suffering as I have never seen him before. We cannot know the full extent of the pain to come, but a dark dread pervades this summer morning.

Jon continues working his job at the Spillway and taking pain pills, although I do not know about the pills. Writing later, he points to this time as important in his slide into true addiction. "Opiate pain drugs. Wow. Especially with a beer or two. I did them off and on for years never quite getting all the way addicted...After Diane took Eddie...I used pills more frequently. The thing about opiates is they...would lift me up. Fill up my spirit. I truly fell in love [with the pills]. They had my mind but they also had my soul." It is early 2004, the same year that the U.S. Government Accountability Office (GAO), a federal watchdog agency, publishes its first report on, "OxyContin Abuse and Diversion."[50] Focused on our daily working lives, we are unaware of the report and of Jon's growing dependence.

Over the winter, he spends lots of time with us and seems to adjust reasonably well to the discovery and waiting periods involved in Eddie's legal case. Evan and I sometimes go to dinner at the Spillway Bistro and delight in watching Jon's smooth charm, his easy manner with customers, his megawatt smile, and the deft coordination of his long, trim body maneuvering and bending among the tables. During this period, he spends some of his time alone at his home designing inventions, making detailed drawings, and registering them with a notary public. He is paying child support to Diane regularly, as ordered under a temporary judgment.

In late winter, Jon begins seeing a sweet single mother named Lisa Norton, whose son is about two years older than Eddie. In the spring, he plants a garden in the yard of his rented home, builds a beautiful set of shelves in the main bedroom closet, and fixes up other areas. When a planned trip for Eddie to visit Richland is suddenly cancelled, I drive to his house to comfort him, but he is abnormally accepting and not even as upset as I am. *Why does no one tell me he has taken more pills? Why don't I see it??*

The court-ordered mediation to determine Eddie's physical custody takes place in June 2004, and the court finds both parents to be loving and responsible. Despite the fact that they live 2,000 miles apart, a back-and-forth custody arrangement is ordered wherein Eddie will live with Diane for two months, then Jon for one month, on an ongoing, repeating basis. The court is unconcerned with the financial aspects of making the agreement work. Both parties are to split the costs and manage the logistics. I am vacationing with Evan on the island off the Washington coast, the same place where, two years earlier, we had hosted the very pregnant, very much in love Diane and Jon. When Jon calls me with the news, I stand far out on the beach where phone reception is best and begin screaming. I am crying, congratulating him, twisting my back against the wind to hear him better, and already wondering how the new arrangement will possibly work. That night, Evan and I sit on our porch watching the sunset and quietly discuss the news. It's probably physically and financially impossible to implement the order, we agree, but it represents an important victory in the Wisconsin court's recognition of Jon's rights. At least some form of back-and-forth probably can be arranged, even if not as often as the court has stipulated. This development seems to bode well for the future.

Eddie's first custodial visit to Richland occurs quickly. I care for him while Jon goes to work in the evenings, and we all delight in watching him play with our dogs, wade in a neighborhood pool, play with plastic cups and dishes, and move around the magnetic letters on the refrigerator. We especially love seeing Jon's enchanted face as he lifts and holds his little boy. Father and son spend much of their daytime hours at the Columbia River shoreline, throwing stones, floating sticks, building small sand dikes, and catching minnows.

Soon after Eddie leaves, however, important things begin to go wrong. The Spillway Bistro is experiencing financial difficulties, and the manager has begun some slippery bookkeeping. For one thing, he has been withholding Jon's child support funds from his paychecks, but not paying it to the Wisconsin state agency responsible for providing it to Diane. In late summer, Jon receives a notice of delinquency from Wisconsin and is dumbfounded. This development jeopardizes scheduled visitations and places the whole shared custody arrangement in limbo.

Jon has been taking a lot of pain pills and his emotional balance is precarious. He would recount later that "I thought I was doing okay but what I didn't see through all that fog was that a freight train was coming and I was standing on the tracks. I remember where I was when it hit me. I was in Eddie's empty room. It had been just over a year since he'd been gone. I've never in my life felt pain so powerful, so overwhelming and so devastating. I realized that I was completely hollowed out inside. A year's worth of undealt-with grief had eaten my heart, my guts and my soul. I decided right then and there to bite the bullet and move 2,000 miles away to Madison. But by that time I was hopelessly addicted to pain drugs – mostly OxyContin."

Elliott sends Jon to Wisconsin in October to consult with a local attorney. He obtains fifty-fifty physical custody there. The Spillway Bistro is closing, and Jon is given fantastic recommendations to take with him to future jobs. I help him hold a garage sale at his house and, even though the weather is turning cold, customers come, and he does well. When Elliott contacts me to tell me Jon cannot pay his final electrical bill and has asked for funds, I am speechless. Just seven months earlier, I had distributed to my three children a few thousand dollars each from the final settlement of my mother's estate. Jeff had saved his, Dori had used hers to pay bills, and Jon's was gone! With the money he had made at the restaurant up until late fall, and profits from selling a used car I had given him, he should not be broke. Where has the money gone?

His departure is scheduled for the last week of November, and for about a week, I do not see him. No one does. The blinds of his house are shut tight. Finally, early one morning, he calls and asks me to go for a walk. I go to his house, and we start out in the late November chill. He has been sick for a week, he says, with severe chills, fever, vomiting, diarrhea, itching, and other really nasty symptoms. Tentatively, glancing at me sideways as we walk, he tells me, "I took some pills because I was sad about Eddie. I guess I took too many and I got addicted." The word hangs in the damp, darkish air. I breathe in sharply, my heart wrenching over and downward into a contorted position that will become sickeningly familiar to me over the ensuing years. It feels like a lopsided pita pocket, folded over impossibly on itself, painful, thudding into an unnatural position. Yet, the word is only a verb – addicted. It is not a noun – he did not say he *was an addict*. He asks if I will help him find a doctor who will treat him. "Of course," I say, keeping my voice steady although I know nothing about this subject. "Let's get busy." We head back to his house and tear out a phone book. Although my hands are shaking, I call several physicians. Many are just too booked, but I keep calling until, amazingly, I get three appointments. I tell Jon to postpone picking up his rented moving truck, as we will need a few days to work on this problem. He does so, and we set a new date for him to leave in early December, on my birthday.

We then start a day-long trek that will begin my education into the stigma, shunning, and utter lack of good alternatives for people who have become addicted. We go to the first waiting room, where the receptionist casts down her eyes and refuses to look at us after Jon states the reason for his visit. The doctor cannot help, he says when we finally see him. He knows of no treatments and has no advice. The experience at the second doctor's office is much the same. By this point, I think we better go on the internet and call some addiction help lines or treatment centers. One phone line suggests methadone, a maintenance drug that allows addicted people to function without the symptoms of withdrawal sickness or cravings for more of the opiate pills. That's all I know. I have so much to learn. However, at that moment, the suggestion sounds good.

We arrive at the third doctor's office, a group practice with a sound reputation and a cheerful, welcoming waiting room. The doctor we see is young and idealistic. Jon tells his story and his symptoms and asks for help. Leaning forward, concerned, anxious to help, the young doctor says he has never worked with an addicted patient before and will consult with his partners. It's getting late in the afternoon. Jon asks for a quick decision, and we leave. Soon the phone rings. The family practice cannot help us, a nurse tells us, and also doesn't want to get a reputation as a place where addicted people go. Helping addicted people would change the practice in ways that the partners don't want, she says flatly. Thus completes the first day – we experience for ourselves the prevailing view of the medical profession that addicted people are dirty and disgusting, not deserving of treatment as patients suffering a debilitating illness.

It's almost evening, and it's already dark. Jon tells me he will have to use pain pills that night, although he doesn't want to do so. There it is. I stare at the looming dread I will face so many times later. The thought of him putting more poison in his body buckles my knees. *I am his mother* but I cannot fix the problem. A parent's job is to help and protect, and I have failed to help him. I am powerless and I am scared. The Demon begins to uncoil his long, repulsive body. His interest is piqued. A hungry drop of saliva slides off his blistered tongue.

The next day, I make endless calls and finally learn of a methadone clinic in Yakima, about seventy-five miles away from Richland. It's part of a national chain, and even has a clinic in Madison, Wisconsin. Jon gets an appointment, and my heart starts to beat normally for the first time in more than forty-eight hours. It has been racing and periodically doing that downward pull to the side – the folded pita move – but less dramatically than when I first heard Jon tell me he was addicted. Jon goes to the clinic in Yakima on Monday, undergoes physical tests, and is given an initial dose of forty milligrams (mg) of methadone. He is told to come back the next day, and, having tolerated the dose well, is given a "carry dose" in small vials for a week's worth of the drug, and an appointment at the Madison clinic upon his arrival there. While he and I race to pack up his house, he talks philosophically about how much he will miss us and shyly asks my opinion about his decision to go. "I gave you life so you could go live it," I say, hiding my sadness. "So go live it with your son!" He has asked Lisa to take her son and live with him in Wisconsin, but she will not. However, she agrees to make the drive with him. Evan has a business trip to Las Vegas and is scheduled to leave on the same day Jon will depart – my birthday. There will be too much leaving for me to absorb, so we decide that I will go with Evan on his trip. I cannot watch Jon's rented moving truck drive away. On the scheduled day, we each go our separate ways.

Their road trip takes Jon and Lisa through Chicago, where they stop for an afternoon and night to walk along the Miracle Mile, take pictures at Navy Pier, and ascend to the top of the 110-story Sears Tower. Jon tells me later their trip was bittersweet. The fun and adventure were tempered by the knowledge they would soon be apart. Lisa flies home the day after they arrive. Jon has rented an apartment near Diane, in a small town about thirty miles west of Madison. He is filled with positive energy and writes me four long letters in December alone. He laments missing my birthday and states that he wishes he hadn't had to move away from us. "But here's the thing," he writes. "I'll be fine. I will flourish with my little man at my side. I can't picture a happier scene. Eddie united for good with his Dad, being helped along and experiencing real love...I couldn't stay anywhere without Eddie. We need each other...Eddie and I will thrive." He acknowledges being, "pretty lonely and a little sad," but says that his joy in seeing and being with Eddie "makes it worth it."

He describes their games, coloring, wrestling, building and knocking down things, and says that just eating cereal together fills him with a deep contentment. "I have completely immersed myself in that little boy...Eddie is the best stress relief...period. He really is quite remarkable. He's playful, intelligent, fun, energetic, attentive and just plain wonderful." Jon says he especially enjoys it when Eddie imitates him, even in things as small as stirring his cocoa: "This little guy learns from absolutely everything I do. I can't think of a better motivation to try to be a good person. I wish I didn't smoke – especially if he's gonna try to be so much like me. Maybe he'll help me quit." He flatters me immensely by stating he learned family values and family love from me. "You are the hero of this story Mom...I love you so much." He tells me repeatedly I should not worry about him, he will stay strong. "You didn't raise a sissy...I can do this Mom. I've got my head up, I'm seeing clearly, and I'm finally on the right path. I'll do well."

Jon's main frustrations in Wisconsin center around searching for a job, missing Lisa, missing us, and difficulties making friends. The town is small and insular. Most of the people living there were born there, and, as a newcomer, Jon is an anomaly and doesn't fit in. In truth, the town is a world away from Madison, where a major university and businesses bring thousands of newcomers who forge connections with each other. Later, after things have crashed for Jon in Wisconsin, he will say that, had he lived in Madison itself, his whole experience might have been different. Clearly, he has a lonely Christmas in 2004, even though he puts up a scrawny evergreen tree for Eddie, buys him presents, and builds snow forts with him.

After two anxious months, he finds a job at a nice restaurant. He buys a poor excuse for a car for 500 dollars and begins work. He remains cheerful on the surface. I fly to Wisconsin in May 2005, to visit Jon and Eddie. By this time, Jon has moved from his first apartment into the second story of a funky old house in a tree-lined, somewhat deteriorated neighborhood. He has more space, a driveway where he and Eddie can paint with water and chalk, and a small back porch where they watch birds. The odd-shaped rooms carved under the steeply pitched eaves of this old place suit Jon better than the squared off, white-walled apartment. He has always favored quirky. We take Eddie to miniature golf, the zoo, and bumper cars, and we ride a small local ferry boat. We eat in child-friendly places like Pizza Hut™ and McDonald's™, letting Eddie leave his seat and play endlessly. I bring a child-size plastic apron and Eddie delights in "washing dishes" (his own plastic cups) in the soapy sink. He smiles broadly amidst huge, outlandish butterfly and bumblebee pictures Jon draws for him with chalk on the driveway. When I ask Jon how he is seriously doing, he answers, "I wouldn't say I'm flourishing, but I'm making it. I'm holding some ground here, and I'm happy to be actively raising my boy."

In mid-summer, Jon writes that he and Eddie are, "up to our usual: strolling around the town going to parks and the [Wisconsin] river all day." Jon dives into the river and catches small turtles they bring home and keep in terrariums. Every turtle is named Tuck and every one of them dies after just a few days or weeks. However, Eddie is happy to watch them endlessly and tap on their glass homes. Jon reports that Eddie is, "testing his Dad's limits, but it's so hard to be mad at a little marshmallow like Eddie, even when he's deliberately destructive. He's just so cute and harmless. When I confront him he tries to change the subject. I'll kneel down so we're eye to eye and I'll say: 'why did you do that?' He'll go: 'cause, um uh, cause um, go to park?' Yup he's pretty slick...he's fun." Jon expresses it still is hard to make friends in the town, and he just doesn't feel he will ever fit in. "I'm dreading the long cold winter season," he admits.

In August, we fly Eddie and Jon back to Washington State for a visit. It is glorious. At the airport, I watch their airplane swoop down, brake, turn, and hurry toward the terminal. It looks like a scrawny little bird, too small for the precious cargo it holds. My heart is full. Jon brings a small box containing his doses of methadone – red liquid inside tiny clear vials. I ask him how he is doing in reducing the dose and he says the situation is fine. Throughout the twelve days that Jon and Eddie are with us, we picnic often along the mesmerizing, always-welcoming Columbia River. Eddie, wearing a long life vest with a strap stretching between his legs, draws endless lines and circles in the sand with sticks. He and Jon build sandcastles and lavish sand dikes, tracing new paths for streams at the water's edge. Eddie stands at our garden fence amidst thick grape vines and launches water from a squirt-gun into the mouths of our dogs. Not quite three years old, he often falls asleep on his father's lap or in his highchair during dinner or moonlit evenings on the deck. Uncle Jeff comes over from Seattle to see him and give expert Frisbee[51] and squirt-gun lessons. Lisa is with us most of the visit, and she and Jon seem close. Still, she will not move to Wisconsin to be with him.

That same month, Dr. Gary Franklin, Director of the Washington State Department of Labor and Industries (L&I) office, along with Jaymie Mai, PharmD, also working at L&I, and four other epidemiologists publish an article pointing to an increased death rate from opioid prescription drugs among L&I clients (i.e., those receiving compensation for work-related injuries). They note prescriptions for the most powerful opioids (drugs known as Schedule II, III and IV narcotics) have doubled in their client base between 1996 to 2002. Sprains, strains, and injuries resulting from falls are among the most frequent types to come through the L&I office – injuries formerly treated with physical therapy and rest, but more recently treated with opioids. These researchers are some of the first to notice and report the correlation, and suggest that prescribing guidelines would be a judicious step.[52] Of course, since we are not scientists who subscribe to such journals, we know nothing of the menacing pattern that is noted.

EIGHT

TRANSITIONS: TIMES GET HARD

My work sends me to Ohio in early December 2005. I let Jon know I can extend my trip to visit him for a three-day weekend. He is happy I am coming, but tells me his car isn't running and he will have to find a friend to pick me up at the airport. It's bitterly cold on the evening I fly into Madison. Jon isn't there, but calls to tell me he thinks he has a ride for me in about an hour. As I watch the kiosks and rental car booths in the airport close for the night, I feel forlorn and have a sense of foreboding. Finally, Jon and his friend Julie arrive with Eddie, and we ride back to his place, listening to the frozen snow crunch beneath her tires. When the sun comes up the next morning, I glance out the window to see the hood of Jon's car propped fully open with several inches of snow lying on the engine. The sight is disconcerting. It doesn't look like the car has moved in a very long time or that anyone has been trying seriously to fix it.

I have brought Christmas cookie cutters, a plastic apron, and bottles of red and green sprinkles. The next night, with Jon at work, Eddie and I buy the ingredients and tools we will need to bake cookies and set about our task. I place a pair of red felt antlers on my head and Eddie looks at me quizzically. Deadpanning, I tell him antlers have to be worn for the cookies to turn out correctly. He wants them on his head, and I gently place them there. He is as thrilled with the blending, rolling, and sprinkling procedures as Jeff and Jon used to be when they were little, and seems awestruck when actual cookies result from our efforts. Of course, he eats lots of the ingredients, but that is to be expected. He even loves washing the dishes afterward, head down, concentrating on his scrubbing duties. We carefully lay out a plate of cookies for Dad, with a note that Eddie scribbles. His pride in his part of our accomplishments is evident on his beaming little face.

After another day and a half, I must leave. Jon has told me several times the cold, dark season depresses him. To cheer him at Christmas, he is counting on Elliott's promise to come to Wisconsin and take him to a gathering of his extended family a few hours away in northern Illinois. At the airport, I watch Jon and Eddie ride up and down an escalator three times, as Eddie has insisted. Fully erect, he reaches not quite up to Jon's waist. Their rounded faces look remarkably similar, Eddie's peeking out from a dark wool cap and Jon's fully exposed beneath a backward ball cap. Eddie is holding a banana, and when we tell him to stick out his tongue, he does so gently, curling his small back into his father's lap. As always, Jon says they will be fine. He is a good faker.

The Christmas plans with Elliott never happen, and Jon's Christmas is very lonely. In February, we fly him and Eddie to Richland for a visit, where Eddie follows our eleven-month-old puppy everywhere and relishes attention from Uncle Jeff, Aunt Dori, and the rest of us. Again, Jon brings the tiny vials of red methadone. I ask whether he isn't about done with that stuff, and he says, "yes, almost." I tell him I am glad because I have talked to addiction counselors who have told me methadone has some strong drawbacks.

Synthesized by Nazi doctors on the eve of World War II so that Germany would have a self-sufficient supply of opiates, methadone is essentially man-made heroin. The word heroin is derived from the German word "heroisch" (heroic), because the Germans said it made men feel like heroes. The Nazis needed heroes as they sent young men by the thousands into freezing campaigns to try to capture Russia or to butcher innocents in forest pits and death camps. Methadone is a Schedule II drug, meaning it is part of a group of substances with high potential for addiction, but with some beneficial uses, according to the DEA.[5] It contains a number of hydrochloride salts and can produce

---

[5] In contrast to Schedule II drugs, Schedule I drugs are those with high addictive potential and no known beneficial uses.

side effects including nausea, vomiting, diarrhea, constipation, loss of appetite, and other symptoms that create a perfect recipe for agitated depression. A wide variety of addicted people in recovery, as well as addiction counselors, including Congressman Patrick Kennedy[53] and Joe Herzanek, chaplain and founder of the Changing Lives Foundation, [54] have said methadone is more addictive than heroin, in part because of its timed-release quality. The withdrawal is prolonged, making it hard for addicted people to remain determined to quit. I have no idea of this phenomenon.

Soon after the February visit, Jon writes to me, opening up about some of his unhappiness in Wisconsin. "Sometimes I really hate it here. I get homesick often. I can't wait to return to the Northwest...I really feel like my life is on hold...Right now I'm in limbo or some sort of purgatory. And when I get back to Washington, only then, can I begin to live my life. This current situation doesn't feel like any sort of life at all."

His letters get further and further apart. I visit him and Eddie in April 2006, and we spend lots of time at the zoo and in Madison's parks and playgrounds. Both of them smile in the sunshine. Eddie makes impish faces while he contorts and clowns for us. They take me to the river shore where they will begin catching turtles as soon as the weather warms a bit, and Eddie tells me every bit of turtle information and lore he knows. I ask Jon about diminishing his dose of methadone and he tells me it is down to ten mg per day. He adds the last few milligrams are the hardest to drop. He asks me to enlarge photos of the Richland docks and marinas and send them to him to post throughout his apartment. His throat tightens as he speaks. He is visibly homesick.

In June, he writes an anguished letter: "I'm not exactly miserable. I'm unfulfilled...Yes, unfulfilled is the word. I'm just not finding the usual even minimum happiness I've found other places...This place is impossible...It's wearing me down. It doesn't feel any more like home than the day I arrived...I've never been so utterly and completely unhappy...This stuff has been pouring out of me as fast as I can write it." I'm not sure what I can do. Whether he leaves Wisconsin or stays, the stakes are high. It is his life, and I dare not advise him. There are times when the best thing a parent can give is just a listening ear. I call to tell him that I love him, I always will, I trust his judgment, and I know he will think carefully. I do not realize that his circumstances are not normal, he cannot think clearly, and he is in grave danger.

It is the third week of July 2006, about noon, and I am in a briefing room at work preparing to be a lead speaker on a boat tour the following day with Washington State's governor. I have spent much of the spring and summer working on the project she will observe, and it is important. By now, we all have pocket-sized cell phones. My phone rings and I step out to answer. It is Jon's phone number, but I hear nothing. Finally, after several seconds, I hear a noise that sounds like a deep hiccup. "Jon??" I ask frantically. I hear another choking hiccup I now recognize as a sob. My heart wrenches down painfully on one side, pita-style. "Mom," he is mumbling. "Mom I'm really sick and I got fired. I can't do this anymore." My mother self takes over. Tamping down my panic, I make my voice soothing. "Everything will be okay," I say, "Just tell me what's going on." He stumbles through a few more phrases, and I ask where he is. "Home," he says. I ask whether he get to the clinic. I say will call them and have Kelly [his counselor there] meet him there. "If you can't get there, tell me and I will send an ambulance," I say. "I'm going to hang up briefly and then call you right back. You *will* answer, won't you?" He chokes out an "okay" and the line goes dead.

God is with us that afternoon. I reach Kelly and tell her Jon is very sick. She takes a deep breath that is audible over the phone. "I have been worrying about him," she says. "His dose is up to 189 mg per day and he hasn't looked very well." This time, the thud in my chest nearly knocks me over. I sink to the floor where I am standing, my chest bending forward over my stomach. My pita pocket heart has turned into a millstone and feels as if it is pulling my throat down into my intestines. I'm not sure I can keep breathing. Somehow — I don't know how — I tell her he has crashed totally and he needs immediate help — what can she do? She goes to him right away and takes him to a hospital where he is admitted for acute detoxification. He doesn't resist. Meanwhile, I call him back and stay on the phone with him until she arrives. I tell him I will be there as soon as I can. Still on the floor in the hallway, I start calling airlines. There simply are no flights for me the next day, but I can leave early the day after that. I book a one-way flight. I don't know when I will be returning home. I call Jon back to tell him I will see him in forty-eight hours, and despite his embarrassment in front of Kelly, he cries hard. "Thank you, Mom," he says over and over between choking sobs. We have crossed a line. It is the first time addiction propels me into instantaneous and total panic, but it won't be the last.

I will learn later that Jon's dose of methadone had been increased steadily, with his own collusion and that of the staff. Payments in Wisconsin were covered by Medicaid. Jon never saw a bill, and the clinic was happy to invoice the federal government for larger and larger amounts over his nineteen months of use. The dose was staggeringly high, given that the average therapeutic dose for opiate withdrawal in adults is eighty to one hundred mg, with the high range extending to only about 120 mg. Subsequently, Jon would recall that in Wisconsin he, "learned it [methadone] is harder to kick than the drugs that brought you there." Worse yet, as Jon's depression and loneliness deepened, he wrote later, "I started drinking so heavily I contemplated suicide. I was happy when I had Eddie over but drank myself to oblivion when he wasn't there. I started…[messing] up at work. Got much worse… Eventually everything fell apart." I learned later that the combination of his huge methadone doses and heavy drinking might well have killed him. Respiratory depression, irregular heartbeat, drowsiness, and eventually coma can result from combining methadone and alcohol. At the levels that Jon was consuming, he probably was saved only by his youth, his hardy constitution, and the grace of God. The outcome in Wisconsin could have been very different.

My tour with the governor is surreal on the day after Jon's crisis emerges. The day is gorgeous and bright with the desert showing off its serene glory. To see the photos, one would think I am just fine. I smile and pose with the guest and deliver my lines about the project with seeming ease. I interject little stories and jokes, shake hands with the facilitators and helpers, thank them for being part of such a great team, and restrain myself from looking at my watch and phone whenever I can. Apparently, I am nearly as good a faker as my son. I also am just as desperate. Whenever I can steal a minute, I call him. Each time he answers, I feel the tether. We are connected, we will work through whatever comes, as long as he doesn't give up – as long as he picks up the phone.

As I pack that night, Evan asks me when I will return. I tell him I have no idea. The next day, as the airplane banks above Madison, I look down at the dense green cover. I have never been here in midsummer before. I lean forward in my seat, craning my neck over the city, trying to trace the route to the hospital I have drawn carefully on paper and in my mind. On the ground, I rent a car and move swiftly through the quiet, early evening streets. I park two blocks away and make precise notes of my location on a small paper. My heart is beating so fast I don't trust myself to find my way back to the car without this tiny map. I walk to Jon's ward and ask to see him. He breaks into an outlandishly huge grin when he sees me, leaps up, and wraps me in an enormous hug. I feel like I will disappear into the hollow curve of his body. He is so thin. "I've gained two pounds in two days here!" he says cheerfully, though the slight catch in his throat tells me he is as close to crying as I am.

Soon the staff bustles in and informs me Jon has been admitted, voluntarily, with a dual diagnosis of alcohol and methadone addiction. Do I really want to discharge him and assume responsibility for him, they ask? He looks at me and nods his head emphatically yes. "He is mine," I say. "Of course, I will take him." Am I foolish? Naively arrogant? Obviously, I don't know the immense power of these addictions. Obviously, I love him. Obviously, love is not a prescription for advanced addiction. Right or wrong? At the time, it seems so right to wrap him up in my care and take him. Lee Woodruff, a mother of four who was tasked with informing her children their father had been blown up by an improvised explosive device in Iraq, writes, "It is a parent's deepest desire to be the human shield, the lightning rod, the four-leaf clover, the lucky rabbit's foot...[to] absorb all the pain for them."[55] I want to shelter Jon and keep him safe from the obscene Demon who stalks him. We leave the hospital, get some takeout food, and return to his place. It is indescribably messy, but I know I can fix that aspect. Suddenly, absolute exhaustion hits us both. I represent security to him, and he represents to me the tangible balm on all my fears. Both of us sleep long and hard, although we know we will awake to many trials. Peace, briefly, descends.

In the morning, I take a good look at Jon. Deep black circles hang below his eyes. He sees me looking at them and begins to talk. "I was in the bathroom at work one night and another server came in and looked at me and said 'Man, you look terrible! Your eyes are totally black and they look like they're sunk a mile into your head!' I looked and he was right. I kept having to go in and throw up. I lost nearly thirty pounds. My boss noticed too. He's a nice guy but he said he had to can me." He continues, spilling out. "I thought of killing myself all summer. I was going to drown myself in the river and make it look like an accident so you wouldn't be hurt." My eyes widen. *Wouldn't be hurt???* "I practiced lots of times when Eddie and I were out catching turtles, but I couldn't hold my breath." I stare and stare at him. My heart does its folding and thudding pita pocket thing many times that morning. This wrenching has occurred so often in the last few days that my chest is actually sore. We hug many times. There seems to be a tacit understanding between us that he must come home to Washington to recuperate. Talk imperceptibly turns toward renting a moving truck and driving home with all his possessions. We never state he won't be coming back to Wisconsin to live, but a mute understanding leads us in that direction.

Soon we get busy. We have to see the clinic so they can evaluate him and slowly start lowering his methadone doses. We have to notify Jon's landlord, contact Elliott, pay bills around town, clean out and paint the apartment, hold a garage sale, and seek a letter of recommendation from his last employer. We have to spend time with Eddie and prepare him for Jon's leaving. We have to make arrangements with the methadone clinic in Yakima. We have to clean the gross refrigerator, prepare healthy meals and get through each day on club soda. Sometimes we work together and sometimes separately. I sort two gigantic boxes of old mail and papers of various kinds. Apparently, Jon long ago gave up opening any mail that wasn't from family. One day, in the midst of painting, he begins speaking, saying his first sentence *very* slowly: "The absolute worst part of everything was looking in the mirror and admitting I'm an addict – not just addicted but *an addict*. It was the hardest thing I've ever had to do in my life. I hate it. I don't want it. I should be strong." Now we have reality. We have passed the verb and reached the noun — the label. The potential now has become actual. Like most addicted people, Jon never saw it coming. Now, there is the stigma, the shame, and the important failure of both of us to recognize he has a disease that has changed his brain. It really has nothing to do with not being strong. Research to prove this fact is beginning, but is nascent and not known outside small academic circles. I just listen. I don't contradict him. Neither one of us understands addiction. *What if I had known that it is a disease?* What if I had reassured him that he was a strong man with a terrible illness? Seventeen years later, I can't go there – the "what ifs" will kill me.

Wisconsin is cold most of the year. Somehow, we have picked the hottest, stickiest week of the year to paint, sort, pack, and haul. One day, I shower and dress in the best clothes I have brought and go to visit Jon's last employer. The restaurant, an old-fashioned mansion that sits on the bank of the Wisconsin River, is well-kept. The owners, a married couple, greet me pleasantly. I sit down and ask them about Jon's performance with them. It was great, they say, and the customers loved him...until recently. Parent-to-parent, I look straight at them. "He is very sick," I say. "I have come to take him home where he is much loved and make him well. A favorable recommendation for the majority of the time he was here would help a lot in his future." They reach across the table to grasp my hand. "Of course," they both say. "Godspeed to you. He is a good man." I pick up a highly complimentary letter the next day. There are good people everywhere.

Eight days later, Elliott arrives in Wisconsin to help Jon through his last few days of packing and I fly home. They drive a rental truck home to Washington State. I do not witness Jon's goodbye to Eddie. The Demon is disappointed. In Wisconsin, isolated and lonely, Jon was falling fast. Now the vile creature will have to wait for another opportunity to devour my son. Were Jon's brain and body changed by the addictive drugs he had taken? Without question, yes. Was he addicted? Yes. Was his condition recoverable? Perhaps yes, if the drugs were stepped down and stopped and abstinence maintained over time. The Demon coils his scaly body into a tuck and hunkers down to bide his time, one eye open with a bead on Jon. The reptile is not sure of his odds, but he knows he's getting closer. This one is vulnerable and may yet be claimed.

NINE

THE GEOGRAPHY CURE

Many addicted people speak of, and have tried, the "geography cure." It refers to moving from place to place or situation to situation to try to escape drug use and habits. It almost never works, because people bring themselves and their proclivities wherever they go. Jon writes of this condition later, saying, "I moved many places to start fresh, but I always let in the darkness…I've moved all over this land in attempts to find the good in me…I moved to places where I didn't know anyone. I've been lonely and heartbroken. So many things in this fight in an attempt to save my soul." When Jon arrives back in Richland in August 2006, he begins an odyssey of new places and situations that will last more than eight years. We approach each new step with belief and relief, imbued with hope and soaked deeply in our desperate faith. Something *has* to work, it simply must. Failure is not an option.

Jon is elated to be back in Richland. He writes to a friend in Wisconsin, "It is so good to be home…it's more beautiful than I remembered…blue skies, green orchards…the other day I could clearly see Mt. Rainier more than one hundred miles away gleaming white with glaciers and snow fields. It's one hundred degrees but doesn't feel that hot…the river is so pretty here." Several of his friends host a barbecue to celebrate his return, and he tells them he is back to stay. "There was volleyball," he tells his Wisconsin friend, "kids runnin' around, girls, tons of food, and most everyone turned out to welcome me home… every single one of my buddies is a genuinely good person, and I missed them terribly."

Elliott has taken a job in Portland, Oregon, and left his house vacant in Richland. Dori maintains her room at our house, but usually stays at Elliott's empty house. Jon decides to stay there too, but to me it is not ideal – not by a long shot. Soon he tells a friend that his living situation is, "too easy…My sister and I have a free place to live…A free, nice big house…I've done my share of playing…Wakeboarding a lot. However I won't go again until I've found work. I feel guilty." To make the living situation even worse, Elliott has given Dori and Jon the use of a fast waterski boat. This boat becomes the scene of activities, certainly dangerous and probably illegal, that we hear about, but are powerless to stop. Time on the Columbia River, which always has been so soothing and positive for our family, now seems sinister.

Within days of arriving back in Richland, Jon gets into a bar fight and ends up with two black eyes and multiple bruises. It doesn't comfort me when he tells me the next morning, "I gave as good as I got." I am picking him up to drive to the methadone clinic in Yakima. We have decided to ride together to talk over next steps. His behavior shows the promise of problems to come. When we arrive at the clinic, his appearance prompts blood and breath tests. Soon the counselor arrives in our consultation room with grim news. Because Jon has been drinking alcohol, he cannot be given any more week-long carry doses. The clinic's liability is too great. He will have to appear in person each day, be tested, and be given only one day's dose. The dose will be decreased one mg per day until he is weaned from the substance. He panics. This situation is not workable, he protests. We live seventy-five miles from the clinic, and he doesn't have a job yet. The counselor is not moved. Those consequences should have been obvious, she says. He should have thought ahead. On the way home, he asks me to pull over the car so he can vomit along the side of the road. "What am I going to do?" he asks over and over. The Demon smiles, as a low whistle – almost whispered – escapes his cavernous mouth.

Jon's decision is quick. By day's end he tells me he will quit cold turkey, go through an intense but short withdrawal, and be free of the methadone once and for all. He asks me to get him chewing gum, lots of club soda and water, and various over-the-counter remedies for nausea, fever, diarrhea, and other expected symptoms. He asks me to visit him every day. We think the withdrawal period will be like those we have seen in movies. It is late August, and we expect him to be finished with the worst of it by mid-September. As requested, I visit each day after work and we go for slow, halting walks on paths through the sagebrush. The September sky is clear and azure. He is very weak, but not violently sick. The process moves slowly. We do not understand. We also don't realize that sudden withdrawal from doses as large as his could kill him. September edges into October, and Jon still is too sickly to look for work. By this time, Diane has filed court papers for his child support to resume. It had been suspended during his time in Wisconsin because they shared Eddie's care and housing.

One day, I'm working late in my office after all my co-workers have left. Jon calls. "What am I going to do, Mom?" he asks. "It's mid-October and I still feel too rotten to work and nothing is moving forward." I am busy. I have deadlines and many work responsibilities on my mind. Jon and I have visited a few doctors to ask for some help, but received only benzodiazepines. These prescriptions, once mistakenly thought to assist addicted people get off drugs by easing withdrawal, only prolong and compound his addiction. Now, I don't have any good ideas. I promise to think and do more computer research that evening. When we hang up, I know I haven't helped him. Just as I walk down a long corridor to the copy machine an idea strikes me flat out of the blue. I run headlong back down the hall to my office and call Jon. "Move to Portland," I nearly scream into the phone. "That's it! Live with your father. There is a methadone clinic there and you can resume a moderate dose and step down gradually from there! As soon as you're off completely and not sick, you can decide what to do next." He begins yelling back: "Thank you Mom!!! Yes that's it! What a great idea. You have saved my life!" (It's just a metaphor, I think...maybe.) Both of us are crying now...relief, belief, hope. The Demon swallows noisily and grins slyly. Thwarted once again, he can wait.

Elliott agrees and Jon's move occurs quickly. Elliott's high-rise apartment on a hill overlooking the city has just enough room for both of them. They settle into an easy companionship. Very soon, Jon is in a methadone step-down program and finds a job in a small bistro in a fashionable, renovated district of the city. Things seem quite good. He will write later that as soon as the withdrawal sickness eased, his longing for Eddie set in. Being a good faker, he hides his depression well.

In the spring, I visit him in Portland. He has spent his spare time exploring the beautiful Rose City and leads me on long treks through leafy neighborhoods. Flowers seem to bloom everywhere. We have lunch in the charming, restored Pearl District downtown, and stroll on the broad walkways in McCall Waterfront Park watching boats in the Willamette River. I ask him about his methadone step-down and he sighs, saying it is awfully hard to go down past a certain level. The last milligrams are the hardest to give up. I inquire about Eddie, and Jon is very discouraged. Diane and Eddie have left the Madison area to live with a friend, and Jon says he feels "a million miles" from Eddie. His face looks absolutely forlorn. We soon schedule a weeklong trip for Jon to Wisconsin.

At nearly the same time, Dori abruptly decides to visit Portland and then moves into Elliott's apartment. Within a month, the apartment proves too small for all of them, and Jon moves back to Richland. I want him to live with Evan and me, but the lure of Elliott's vacant house is too strong, and he chooses it. Soon afterward, I find myself with Jon in my car, doing an errand. I detour toward a very poor area of the region, replete with streets flanked by small, decrepit houses with failing fences and tools scattered in yards. We come to the block where our area's homeless shelter sits across from an empty lot. The buildings here are old brick or concrete, flat, sometimes painted garish colors and advertising payday loans, pawn services, or adult entertainment. Piles of broken appliances, parts of fences and cars, busted concrete blocks, and ordinary litter sprout everywhere. A mournful train whistle sounds on a nearby freight track. Finally, Jon notices. "What are we doing here?" he asks. "This is where people end up who keep using drugs," I tell him. "This is a dead end, and it can really happen," I say with a meaningful sideways glance. He is nonchalant. I know I am unconvincing. Neither one of us really believes Jon will come to such a place. It is still easy to dismiss.

He finds a doctor in Yakima licensed to prescribe a new addiction maintenance/step-down drug called buprenorphine. Approved by the federal government in 2000, it is tightly restricted and can be dispensed only under strict clinical conditions by physicians who have special training. It is combined with naloxone, an agonist that blocks the high of opioids, in a medication called Suboxone.[56] As far as we can see, it seems to work well for Jon. At nearly the same time he moves back to Richland in 2007, Purdue Pharma pleads guilty to a federal criminal charge of misbranding OxyContin as non-addictive, with "intent to defraud and mislead the public." It pays 634.5 million dollars in fines — a small portion of its sales from the drug. Three of its executives pay insignificant parts of this fine and are convicted of misdemeanors. As part of this settlement, Purdue signs a corporate integrity agreement with the government, pledging the company to monitor and report doctors suspected of overprescribing.[57] Purdue also settles a lawsuit by twenty-five states including Washington and the District of Columbia, alleging it sought to increase its sales of OxyContin by downplaying risks, and has failed to monitor and report suspected "pill mills" discovered by its sales staff. The company admits no wrongdoing, but settles for nineteen and one-half million dollars, of which Washington State receives $719,500.[58] At the same time, the company spins off Rhodes Pharmaceuticals, a wholly-owned subsidiary, to sell immediate-release oxycodone.

In May, Jon travels to Wisconsin for a week, but doesn't get to see Eddie as much as he hoped. On this trip, he begins drinking again. Afraid that he will lose contact with Eddie, Jon files court papers to establish mandatory visits, including phone visits with no supervision by anyone. The court appoints a Guardian Ad Litem to evaluate both of Eddie's parents.

Back in Richland in late summer, Jon searches for work. I fly to Wisconsin to visit Eddie. I haven't seen him in a year, and I miss the little doll. His mother agrees that I can have him for a three-day weekend, so I rent a residence-type hotel and sweep him up. We play hard! We play miniature golf — his favorite activity — each day. We also visit the zoo, eat at fast-food restaurants with play areas, and wander the neighborhood and rivershore where he used to live and play with his father. I ask about the things they did together. Climbing on a large fish statue near the river, Eddie, not quite five years old, lowers his head and tells me softly, "I'm sad because I don't see him." Late in the afternoon on the day before I leave, his mother needs him back and I am left alone in Madison. I feel an awful, yawning loneliness. I wander through a shopping mall and look at all the people who know each other, but I know none of them. The minutes tick by slowly. I cannot wait for morning to come so I can fly home. Is this just a fleeting taste of the desolation Jon felt when he lived here alone? The thought becomes visceral; it has flesh on it. It makes me ill.

By the time I return to Richland, Jon has obtained a job, and I agree to co-sign for the financial responsibility for a small, nearby apartment for him. He moves into the new place in November. At Christmas, his smiles are wan and dutiful. There seems to be no joy in them. The year 2007 finally, thankfully, exits. Evan and I have a New Year's Eve tradition of telling each other the top three things that we loved about the previous year, the three things we most disliked, and the three things we hope most for the coming year. This New Year's Eve, it proves a hard exercise. We feel browbeaten, baffled, exhausted. We even feel incompetent as parents. Is Jon on a good path? Maybe a better one than a year before, but we know he misses Eddie desperately and we have no idea how this situation can be resolved. Things are janky, not working right. The Demon is close. There is so much we do not know.

By this time, Elliott and Dori have moved to California. Jon is drinking more and more, but I don't realize the extent of his gathering storm. Early in the new year of 2008, I invite him to the local community college to visit the machine shop. He is visibly excited about the machinery and the possibilities for making and/or inventing things. Afterwards, I offer to walk straight to the Admissions Office and sign him up as a student. He demurs. He is polite, but shrugs against a pillar under a campus walkway and seems to shrink into himself. "Not now," he says. The Demon is there, stretching his serpent's body around Jon, but I do not see or sense it. Blithely, unawares, I point out the endless benefits and fun of learning the skills this shop can teach. "No," he says, and pivots away. He just wants to go back to his apartment.

As he later described his condition in early 2008: "I fell into an alcoholic state of constant drinking day and night. I became very sick. I no longer was drinking to suppress the pain of missing my son. I was drinking just to function. Then I found pills again." During this period, he writes a melancholy poem about wanting to "start things over." Like many addicted people, he begins to personify the addiction, viewing and writing about it as a person or creature that stalks and shadows him. The Demon, he writes, "shrouds every step I take...making every promise empty, breaking everything around me." He continues, writing as if the Demon is speaking: "Trust in me and fall as well; I will find a center in you; I will chew it up and leave; I will work to elevate you; just enough to bring you down."

Alarmed at his own situation and intensely unhappy, he decides in March to move to California and start fresh near Elliott and Dori. Quickly, he finds a job as a bartender at a large, gorgeous restaurant set in a vineyard and rents a room in a house with three other young men. Soon, he feels stronger and better. He tells a friend that "California is as beautiful as ever and I've been doing quite a bit of exploration. The city [San Francisco] is awesome. The coastal forests of northern California are full of well-maintained trails and there are...loads of outdoor things to do." He has decided to stop drinking and relates, "I can't begin to tell you how good it feels to be getting my health back. I have energy now. I get pumped about hiking and climbing...I feel good. I feel strong." He states he misses Richland and his friends there, and of course, Eddie.

Jon's custody and visitation hearing is scheduled in Wisconsin, following the Guardian Ad Litem's report. In April, he borrows a three-piece suit from Elliott and appears in court in Wisconsin looking terrific. He is handsome and well-spoken. The investigations have shown Eddie misses him, loves him, and wants time with him. The judge commends him for his long and consistent efforts to seek time with his son: "I see too many cases where fathers must be coerced into spending time with their children. The opposite is true in this case." The court awards Jon three weeks of time with Eddie each summer, and Christmas and spring breaks every other year, with the summer periods elongating each year until they stretch to essentially the entire summer by 2012. It also grants him two telephone calls with Eddie each week, with the calls not being on a speaker phone or monitored in any other manner.

Best of all, Eddie is brought to him immediately and they spend the rest of the day together.

Jon flies back to California feeling elated. He tells a friend that "I didn't get everything I wanted but I'm still relatively happy with the outcome...[Soon] I'll be taking him [Eddie] home with me for summers and spring and Christmas breaks. So I can finally get back to raising my son. And this time on my home ground near my family so I am pretty happy."

In Richland, I sublet his apartment for the remaining few months of his lease, clean it out, and place his meager furniture in a storage unit. Once again, his papers and mail are in a jumble, and I sort them over a weekend at home. Evan is fed up, angry and resents the drain on my time and efforts. We spend the weekend in stony silence. I write a letter to Brett, a "shadow child,"[6] expressing sorrow that my preoccupation with addiction problems have caused me to neglect my relationship with him. I haven't visited him or helped much with his moves or home furnishing projects. He answers with understanding at a depth beyond his years. "People have different needs," he says. "We all know where your efforts need to go...and we know it drains your energy."

In the late spring, my company sends me to a training seminar in San Francisco, so I go eagerly, extending my trip for two days. Jon seems to be doing very well. He seems happier, more content, and more "like himself" than I have seen him in a long time. He has bought a used Ford Explorer SUV from a co-worker and camps in nearby woods with it whenever he wants. Later, he recounts that during this time, he "found that staying clean felt good. Everything started coming together. My life was good again...I was alive again." He is a generous host, driving me all around the hill country near San Francisco, and showing me his explorations of the coast and coastal waters. We feast on seafood, hike through Muir Woods, and climb Mt. Diablo, smelling the verdant forests. In August, he flies to Wisconsin for a week's visit with Eddie, this time getting ample time with him. He and Eddie swim, visit the

---

[6] Shadow child is the term applied to siblings of addicted children, who are ignored while the family focuses on the addicted ones.

zoo, trek around, color, work puzzles and watch silly movies. When Jon returns to California, they talk on the phone twice a week.

In very late summer, I fly back to California and stay with Jon for a few days. One night, I join him in mid-shift at his work and sit at the bar eating dinner and watching him work. He is smooth, competent, friendly, and capable of giving a warning scowl to patrons getting too drunk. Sometimes, he refuses to serve them more alcohol, and they back down. He is a big guy with a firmly set jaw. Every female in the place flirts with him, even older women. By now, he is managing the whole bar, which encompasses large indoor and outdoor areas. The outdoor space is replete with grape vines growing up and over trellises. Twinkling lights are strung among the trellises and trees, and birds flit and call in the midst of the enchanting scene. Jon tells me the birds feed off tiny lizards that dart through the greenery, unseen by most patrons. He has caught several of the lizards, and they are living in a terrarium at his house. Late at night, at the end of his shift, we sit together totaling his cash, electronic tips, and the register take for the night. He carefully sets out a percentage of his tips to give to employees who expedite service but receive no tips.

He has two nights off, and we drive off exploring throughout each long day. I am amazed at how well he knows the whole, complex Bay area. We visit and walk the hills of downtown San Francisco and tour through the World War II submarine USS *Pampanito* and the Liberty ship SS *Jeremiah O'Brien* at Fisherman's Wharf. From a deck of the O'Brien, we take several photos, one of which becomes Jon's favorite of himself. He stands at the ship's rail with Alcatraz Island in the background. We walk through the Haight-Asbury district, an area that became famous in the 1960s as the birthplace of the counterculture movement. After the Psychedelic Shop opened there in 1966, offering marijuana and LSD, the area saw surges of addiction, homelessness, and torment. Singers and groups who romanticized the drug culture in songs, such as Janis Joplin, Jefferson Airplane, and the Grateful Dead, also lived nearby. Jon and I see many homeless shelters, storefront churches, detox centers, and preposterously skinny and addicted people. I remark on one man, truly a walking skeleton, and Jon says, "When you're that far gone, you don't care what you look like."

We drive and hike through the Presidio grounds and then around Golden Gate Park. Jon tells me he might like to live in that colorful neighborhood with Eddie in the future, and I feel a stab of sadness because he might settle so far away. I know I would miss him. Then we cross the Golden Gate Bridge and walk around Sausalito, poking through charming shops and eating wonderful seafood on Bridgeway. Again, we take several photos, some with Jon on the beach and some along a seafront walkway, sun in his eyes, jacket casually flung over one shoulder. One of these photos later will sit at the centerpiece of his Memorial Service. I have no idea.

I fly home feeling as close to content as I have been in a long time. I think back to flying into Wisconsin to rescue Jon two years earlier – me so scared, him so sick. He seems so far from that time and place and circumstance. He has been off drugs for nearly six months now and seems healthy. I don't know old longings are calling to him. As he admitted later, "I found myself seeking the high that opiates held." The Demon has uncoiled his snaky body and winds it surreptitiously around Jon. Is my son prompted by missing Eddie even more, after just seeing him in August? Or does longing for Eddie have nothing to do with his drug cravings? He finds a supply connection through his work. This time, he tells himself, he will keep his drug use, "under control. I decided to just stick to Vicodin ten mgs. Nothing bigger because of course if I did that I would get addicted. Right? Wrong. It wasn't long before I was [taking] OxyContin eighties."[7] William Moyers also recalls hoping he could, "learn how to get high and do it right, avoiding the consequences."[59] However, it never worked.

I don't know Jon is using drugs again, so I agree to set up a winter visit to Eddie. In February 2009, Jon and I each fly into Chicago from different cities and then drive north to Wisconsin. I rent a residence hotel and we have five wonderful days. We play indoor miniature golf, build giant spaceships and rockets from Legos, hike through the

---

[7] OxyContin pills were manufactured in doses of forty or eighty mg per pill. Those containing eighty mg were known on the street as "eighties." For a brief time, pills containing 160 mg were manufactured. The street value of an OxyContin pill was usually one dollar per mg.

wintry zoo, work puzzles, and swim in the hotel's indoor pool. Jon draws incredible pictures for Eddie to color, effortlessly sketching life-like animals, as well as fanciful, incongruous creatures. He lifts Eddie high in the air, hugs and snuggles him, and reads to him as Eddie falls asleep. Apparently he is forcing down his drug use, or else concealing it masterfully, because I never see it and I am with him constantly.

Back in California in late winter, Jon's employers notice his pupils are pinned, and his behavior is getting irresponsible. He is often forgetful. He later explained: "Having steady employment and plenty of hook-ups I was rarely out of dope." His habit gained weight: "I eventually had a habit of enormous proportions and upwards of 250-300 dollars per day. Or more." He is taking the equivalent of 250-350 mg of OxyContin per day, depending on the bulk price rate he can negotiate with his supplier. On the telephone, to keep secret their dealings, they refer to OxyContin eighty mg pills as "beans." Soon, he begins padding the register at work. He ultimately recounted: "It wasn't long before they called me out. My boss knew I was on dope. We had a great relationship but after a few stern warnings her hands were tied. They let me go. Now I had a huge habit and no income. I was already behind on rent and had no way of coming up with the money. It became clear that I had to make another big change." Addiction has taken hold and dug in. Near my son, the Demon is stretching his reptilian limbs. He begins to sing in low, guttural tones. Nationwide, legal sales of OxyContin now surpass two and one-half billion dollars per year, and overdose deaths from prescription painkillers have almost doubled in the eight years since 2001, from approximately 18,000 per year to 37,000 per year.[60]

Jon does not tell his drug supplier he has lost his job. Because he is a good customer, he persuades the dealer to front him some methadone. He packs his SUV and leaves California in the middle of the night, arriving in Richland in mid-spring. It has taken just over seven months from his "experiment" with Vicodin tens to reach full addiction to OxyContin eighties. Using drugs is different from abusing drugs, and the distinction is about control. In the latter case, the element of choice is gone. However, the abuser is often the last to know he has lost command.

Jon stays at our house for a few weeks while he decides his next steps. He has painted his seventeen-year-old SUV a dull black. One day I mention to him that as soon as he does some chores for me and makes some money, he can paint it a nice shiny black. "Oh no," he tells me. The car's color is called "stealth black" and it is just the way he likes it. I don't recognize this preference for its camouflage value, and I don't know why he has left California. However, Elliott soon reports he has found several notes taped and tacked to Jon's bedroom door, demanding money.

TEN

DEEPER AND DARKER

In Richland that summer of 2009, Jon runs into old friends. One named Jess has been working summers as an on-call, wildland fire fighter and offers to help Jon apply. Jon is intrigued by the rugged sound of the job and the possibility of a lucrative summer. He forces down his drug use. His body is still powerful, and he passes the rigorous fire-fighter tests. In the dreaded "pack test," he carries a fifty-pound pack for three miles and finishes fourth in a class of fifty-six applicants. He borrows money from us and rents a small apartment with Jess, just a few blocks from a boat launch. Jess has bought a used boat, giving them access to fun on the river. Jon later recalled he was almost drug free, and "life was good again." On July fourth, he comes to our house for dinner before going boating with Jess. They are meeting friends on an island to set off fireworks. He is as elated as a little kid. That night, at the island gathering next to the sweet-smelling Columbia, he meets Lara. She will become the defining love of his life. Later he would recount: "I liked her immediately...I was higher than a kite!"

Mercifully for the western forests, but unfortunately for Jon's fire-fighting career, there are very few fires in Washington, Oregon, and northern California that summer. His team is called out only twice, and he makes very little money. He brings in some small income by doing odd jobs at our house and yard and at the properties of a few of our friends. Lara works hard at her server job. She is small but strong, with long, thick blonde hair and a sweet, caring disposition. Jon, who is nearly a foot taller than she, calls her Peanut. They often float the Yakima and Columbia rivers in our old red canoe or on tubes and small rafts. They share a love of the outdoors, and often camp out, taking along one of our dogs or Lara's dog. Like almost everyone who meets Jon, she is drawn to his curiosity about everything, his ebullient talkativeness, his sharp intellect, his headlong, enthusiastic embrace of life. Soon they are a couple.

In late summer, Jess crashes his dirt bike and is injured. He is prescribed a bottle of pain pills. Jon begins sneaking some of the pills and quickly escalates. By the end of a week, he has stolen most of them. He and Jess argue, and their relationship becomes stiff, guarded. Jon recalled later that during that summer, "I swore I wouldn't use often enough to get strung out." However, during the autumn months, he drives a huge circuit around much of eastern Washington and northeastern Oregon, visiting hospital emergency rooms with feigned injuries and illnesses, seeking pain pills. He is successful at many of the places. Insight and promises take a back seat to the voracious physical forces that propel him. Later, he will tell Dori that when he was on his way to get pills from doctors, "I felt so driven...I mean I felt like something else, some machine, had control of me and we weren't going to stop for anything until I was holding drugs in my hand."

I don't see Jon's desperation. Evan has taken a work assignment out of town for several months, and I need lots of help with our big yard. Jon trims trees, pulls out the dead stalks from the garden, and cuts the grass. We often work together, me loving his cheerful company and the big steaming mugs of coffee we set on the roof of the dogs' house while we work. Unless Lara is free, he often stays and eats dinner with me. I notice only that he seems to have almost a "cut-off switch" – a time early in the evening when his energy just drains away. He is heading for a collision with the choices he has made, but I don't see it coming.

At Halloween, we visit Eddie in Wisconsin again. Jon decides he wants to make a costume replicating the Transformer[61] character called Bumblebee. It is a yellow, black, and silver robot with a large, angular head. We gather supplies: cardboard, yellow and black paint and tape, silver duct tape, and lengths of silver clothes dryer hose to make flexible knee and elbow joints. We measure, cut, paint and tape, with Eddie helping and jumping around as the pieces are tried on him. When Halloween comes, I paint my face and place wiry bug antennae on my head, and we go trick-or-treating at a shopping mall. During the week, we also do our accustomed activities, including visiting the zoo, swimming, building with Legos, playing indoor miniature golf, and assembling puzzles. Eddie watches Jon shyly, almost constantly. As Jon slips his long body down into the hotel pool, Eddie's eyes rivet on him. "You're huge," he whispers softly. As we return Eddie to his mother at the end of our visit, I photograph Jon and his son. Eddie is seven years old. His little face is thoughtful, quiet, somber. There are no smiles.

Back in Richland in late autumn, Jon is hired at a brewpub/pizza restaurant. The lively place makes its own beer on the premises, visible in large gleaming vats behind a glass wall in the dining area. Quickly, he masters the brewing machinery – measuring temperatures, yeast, sugar and froth levels, and pressures. Soon, the owner says Jon knows the equipment better than he. Jon also learns how to carefully regulate the temperature in the large brick pizza oven, chopping and adding just the right sizes of wood from a large collection outside the building. Of course, his friendly grin and easy banter also charm the customers when he waits on tables. However, he can't pay his rent. I stop over at his apartment one afternoon with some things he has requested and halt dead in my tracks. There is a formal eviction notice bearing his name tacked to the door. Thud. Wrench. My heart. The same downward, sideways pull. It hurts. I go home. I say nothing to Jon, but wait for him to tell me what he will do next.

A week later, Jess pulls his truck into our driveway. He is angry, but not at me. Out of the truck window, he hands me a fat bundle of envelopes wrapped in a rubber band. "These came for Jon," he says. The envelopes are bills from the hospital emergency departments Jon has visited throughout our region, some more than one hundred miles away. Some are duplicates – they have been sent many times. I open just one, but I already know the contents, and my heart folds down and sideways into a hard wrench. "Patient reported pain from a sprain, prescribed Vicodin" or Percocet, or hydrocodone...on and on the accountings read, monotonous, awful. In 2012, Washington State will establish a prescription monitoring program, creating a database shared among hospitals and prescribers, identifying people receiving prescriptions for opiates. In 2016, the law will become even stronger, mandating referral to treatment for persons continually seeking opioid prescriptions. None of these protections are in place in 2009, as Jon continues harming himself. By this point, addiction has implanted itself firmly in his brain. It snakes like a poisonous vine, hijacking and hyperactivating reward circuits and deadening inhibitions, planning, judgment, and logic. His brain has changed. It is diseased, and none of us understands it. The Demon's low song becomes shrill, but not yet full-throated. He hunches his back to contain it.

By early December, Jon has solved his housing problem himself. He rents a bedroom in the house where Lara is living with her aunt and soon-to-be uncle. The situation seems like a good fit, as Lara's aunt Kathy is only three years older than she and two years younger than Jon. Clark, the man who will marry Kathy, is just four years older than Jon. The two couples soon become compatible friends. Kathy's son Miles, a gregarious five-year-old, lives with the four adults in the spacious house, and all take turns caring for him. Jon and Lara also help with the house and yard work. Kathy later described Jon as such a friendly, positive guy that he was a joy to have around. "He was almost airy, floating," she said, "but not in any stuck-up way, and certainly not effeminate. He was just warm-hearted and sweet. Everyone was happier when he was in the room."

Continuing to work at the brewpub, Jon is having difficulty finding opiate pills in Richland, despite his excellent connections. The nationwide trend to restrict open access to these pills is just beginning. However, as he later admitted, "there was plenty of heroin, and it was cheap. I went to it because I really couldn't afford the pills anymore." It is a familiar tale. In the years that followed Jon's switch to heroin, the National Institute on Drug Abuse (NIDA), CDC, and many other expert sources have emphasized that opiate pill dependence became the chief route to heroin use in the early years of the twenty-first century.[62]

Heroin – horse, smack, goat, night train, kamikaze, scag, TNT, mud – is a venom of a thousand brutal names. It is three times as potent as morphine. Sam Quinones calls it a "take no prisoners drug." It "stunts and ends lives," literally "brainwashing" people, causing them to act contrary to their own self-interests. It is like a lover, in that it provides intense pleasure, then "hooks people and punishes them mercilessly when they want freedom from it."[63] Dr. Grisel agrees: "Smack is all you care about as the intimacy you shared gives way to hopeful longing and then to deep grief and finally to bleak isolation."[64]

By the time Jon tries it in late 2009, Mexican brown tar heroin, a thick and sticky substance that looks like tootsie rolls or rat excrement, has made its way into essentially every part of the United States. In fact, Mexican producers have increased their output steadily every year since 2006. The brown tar heroin is a semi-processed opium base cooked from the milky goo collected from the seed pods of ripe poppy plants. In the cooking, it is mixed with lime, sodium carbonate, hydrochloric acid, and charcoal, turning it dark. Some people call it black. It is meant to be smoked or injected. Jon begins by cooking it down in a spoon and squirting it up his nose using a syringe. The feeling, he said later, was "god-like, zen-like. I was in heaven. There was no pain. Cloud Eleven." He experiences the warm, soothing rapture that many addicted people describe as the chief appeal of early heroin use. There is a sense of floating, drifting in perfect peace, all cares erased. His doomed love affair has begun, and he is captivated. Maia Szalavitz, a journalist now in recovery from addiction, describes her feelings during her first experience with heroin: "I just didn't care [about anything]. I needed nothing and no one. It was complete satisfaction. All desires extinguished. Instant Nirvana...Every molecule of my body felt nurtured. I was home...I felt safe, wrapped in a cozy, protective blanket."[65] William Moyers explains, "Drugs stopped time...when I was high, time became irrelevant, and the future held no threat. All that counted was the feeling of floating away, rising above and beyond my troubles, being at peace."[66]

Jon's early heroin use also includes "chasing the dragon" – inhaling the fumes of brown tar heroin that has been heated to melting temperature on tinfoil and "chasing" them through a straw as they vaporize away. He swears to himself he will never shoot it into his veins, even though he has needles, and he has heroin. He later recalled his thought process: "I'm not the kind of person that would ever stick a needle in my vein. Period....I swore I would never shoot it. Everyone told me it was the best way but still I resisted." However, the dictates of addiction can demolish inhibitions when cravings and promises of the next – or best ever – high take hold.

And so it is with Jon. Around Christmas, he cooks up, ties off, finds a vein, and pulls the plunger back out to make sure he has hit a vein.[8] A small amount of red blood backs into the needle as he pulls back. He tells me later that "I was shaking and I had tears in my eyes. I was breaking one of my own life or death rules. I figured myself for a goner...I was a junkie now and headed for ruin and eventual death. It was horrifying." Nevertheless, he pushes three-quarters of a gram of Mexican tar into a vein in his arm. The technique is called "slamming." He joins the darkness. The Demon throws back his head and begins to whirl and dance. His song has become a shriek. It pounds in Jon's head.

The winter progresses miserably for Jon. He later tells Dori that "I just managed to support a habit of mostly...Mexican tar, subs [Suboxone pills or a variety called Subutex] and alcohol. I felt like a vampire trying to subsist on a diet of rat blood. I wasn't alive but I wasn't all the way dead either. I had no real emotions and I couldn't understand how people could care about me, why...anyone would waste energy worrying about me. After enough time and money had been wasted I was barely even getting high...I remember hating seeing old pictures of me because they reminded me of how happy I used to be. I would wonder what... happened to that smiling kid who used to lust for the adventure of every day." Like the experience of all addicted people, the early highs of drugs use are gone and he uses just to avoid the miserable symptoms of withdrawal. Now, everything, including physical and relational harm, takes a back seat to the pull of addiction.

During that winter of early 2010, Jon lies to Lara constantly, but she almost always knows when he is high. They are in love, and argue almost never, except about drugs. Joe Herzanek would understand. He writes that in the throes of his addiction, "other people's feelings were their problem. Being honest became less and less important; I could look a person in the eye and make up any excuse, or lie on the spot, if

---

[8] Drug users want to make sure they are not injecting into muscle tissue, called "muscling," because abscesses can develop rapidly.

it suited my needs."[67] William Moyers adds confirmation when he says that "we [addicted people] lie repeatedly, and we are incredibly inventive with our deceptions and obfuscations, turning and twisting them to fit the situation...we have to lie to keep using and we have to keep using because our bodies literally need the drug to function."[68] Bill W. adds that alcoholics make "the invention of alibis a fine art."[69]

As the winter goes on, Lara and I talk more and more frequently about Jon's drug use. I don't know it is heroin, but I know it's serious. Lara tells Kathy and Clark to watch for certain signs in Jon's behavior when he is high – noticeably, pinned eyes. Kathy observes that when his eyes are pinned, he is extra fidgety. In March, Lara and I hold a mini-intervention with Jon in my kitchen. He is adamant he can handle himself and won't go into treatment. Struggling to control himself, he sees our offers of help as taking away his dignity and trying to coerce him.

That winter, Jon's voice is a husky rasp, and he looks unhealthy. His skin is dun-colored and has a strange greasy appearance, as if it has been smeared with tallow. His body and clothes give off an acrid, pungent smell that doesn't go away even when he is freshly scrubbed. There is no light in him. Lara and I share phone numbers of dealers and suppliers we know and agree to stay in close touch. Each of us thinks the other has more power than she does. Jon says later, "I tried to keep it [drug use] to a minimum, even quit for short periods. Tried to stay clean. Wanted to stay clean. I didn't hang out with other junkies, but I was rapidly losing clean friends. I became very isolated and soon Lara was pretty much my only friend. No question she was having trouble living with a heroin addict." He will write that during this period, he "shot ridiculous amounts of street black into my blood stream."

In April, I fly to California to visit Dori, who still is living there with Elliott. She and I visit the beautiful restaurant where Jon had worked. When we identify ourselves, many of the staff greet us with big hugs. They invite us to sit and chat. Everyone, it seems, loved Jon and hated to see him go. Most of all, they hated to see him so sick and addicted, and they want to know how he is doing. I tell them he is in adamant denial of his addiction, working at a small pub. "Let him prove to you he isn't addicted," says one young waiter. "Make him submit to random tests. Better yet, make him go to treatment," says another. "Is he attending NA [Narcotics Anonymous] meetings? Does he have a sponsor?" asks yet another. Clustered around us, they are vehement. To a person, they believe he has a huge drug problem, and they probably know even more than they are telling me. They are worried about him. I don't know about his heroin use, but, after listening to these good and sincere people, my concern mounts. My heart doesn't wrench, but it flutters, and not in a good way. I fly home with a heavy heart, determined to press Jon even harder to accept treatment.

Later that month, Jeff visits Richland for his birthday. We hold a big family dinner. Late in the evening, after much fun and banter, Jon and Lara leave, and we all go to bed. The next morning, Jeff can't find his cell phone. I pull out the scribbled list of suspicious phone numbers Lara has given me, and tell Jeff to bring up his mobile phone account on our computer. Sure enough, three phone calls were made from his phone to known drug suppliers at times near midnight. Soon after this discovery, Jon and Lara burst through the front door, cheerful and ready for brunch. I stare at Jon. His hand flies to his pocket and he smiles broadly. "Oh my goodness," he says, "I accidentally took Jeff's phone last night. Here it is." I point at the door. "Get out!" I bellow. He protests that taking the phone was just an oversight. I rattle off the offending phone numbers and the midnight cluster of calls. Lara backs him out of the door. As Jon and Lara drive away, there we stand – all of us sad, stricken, shaken, and trembling with the shock that our family has been brought to this brink. Confrontations, anger, fear, shame, shunning – the detritus of a family twisted and confounded by the addiction living in our midst. We have been poisoned and stolen by an unseen, hideous force – just like Jon's addicted brain. The pathways on which we used to relate to each other normally have been re-routed, like the errant trails in Jon's brain that flash craving and desire and steer him into unreasoned, self-destroying actions. We know so little. We hurt so much.

In May, Jon is obviously worse, and is fired from his job at the brewpub. He can't pay his rent to Kathy and Clark, so Clark brings him to work with him at his construction site. Jon is humiliated, doing menial clean-up work, but he understands he must contribute. The relationship shifts from a friendship basis, putting Clark into a parental role that is awkward for both him and Jon. AA wisely advises that "you are only as sick as your secrets." Congressman Kennedy, addiction advocate and man in recovery, says, "It is the lies and the secrets that eventually kill you."[70] Jon is keeping a big secret that winter and spring, and it is growing bitter fruit. His SUV runs out of gas frequently and needs repairs he cannot afford. He learns to kick-start it by pushing with his long leg out the open door and popping the clutch. It's heroic and pathetic to watch.

Lara and I capture him in another intervention in my kitchen, but Jon is stubborn. He is fighting us hard. There is pride – the belief and hope that he can handle the problem by himself. He would rather be defiant than helpless. William Moyers describes feeling the same way: "We [addicted people] can convince ourselves that we're in control at the very point we are beginning to lose it."[71] Congressman Kennedy understands. He writes, "Most people think they are hiding things much more brilliantly than they actually are."[72] I continue my familiar methods of coping – prayer, long walks and talks with my Labrador retriever Mountain, with God and even with the Columbia River. The river, azure and growing full with spring run-off, rushes past, busy with its tasks of nurturing and replenishing the region.

We learn later Jon is getting desperate at this point. As Maia Szalavitz describes this stage, he has gone from "freely choosing to get high to feeling more and more compelled to do so."[73] Congressman Kennedy explains further, "The level of self-delusion and pretending that goes on…is really astonishing…The denial is so huge, the self-perception so skewed. And the problem worsens so gradually that it's like being in water and you don't notice the temperature is rising a degree at a time until you realize…*it's boiling, and I'm cooked!*"[74]

A year later, Jon explained: "It was surreal for me, living with this budding, striving young family [Kathy, Clark and Miles], watching them grow and strive for success while I was slipping backward into an ever more unmanageable and meaningless existence…I didn't want to go to treatment because I knew there wasn't much someone like me could possibly learn about drugs that I didn't know all too well. Let's get real...I have the equivalent of a Ph.D. in opiates, alcohol and other mind-altering substances. Besides I have my own methods of getting clean, and they didn't include Twelve-Step plans and total abstinence and all that garbage. I also thought maybe I was beyond help. After all I didn't want to be an addict but for all these attempts, all the times I've thrown all my willpower at it, really wanted it and meant it, here I was a half-functioning drug addict."

In June, Eddie is coming to Richland for a visit. Just before he arrives, Kathy finds a rig[9] on a shelf of the garage, behind some tools. She and Clark have no choice. They confront Jon and tell him he cannot continue to live at their house unless he stops using drugs. "This is a selfish act," Clark says of Jon's drug use. They recommend he go to inpatient treatment. Out of options, Jon agrees. I call Elliott and we, both relieved, get busy researching treatment centers, searching for a reputable one that will last several months. With Jon in a compliant position, we let him know a one-month treatment program won't be sufficient. His addiction needs to be confronted, treated, and put to an end, no matter what it takes. Elliott finds a place called Fresh Directions that seems ideal in the San Francisco Bay area. Patients there begin with one week of detoxification medically assisted with Suboxone; then they enter either a one-month or a six-month treatment program. We consult with Jon, and he accepts the B Pod (six-month) program to follow detoxification. Eddie's trip is scheduled for June eleven through twenty, ending on Father's Day.

Eddie's trip is wonderful. He and Miles become fast friends, staying in Kathy and Clark's house, which is full of preparations for their wedding. One day, sitting among sets of paper flowers, Eddie and Miles grin slyly at me and whisper that Jon and Lara are going to get married someday. "Then we'll be brothers," says Miles, "and you will be my grandma." During Eddie's visit, we all swim, climb around playgrounds, color, draw and paint with chalk and water all over our driveways, sail

---

[9] Heroin use paraphernalia. Also known as "works."

miniature boats in plastic tubs in the yard, have barbeques, and let the boys stay up late during overnights at both houses. They hug and sleep with our dogs and laugh with abandon.

Jon and Lara take the boys hiking on nearby sand dunes, and they carve their names in the grit. Eddie writes "Dad" with a big stick and tears roll down Jon's face as he photographs the scrawl. Later he will admit he "tried to stay straight" throughout Eddie's visit, but wasn't entirely successful. "I was sick a lot," he confesses. Three days before Eddie leaves, unbeknownst to us, Jon stops using drugs entirely. On their last day in Richland, we all meet for a Father's Day lunch. The boys hug each other, me, Jon, Lara, and the dogs. "Make this count," Evan says to Jon, looking deep into his eyes and hugging him in a rough, manly grasp. I cry openly as Lara, Jon, and Eddie drive away. The parents of every addicted person cry these tears at one or many times in their journey through the twisted path of addiction. They are tears of utter deliverance. For one moment, at least, the knee-buckling fear and dread are put to rest because treatment is imminent. There is, just for now, a chance to breathe.

Jon realizes he needs help. On his last night with Lara in Seattle, he tells her he knows if he continues in his current pattern, he undoubtedly will have a "short, miserable life." Believe it or not, he says, a part of him is "ok with that." However, he tells her she makes him feel stronger and makes him want to live a long and happy life. The next morning, Lara deposits father and son at their respective airplanes in Seattle. Eddie flies back to Wisconsin.

Why does Jon climb aboard his airplane to treatment? As he recounted later, "I don't know what finally motivated me. I guess I just wanted to be done. I knew that my very existence, or even just the thought of me, hurt the people I love, and I didn't want to hurt anyone anymore. I guess I wanted to actually chase down a dream or two... salvage what time is left and what remains of my health and youth and rejoin the world and maybe even contribute something to it. This is, after all, a wild and wonderful thing we call life...I was realizing that never in the last ten years had I ever truly achieved freedom from this affliction...I've started my life over more times than I care to count.

I've sacrificed. I've lost. I've fought with everything in me. I've cut all ties and run for my life, yet here I was beyond help. It became clear to me that I've been an addict in some form or another, active or dry, for almost a decade...I guess I just wanted to jump back into life."

ELEVEN

HOPE AND TERROR

A car service Elliott has hired picks up Jon at the Oakland airport and delivers him to San Francisco on a beautiful, sunny morning. Jon stands in front of the Fresh Directions campus and ponders whether to go wandering around the city or go in. Later he says he probably would have gone exploring if he hadn't been so "miserable" from drug withdrawals. He walks in and is searched and assessed. When the intake counselor asks him why he wants to be at the treatment center, he answers he wants to stop hurting the people he loves. To his own amazement, he nearly cries as he says these words. "I can't believe how emotional I am right now," he writes in a journal he begins that night. "I haven't been this broken up in a long time. I'm racked with guilt. I feel so inside out." The journal is titled "Dead on Arrival." About six p.m., he finally gets a Suboxone pill and falls asleep.

Jon's week in the detoxification unit stretches into eight days and passes slowly. He has difficulty getting off the Suboxone, so much so that the center increases his dose to one and one-half pills. At that time, reliance on Suboxone - one medicine that is part of Medication Assisted Treatment (MAT) – was considered by most to be simply substituting one drug for another. Getting off of it quickly was a firm goal. Today, many attitudes about Suboxone have changed in the treatment community, as some practitioners now believe a long transition period, or even perpetual access to it, may be the only achievable path for people with severe addictions.

In detoxification, Jon misses our family, Eddie, and Lara most of all, and writes that his time with Eddie right before going in was "magical" and "crucial to" his recovery. He is determined to "stay positive and stick out" the six months of treatment, even though it will be "a long haul." He writes he is "extremely motivated, and willing to do whatever it is they ask me to do. This 'thing' [the addiction] is so daunting, so heavy, so enormous. But it can and has been done. Teach me..." He also writes about his "extremely negative self-image." He feels "so hollowed out. So guilt stricken. So ashamed. So sick. So sad. I hurt everywhere." Searching for something familiar, something that affirms he has a home and belongs somewhere, he sketches mountain scenes from Washington State – Mount Baker and the San Juan Islands with a ferry boat gliding among the islands. Elliott visits him on his fifth day, bringing him cigarettes, shaving equipment, flip-flops, towels, and some snacks. As he is leaving, Elliott says "I love you." Jon doesn't say it back and later that night regrets not doing so. He writes, "I love you Dad" in his journal. He also writes he is, "glad I have some peace and am sleeping better... now that she [Mom] knows I am clean and gonna stay that way." He counts his blessings, acknowledging he is lucky not to have contracted diseases such as Acquired Immune Deficiency Syndrome (AIDS) or Hepatitis C, and does not have felony legal cases hanging over his head. "I guess I can say that I'm extremely thankful that I'm safe and in one piece if for no other reason than so that Mom can feel less worry."

During the first week, Jon works on Step One of the AA program: "We admitted to ourselves that we were powerless over alcohol [or drugs] and that our lives had become unmanageable." He admits he has had an "enormous problem with the word powerless...I'm not a controlling person but it's humbling and even humiliating to have to admit powerlessness over any aspect of my life." Bill W., founder of AA, understands: "Who cares to admit complete defeat? Practically no one, of course. Every natural instinct cries out against the idea of personal powerlessness."[75]

Jon describes his life before coming to treatment, saying he had, "lost my job, couldn't pay my rent and was sliding deeper into heroin addiction. I spent most of my time finding ways to get money and scoring drugs. I waited in parking lots for dealers who took way too long." Now and then, he recalls, he would, "put deals together to try to recoup my money by selling drugs. But I was my own best customer and on several occasions wouldn't sell any." He recounted lying "all the time" to Lara and to "my concerned Mother." He writes, "I tried to stay in control but I was getting lost." Even through the fog of drugs, he realized, "If I kept going I'd lose my girl, the respect of my parents, visits with my son, be homeless and ultimately die. I was suicidal on several occasions." I have no idea he had been thinking of suicide that summer. I continue to think that entire subject had been left behind in Wisconsin.

The Fresh Directions counselors, pulling more information from him, ask Jon why he needs to be in treatment. Summing up, he states simply: "To have a future." Without recovery, he says, "I would have, in the short or long run, died from an overdose or disease or from suicide. But not only would I have died, I would have had to endure losing my girl, being homeless, being miserable, losing friends, possibly having jail sentences...pretty much all the misery life can dish out." He recounts his story to a small group session at Fresh Directions, telling the gathering how he had "rebuilt, relocated, and re-established myself more times than I can count to get away from addiction – only to re-invite the destructive forces of drugs into my life." Now, for the first time to other human beings, he admits, "I truly am powerless over drugs...The only honest, real truth is that I can never do drugs and have a manageable life." He is, he says, "willing to release all my resistance and struggle... [to] find good...inside me." The group feedback is positive. Members believe he has been honest in admitting facts and accepting his disease. Most believe he is willing to change, and they rate his prognosis for recovery from fair to good. They classify him as being in the late stages of the disease of addiction.

On his last day in the detoxification unit, Jon becomes philosophical: "I'm realizing that I never did anyone as dirty as I did myself. I was pretty bad to myself...I'm trying to dig into my past. Find out why I'm me. Why I don't approve of myself. Why I let myself and set myself up to fail." He's not sure whether he believes in a personal God, but feels there is surely a positive energy or force in the universe that loves him and has kept him safe. "I know you look out for me," he writes. "I know you've kept me alive on countless occasions when I've put myself in harm's way. I'm upset with myself though. I got in bed with the devil again, a lot. I don't know if you feel pain. I'm sorry if I hurt you...I don't have a clue what you are. Why you look after people like me who are reckless and dangerous. I want to get close to you. I want to, someday, serve you...Help me get through this. Not to make it easy and comfortable, not for me and my selfishness. But so I can stick it out. Find truth. Find Faith. Be honest. Be faithful. Reap the benefits of this place."

Jon has heard rumors and gossip that the B Pod of Fresh Directions, where he is going for six months, is very harsh and rule-bound, and behavior modification is practiced in the extreme. During detoxification, he is interviewed by one of the counselors of B Pod and finds him to be "a hard dude." Jon writes he doesn't think he needs to learn "a lot of the things they 'teach' over there. I mean...I'm not a hardened criminal. I just want to learn how to stay off drugs."

On Jon's ninth day at Fresh Directions, he moves into B Pod. He gets no more Suboxone, and the next day his withdrawal sickness erupts again. He experiences not only physical symptoms, but the mental and emotional pain that comes from trying to break the nexus between drugs and relief that is deeply embedded in his brain. "I'm scared and I'm lonely," he writes in his journal. "I think about Eddie all the time." In a letter to me, he writes he has heard B Pod is very strict, "but I came here to work. I came here to do something hard. So I'm ready and more than willing. I'm absolutely brimming with confidence. My willpower is up. I'm overflowing with a sense that I can overcome this terrible affliction...I used to feel utterly hopeless. So alone in this. Now I'm confident and I feel my strength returning. I miss you. I love you. Thank you for this opportunity."

Soon, he experiences the puritanical nature of the B Pod program for himself. Corrections are immediate and harsh, making the patients afraid to reveal their true feelings. Brotherhood and mutual support are not fostered. Instead, addicted people are made to feel they are moral failures. "This place is brutal," he writes on his third day there. "This isn't treatment but twenty-four-hour a day torture. But I'm not leaving. I'm stronger than that...My family deserves to have me back."

In the next few days, a man in his group is caught with drugs and evicted. Jon hears the man's parents crying hard as they come to gather his belongings. The sounds, especially the father's sobs, upset Jon, and he again muses about God: "I don't know if God is an organism or just the ball of energy and light that is life -- this unspeakably enormous force that is life and the love that all living things share. I don't know if 'it' acts directly upon us but I'm willing to have faith that it does. I'm going to start praying. I've always been unconventional and gone against the flow. I don't know how I'll pray but I'll find my own personal weird way."

He is still "dopesick" (i.e., in withdrawal), a condition that becomes progressively more severe the more times a person goes through it. He asks to move back to the detoxification unit. The staff refuses, but agrees to get him a Suboxone pill on his sixth day in B Pod. He graphically describes his withdrawal symptoms in his journal: "I got the worst flu of my life. Dysentery. Ebola. My skin is crawling all over my spine. I ache everywhere. My eyes water. I can't swallow. I'm exhausted. I have the most awful foamy diarrhea. I'm suicidally depressed. I'm super sensitive. Overly emotional. My sense of smell is acute, especially for bad smells... I'm freezing. I'm sweating profusely. I can't sleep a wink. My soul is utterly missing. I feel like destroying something. I would if I had the strength."

Jon calls and tells me B Pod is not the place any of us envisioned. Our research was faulty, he says, or else the staff lied to us about the conditions. "I've been to treatment before," he says, "and this is not it." He asks me to get him relocated into the one-month treatment section of Fresh Directions. Maybe I am just exhausted. Maybe I can't think about making more arrangements so soon. Maybe I assume he is feeling so badly just due to his withdrawal sickness. I don't agree to make any changes yet. He vents at me in his journal, but at the end of his rant, he gives me the benefit of the doubt: "I doubt if she knew what this place was like. I don't think she knew she wouldn't be putting me in rehab by putting me here." (He's right – I did not.) His two mg of Suboxone the next day make him feel a lot better. However, he still is very angry at the conditions in B Pod: "Why am I being punished? I'm not a criminal. I have to get out of here. I don't think I can afford another failure...I don't have major behavioral issues. I have a drug problem...I really don't understand how I signed up for drug rehabilitation and end of doing six months of behavior modification which is just a fancy way of saying punishment." It is his first real encounter with a treatment model that believes a person must be humiliated and stripped of dignity to stop addiction. "Trying to humble a person with an extremely negative self-image seems counter-productive," he observes wryly. He requests to move to the one-month recovery program.

It is a few days after the Fourth of July. Jon has been in B Pod for eight days, and Evan and I are attending a fund-raising dinner for a local charity at a beautiful home along the Columbia River. The huge yard contains terraced vineyards, gazebos, and an ornate stone guesthouse. The night is lovely, the air almost velvet. Many of the people we know and work with are there. As we mingle on the lawn, my cell phone rings. Jon is talking fast and urgently, telling me he absolutely can't stay in B Pod. He's angry we didn't do more research, and sent him to a negative place where he feels he is being "set up to fail." He says he cannot endure this "bad energy and torment...Now I'm lost and abandoned. I feel duped. I already never want to do drugs again, but in here I will lose my mind." I walk further and further away from the crowd, until I am off in a far corner of the yard, pacing back and forth, shoulders hunched, phone to my ear. People are beginning to glance curiously at me, then stare. Evan comes to urge me to hang up. He tells me I am being rude to the hosts and making others uncomfortable. *Uncomfortable? Really???* In my slow-motion disaster, I have been in this position so many times – at work, in my yard, out with friends, walking, and exercising. Does everyone but me have a normal life? I am cornered, torn between wondering whether I can really help Jon, or whether I'm being conned and used. I love my son. I can't trust him very much, and I don't know what to do. Finally, I tell him I will contact Elliott and make sure he visits him the next day to discuss options going forward.

The next day, Elliott drives the hour from his house to visit Jon. However, inexplicably, someone on the staff tells him he cannot see Jon, so Elliott leaves. Then another person comes to get Jon for the visit, but Elliott is gone. Jon is beyond angry, beyond frustrated. However, even in the midst of hating his surroundings, Jon writes in his journal about hope for the future. He recognizes the power of drugs and wants to rid himself of the poison. "It really is the little things that kill," he writes. "A dirty little chemical has the potential to completely destroy me. I know I can't control it. It's way too powerful. I need to kick it out of my life for good so that I can squeeze every drop out of life. Climb the mountains. See the world. Raise a family. Have respect. And for better or for worse in good things and bad, <u>feel it all</u>."

The day after Elliott's attempt to visit Jon, Evan and I travel to the beautiful island off the Washington coast where we go every year and which holds so many great memories. We unpack and settle into our lovely seaside cabin. I have no idea what is going on at Fresh Directions. One day later, my phone rings. Elliott and Dori both are on the phone, his voice grim and low, her voice hysterical. They tell me Jon has left the treatment center, and called them. When he received the call, Elliott's first reaction had been anger. He told Jon to "stick it out" in treatment. Jon had hung up on him. Now, his father and his sister do not know where he is. Of course, my heart wrenches violently – over and down sideways, the ravening, lopsided pita pocket pattern that is becoming familiar. There is no more delightful, restorative vacation. There is terror. Dori has been calling homeless shelters all over the area and in Oakland with no results. I tell her to keep trying. I ask Elliott to restrain himself if Jon should call again – to just listen and try to learn where he is. All of us fear he will relapse and just disappear into the heartless streets. Contemplating that outcome, I begin to tremble uncontrollably. My skin is insufficient to contain the fear that grows and grows and grows. I am very cold, but still, I feel that I will explode.

At the same time, Jon has made his way to Berkeley and is taking stock of his situation: "I have no money. None. I am 800 miles from home. I don't know anyone. I have no food. I have no blankets. And the Bay gets cold…at night. Especially the wee hours when the fog gets thick and brutally cold, gets everything including you and the ground you're lying on soaked all the way through. Uh – I have nowhere to go. I don't have a place to store my stuff so I have to lug it around. It's heavy. No food. No money. No body. Lost. Very very cold." Then he lists his assets: "I have clothes. I have books. Oh, big one – I have cigarettes. I have my mind, my body, my spirit. I'm resourceful, capable and determined. I'm topped off with anger. I'm alive. I could let this situation hurt me or I could man…up and move on. What to do, huh? Be a street addict? Not me! I'm proud of my clean time and I'm gonna keep it that way." He calls Lara and tells her he is out of the treatment center and not to worry. He does not know his plans yet. As for me, he writes in his journal, "Mom – she will worry…My heart is breaking for Mom."

On the island, I continue to shiver, and Evan's face wears a forbidding grimace. Once again, addiction cuts its unforgiving swath through our lives. We are no longer ourselves, but prisoners of our fear and love. My first step is to call a reputable treatment center in Seattle, to ask if it has available space for a male if I am able to bring him in. It does, and the staff is very nice as I explain that producing my son at their door is a "maybe" at best. They deal with many frantic parents. I research Al-Anon meetings on the island and find just one. Mercifully, it is scheduled for that night. I wait all afternoon. I cannot bear to go in the boat with Evan, nor take an interest in the things we normally love to do on the island. I sit with my knees folded up to my chest, hoping that staring at the ocean will make me at least numb or lulled, but nothing helps. There is bile when I swallow, I don't answer Evan when he speaks, and I don't know how one human can be so filled with misery and not just disintegrate. I don't come into our cabin for dinner. Saying nothing, I drive away and find my way through the tiny, twisting streets to the Al-Anon meeting. There are just four of us there, but we go through the familiar readings. We recite the Twelve Steps. We introduce ourselves. Even though we are just four strangers, we are soon connected, earnestly pouring out our stories to each other, spilling our tears onto the table that gathers us, intuitively knowing the anguish the halting words convey. Pain binds us. The meeting helps. I drive back in the quiet darkness. Of course, there is no sleep that night.

In Berkeley, Jon makes his way to People's Park along Telegraph Avenue, and sleeps there. The famous old park was the scene of multiple protests against the Vietnam War in 1968 and 1969. In May 1969,

Alameda County Sheriff's officers opened fire on the protestors, killing one, blinding another, and wounding at least 50 people. After that time, the park became a gathering place for hippies and the homeless. Many charities and churches began to serve food to the homeless, and the park served as an informal logistics center for information about shelters, free soup kitchens, and other social services. Jon has memorized William Ernest Henley's famously defiant poem *Invictus*[76], and writes every word of it in his journal that night. The poem speaks of an "unconquerable soul" whose "head is bloodied but unbowed." He is "unafraid...I am the master of my fate; I am the captain of my soul."

Jon identifies. On his nineteenth day since arriving in California, and his second day out of Fresh Directions, he retains a fierce fury: "I'm a crossfire hurricane. I'm a careening freight train. I'm deadly. I'm sober...I'm a survivor. I'm alive...In danger? Not really. I'm bigger than a lot of the guys and I'm brimming with anger." He hasn't eaten in forty-eight hours and still has no blankets. Finding a free food kitchen in an old church, he eats "the most wonderful heaping plate of jambalaya on rice...Yuuum. I wish they did that every day." Later, he will recall the night of the jambalaya: "There were about one hundred of us homeless people sitting around tables in this enormous great room. There was a grand piano in one corner. The most haggard looking...homeless man sat gently at the bench and started playing the most elegant, perfect sonata. It was sad and soaring. The high ceilings carried even the softest notes crisply through the room...The tired. The poor. The hungry in a collective moment of freedom. I will never forget how that made me feel. It was so uplifting. God's house. I was inspired to say the least."

Jon attends two AA meetings that day. He shares his story and people approach him offering advice. He ends the day writing he is "still kinda lost." The next morning finds him back in People's Park. "I'm sober but I'm still lost. I'm sore. My legs are killing me. H.A.L.T. – hungry, angry, lonely tired.[10] It seems to be a perpetual condition." In his journal, he scribbles several verses from the Bob Dylan song *A Hard*

---

[10] H.A.L.T. is an acronym often used at AA meetings. It warns of conditions that are set-ups for temptation and relapse.

Rain's Gonna Fall.[77] He sees his reflection in a glass window and says, "I look…[awful]. My eyes are sunken and drifting. My cheeks are sucked in. I have to force a smile…My dogs are howlin! Ooow…feet tore up. Hard to walk so far…All I can do is soldier on. I'm lost." He attends another AA meeting and speaks. A man there says Jon "looks like pain." He goes to a men's shelter and finds an emergency bed on a short-term basis. He remains drug free and sober, but admits, "it's hard to stay clean here." He returns to People's Park and finds a vegan meal. "The vegans just came and fed the whole park. Couscous and something else. There's something to be said for this place, as dirty as it is. There's something I can't quite nail down but it's…freedom, love, acceptance." He wonders about me: "I'm so worried about Mom. She's probably distraught. She's probably worried sick…But has she gone from worried to angry, just as I have passed from angry to worried?"

That evening, he attends another AA meeting. At the end, a man walks over to him and urges him to call home. He hands Jon his cell phone, and Jon dials my number. I leap from my seat, see a strange number with a California area code and feel my heart nearly vault out of my chest. It wrenches so hard I think it must be torn loose from its position. Of course, I fear the worst – the police must be calling to tell me he is dead. Instead, it is Jon's voice, tentative, not sure how I will react. I am screaming: "You're alive! Where are you? Are you OK? Praise the Lord Jon! Talk to me!" I offer drug treatment in Seattle and tell him his father is ready to pick him up and fly him north. He says he will think about it. "Don't hang up," I beg. "I can't stand not knowing where you are." However, he says he can't stay on the man's borrowed phone too long and promises to call me the next day. After he disconnects, I sit staring at the phone in my hand. It is my lifeline to Jon. I don't want to put it down. The addiction roller-coaster jolts me back and forth. I am so relieved my whole body feels like jelly. I have no solid bones, but am just a heap of matter, defeated, disabled, stupefied. I cannot rouse myself until suddenly, once again, stress and fear and adrenaline and cortisol course through me. What if he doesn't call back? I didn't learn enough information. Why didn't he jump at the chance to come to Seattle? What is he hiding? I hurriedly call Elliott and Dori to tell them the scant news I have received and ask them to investigate specific flights and times in case Jon actually calls back. In the meantime, Evan sits alone. I am no companion, too wrecked to even notice we are together on vacation. He is patient and he loves Jon, but he wonders whether and what kind of life we can have in the midst of such chaos.

That night in the shelter, Jon ponders his alternatives: "I could stay here and rise from the street (or get swallowed up by it). Or I could make my way to Washington for a 28-day treatment stay. I could use it. I know it would be the best thing but I hate to spend Mom's money... what to do?" He sleeps on the question, goes to an early AA meeting, and calls Lara to tell her he agrees to go into treatment in Seattle. "I had a sort of revelation," he tells her, "I still need help. I need treatment." She calls to tell us. My tears of relief come in such a torrent that I am choking, gasping, hiccupping. Evan just holds me. For the rest of the day, while Elliott and I make arrangements for Jon to fly to Seattle the next day, he walks around Berkeley, eating again at People's Park and attending additional AA meetings. The H.A.L.T. conditions beset him – he is hungry, angry, lonely and tired. "I feel like passing out, most of the time. My feet are killing me. I'm ravenously hungry, like a wild animal. I'm so lonely...I've let go of most of my anger."

TWELVE

THE CHALLENGE
OF HEALING

The next morning, Jon flies to Seattle. We have asked Lara to meet him, so I can salvage a bit of my tattered vacation and marriage. He tells her he has "learned so much from this experience I can't even begin to explain...I've learned a lot about the people who care about me and love me. I've learned a lot more about anger...Yes there is an appropriate time and place for anger...Anger can be very useful if it drives you and fills you up with determination...But I also learned how to let anger go." He worries the Morning Hill treatment center in Seattle may be as negative and humiliating as Fresh Directions. However, once he registers, he is relieved. "The staff is courteous and helpful, not suspicious and hostile," he writes. He still has Post-Acute Withdrawal Syndrome (known as PAWS), a condition characterized by depression, some compulsivity, impaired concentration and memory, sleep disturbances, anxiety, and other unpleasant symptoms that ease only gradually as the brain heals from the damage of drugs. Jon recognizes PAWS and knows it will "last awhile," but says he is "sure I'll get better while I'm still in here." He feels so positive he even says he is "sure a month will start to fly by once I'm feeling better."

The following day, he awakes consumed with drug cravings. "I can't begin to explain how badly I want to do drugs right now," he writes in the journal he always keeps with him. "It's eating me alive." He girds himself and bears the torment. One and a half hours later, he writes the craving has passed, but he feels weak and depleted from the fight. For the first time since beginning heroin, he is at least somewhat clear-headed and able to see a pattern. "Wow...when that...gets to driving you you'll stop at nothing...If you feed those urges with your energies and acquired talents for putting together your plan, then executing it, you will knock down anything that gets in your way until you are high. And so begins anew the cycle of regret, into urge, into high." He vows that the next time he feels that "insatiable lust building up and gnawing at me like a ravenous wild beast that...won't stop gnawing at me until I feed it," he will pause and remember – "this too shall pass."

During the next few days at Morning Hill, Jon continues with the discomfort of PAWS, and describes its debilitating depression, low energy, and irritability. He hasn't used heroin in a month. He feels "drained and depressed. Nothing seems all that fun. The future, although it may be bright, sure doesn't look like it from here." He has chills and cannot get warm. He describes "the ravages of this monster... You take opiates away and the body goes code red violently ill...All drug addicts have cravings but nobody has post-acute withdrawal like the opiate addict." The weather is gorgeous, and residents are outside playing volleyball, a game he normally loves. However, he can't picture himself jumping into it. "I need to pray," he concludes surprisingly.

A few days later, with vitamins, a helpful staff, and reasonable sleep, Jon begins to feel better. He still has no cigarettes and has low energy and the emotional dysregulation typical of PAWS. He states, "I might not feel all the way fantastic but I am very positive. I'm comfortable and safe, but good feelings come and go. Sometimes I feel empty...sometimes almost happy...there are so many things I want to work on and I think I may just be able to do that here." Always the individualist, he writes he is "resisting the teachings, the lectures, the groups," but wants to work on honesty and spirituality. "I want to get closer to God, whatever God is. – Help me find you. Please." He also decides to exercise and begins a regimen of pushups and walking every day.

Back at home, Evan and I return to our jobs. Having been flooded for so long with cortisol, the primitive fight-or-flight hormone that causes blood to coagulate more quickly in case of injury, I now have low energy and depression. The relief I feel at Jon's new situation is a slow fire within me, low and sustaining, but nowhere near exhilarating. Thus, the cycle that governs and restricts my life for so many years plays out once again. I am consumed by a crisis, then in recovery from the turmoil, but always watchfully waiting and dreading the next spike of fear. I am one part functional, two parts wary, and three parts desperate. Actually, I don't know how many parts I have, but I know I am not whole. I don't fit with other people. Their lives are normal or even frivolous, and mine is terrifying. Old friendships fall away, visits are refused, plans with other couples are postponed, events in the lives of our other children are ignored, and the sparks that ought to exist between husband and wife wither.

At Morning Hill, Jon alternates between feeling quite positive and returning to the angry, depressing, deterministic sentiments of late-stage addiction. He pens in his journal some of the lyrics of Layne Staley, lead guitarist and singer for the grunge band Alice in Chains. Staley died of a heroin overdose in 2002. Apparently, Jon has learned many of Staley's lyrics by heart, as music is not allowed in Morning Hill. He also writes verbatim some of the lyrics of Anthony Kiedis, addicted lead singer for the punk rock band Red Hot Chili Peppers. In addition, Jon scrawls the lyrics to *Dignity*,[78] *Things Have Changed*,[79] and *Not Dark Yet*,[80] – some of Bob Dylan's most despairing songs – and *Hunger Strike*[81] by Temple of the Dog. *Hunger Strike* was written in memory of lead singer Chris Cornell's friend Andrew Wood, who died of a drug overdose in 1990. On nearly the same pages, Jon again recites the defiant poem *Invictus*,[82] and the complete words to *The Serenity Prayer*,[83] the famous work of theologian Reinhold Niebuhr. The emotions of rebelliousness, despair, surrender, saving grace, hope, and Niebuhr's philosophy of "hardship as the pathway to peace" all agitate within him.

In Morning Hill, Jon confronts the full force of his addiction for the first time. He is open with counselors and his groups about his manipulations of others while on drugs, behaviors he has done and needs to change, consequences he has experienced, and the distorted ways he thinks when he listens to the Demon. He admits to lying to doctors and Lara to get drugs and use them, and lying to me about his expenses. He has driven his car recklessly while high, drunk or sick, and been "willing to go anywhere to score drugs." He has lost friends and has "really hurt my Mom, Dad and my girl." William Moyers and his family were caught in the same cycle. He writes, "For years I lied to my parents, my wife, my siblings and my friends...because...when 'want' becomes 'need,' truth, honor, integrity and decency cease to matter. All that matters is the drug."[84]

Jon's deeds have savaged his own belief that he is a good person. In other words, as he glares openly at his actions in addiction, he sees a different person than the one he thought he was and wants to be. To heal, Jon must regain a belief in his own worth. In the treatment center, he begins this restorative process by acknowledging he must stop lying and being so hard on himself. His self-condemnation, he says, has been huge, but not big enough to make him stop using. He writes of beginning to accept himself, letting go of negative thoughts, and believing in his own strength and ability to direct his life.

Jon describes the Demon's siren song, which is subtle and sweet on the front end. As the monster whispered to him at the start of each cycle, he would begin to rationalize: "I won't get caught (this time). It's not so bad. I won't get out of control this time. What she [Lara and/or Mom] doesn't know won't hurt her. I'm only doing this to me (not my loved ones)." He is facing a temptation as old as time; one that Saint Paul described so eloquently when he wrote, "And no wonder [we are misled], for Satan himself masquerades as an angel of light"[85] (brackets added).

As he did back in Richland in 2008, Jon personalizes his addiction as a malevolent, but most of all wily, adversary. He describes the paradox and power of the Demon that seeks, torments and calls his name: "It approaches as the beautiful stranger or trusted old friend but soon after I let it in I find my world burning and crumbling around me." Confounded, Jon calls his enemy "an evil robot inside me...my opiate android...my...monster." The monster confuses, pleads, manipulates, shadows, offers, and even impersonates Jon himself – trying to convince him the monster's desires are his own. He eventually names him "Ron" (for heroin).

As cancer patients sometimes envision a battle inside their bodies as immune cells fight cancer cells, Jon portrays his war with his Demon: "I'm starving that [devil] and he is not havin' it. He's at me day and night. Takes my strength. Takes my peace of mind. But I continue to starve him...He's fighting back and he's far stronger than I could ever put into words...Now he's bargaining with me. Playing his games and using every trick he's got and yet...I refuse to forget how...powerful he really is. How sneaky too. He cares nothing at all for me. He's seething. But if I feed him he will re-take control in this battle. He wants to kill me. But first he wants to make me watch my passions die in front of my face."

On Jon's fifth day in Morning Hill, he wakes up feeling exceptionally well. In the afternoon, he decides to join a volleyball game in the yard. Late that day, I am in a friend's backyard, helping to host a fund-raising picnic for a local political candidate. It is good to be in the company of friends on this lovely day, participating in an event that makes us feel like a community. The yard is leafy, and a bountiful garden covers a large rectangle. My phone rings in my pocket. It is Elliott, telling me Jon has had an accident at the treatment center and is at a hospital. My pita pocket heart doubles over and twists sideways. It is violent. It hurts. I step away from the group and crouch in a far corner of the yard. This setting is so familiar. It is a different yard, but it is my position – my destiny, it seems. Voice low and urgent, Elliott shares the little information he has received from the treatment center. I ask what I need to do. How bad is it? Can he stay in treatment, or does he need to come home? I leave the picnic in a hurry, once again cringing that my dysfunctional life is on display for all the normal people to see. They will distance themselves from me, I'm pretty sure. Evan will sigh and slump his shoulders when he hears. Will I be in the car on my way to Seattle in an hour? Is it selfish for me even to have these thoughts?

That evening, Jon recounts the events of his accident in his journal. During the second volleyball game, he writes, "I'm playin' center net. I love it. I'm getting my groove. Ball goes up. I tear toward that net like a freight train. My own teammate jumps in my path. We collide – bright flash of light. Stumble. Catch my balance. But something's not right. No pain. But I feel the side of my face and...there's a dent from my temple to my jaw and a bulge under my eye. I have a broken cheekbone. Very obvious...I go to the local E.R. [and get an] X-ray. I wait hours. Now the pain's coming on. Yup, it's broken in two places." Because he is a patient from the treatment center, the hospital gives him nothing for the pain. The emergency doctors recommend a surgeon he can see for further treatment, and he is driven back to Morning Hill. The staff calls to tell me I don't need to come to Seattle, at least not yet. Jon doesn't sleep well and awakes the next morning, hoping the whole episode was a bad dream. Assessing himself, he finds his left cheekbone is "popped way behind my eye…So now I'm disfigured…[and] this isn't going to fix itself…I don't look like me now, and my jaw doesn't work right…I want my face back." He calls several doctors and finds one who will see him that day. One of the counselors agrees to drive him to the appointment. He worries he has no health insurance and that the bill will be "enormous." He has had nothing for pain except a mild, over-the-counter acetaminophen. However, he writes, "I refuse to be miserable. I know I'm tough."

After Jon waits at the doctor's office much of the day, staff tell him he can't be seen because the scans from the emergency room have not been sent over. He offers to wait through the end of the afternoon, but they send him back to the treatment center. He grabs his journal, which has become his solace, and writes furiously. "So, I'm lookin' at another sleepless night. Painful but I repeat to myself I'm…[extremely] tough. I remind myself how strong I really am. With God's help I'm ten feet tall and bullet proof. I try not to forget that hardship is the pathway to peace." Philosophical, Jon writes, "I guess you could call this a bad day. But then again you could call those Hungry Angry Sick days alone on the streets, homeless, penniless and lost bad days, right? Perspective. Outlook. Is everything – everything! You've got to count your blessings. I call it inventory. #1: Living. I'm above ground, no toe tag. Yes I'm delirious with pain but I'm alive. I get to feel the pain. The dead don't feel. #2: I always thought I was tough. Now I know I am…#3: I am still very loved. My family rocks. #4: This too shall pass. I'll be OK…This won't kill me. My opioid android may kill me but this won't."

The next day, after sleeping poorly, Jon pens a haunting original poem about his own personal war on drugs. He writes he is proud of the missive, and that it "filled a place inside me I didn't know I had, or didn't remember." A little more than four years later, I will read it at his burial.

The Front

This is no battle, this is war
I've heard death's rattle at my door
In these dark days like times before
I have to settle this last score

To a parasite I've been a host
Happiness was but a ghost
Grinning from its lonely post
Somewhere out beyond the coast

So once again I'm in the trenches
Stripped of all my best defenses
No defilade behind my high fences
As my enemy advances

I'm standing tall, I'm holding ground
As comrades buckle all around
The bullets scream, the mortars pound
I will not fire one hateful round
My strength will find me safe and sound

Jon spends much of the morning in his room writing and thinking.
He has a lot of physical pain and feels emotional. At one point, he cries,
writing, "it was not in self-pity but in inspiration...My soul is healing.
And that is very good. Painful. But good. This program demands
rigorous honesty." In the afternoon, he goes back to the doctor's office
and is told a pocket of fluid is collecting behind his left eye. The doctor
describes to him very graphically that to fix his cheekbone he would "cut
a hole and push a [medical] crowbar down behind the bone and pry it
back out." Jon has a week to decide whether to have the procedure, but
immediately decides he won't undergo it because of the expense. He
does not tell me this reason, because he knows his father and I would
pay. He tells us instead the doctor says nothing needs to be done and

his face will heal on its own. That evening, he tells his journal: "I'll wear this slight disfigurement like a badge. I'll embrace the pain. I'm on the path."

That same afternoon, a new challenge confronts him. Someone has smuggled heroin into the treatment center, and rigs and a spoon have been found on the grounds. Jon is pretty sure he knows who brought the drugs, and is positive that person has more. With lightning speed, his brain makes the connections, and he knows he could find and use heroin that night if he chooses. His Demon is very close, and, shape-shifter that he is, the reptile presents his most winning façade. Jon warns himself and prays: "Oh God help me. I'm standing on the train tracks. I'm in danger. I may relapse. God help me." Next, he says, the "sneaky [devil]" changed tactics. Jon has been considering trying to fix his broken cheekbone on his own. He has attempted it, but passed out from the pain before he could "pop it out." Now, however, his Demon "makes me a promise. He says if I push some Ron [heroin] I'll be able to stand the pain of fixing my face...He's past kicking, screaming and clawing at my soul. Now he's making promises. Whispering sweet nothings." Jon struggles and dialogues with himself: "Honesty. If I want to change the way I feel I have to change the way I act. And [do it for] long enough until acting right feels. I'm fighting. Lord I'm fighting. Practice, until there is space between the impulse...and...the action." He pens a quick poem to the Demon, telling him:

> "C'mon Satan, you wanna come hit me?
> I'm flowin' with anger since the vampire bit me.
> I hold a blade.
> I'm not afraid."

That evening, he attends an NA meeting in the treatment center, writing in his journal throughout much of it. He says he is looking for strength on this strange, long, hard day filled with "pain...strain... [and] the whispering parasite." He says he needs the meeting to be reminded of "the terrible things that drugs can do. The sickness. The jail time. The loss. The emptiness. The unemployment. The disrespect.

The self-loathing. The way that nothing ever works. The lost dreams. The lost love." He hears NA can stand for Never Again or Never Alone. He takes strength from the constant use of the word "we" in the meeting. He feels the powerful fellowship. "I'm finding the only way to...have any chance at surviving is to stick together. To seek out...those who are fighting the same enemy. Surround yourself...It just makes sense. You are in a fight. You are in grave danger. It's safer if you stick together...The addict alone is in bad company." From common sense and hard experience, he has learned that people who use substances alone, eschewing friends and family to ensure the ability to use, are almost sure to develop problems.

Jon wants to hold fast to hope and to other struggling addicted people, but he also feels despair. "It feels like my life is ending. But it could very well be that my life is just beginning. When I was born I was screaming and naked. Completely vulnerable. Gasping for air. Grasping for life. And here I am again. Don't let me forget this time, how badly humans want life. This terrible affliction takes that away. Takes it all away — takes everything — gives nothing." He ends the night with fervent prayer and writes a poem about addicted people as "misfit toys," finishing by saying he loves every one of the misfit toys at Morning Hill: "You are my people."

The next day, Jon finds one of his prayers has been answered. The person who brought heroin into Morning Hill was caught, and Jon had been right about his identity. "If he'd evaded detection and kept it, it would have been within twenty-five feet of me. Scary! I imagine how I'd feel, oh God, right now, if I'd pushed last night. My android is very upset. But I am grateful." In addition, a larger conspiracy had unfolded in the treatment center the previous night. A woman patient had received money from a male patient and given it to a connection on the outside to score. When the male patient sneaked out to the dark driveway to collect his expected drugs, he found he had been cheated. The substance he thought was Mexican brown heroin turned out to be dark caramels chewed up and packaged to look like "balloons" of heroin. Both patients were expelled from the center. Jon knows the rough justice awaiting these people back on the streets. "There's a code in the dope game," he says. He expects violent payback to the woman and her outside connection.

Throughout the next week in Morning Hill, Jon fights what he calls a "three-front war" against the pain in his face, PAWS, and a case of bronchitis he catches from other patients. He calls it the "camp crud." He also has "drug dreams," in which he vividly experiences the highs and lows of drug-taking – being "peeled back," "blown out" and feeling "absolutely perfect...ten feet tall," and then feeling sick, broke, ashamed and desperate. His huge black eye scares many of the other patients, some of whom don't know how he got it. They think he must be an extremely tough street fighter – maybe even a major dealer – a misjudgment he finds rather funny.

Jon's counselors, seeing he is an avid and articulate writer, encourage him to fully commit to paper the characteristics of his monster and his duels with it. If he gives it all to his journal, they tell him, the narrative will absorb some of the power. This technique is similar to "exposure therapy" in psychiatry and sometimes is used to treat patients with post-traumatic stress disorder (PTSD). Reliving the painful experiences in detail can help those episodes become almost "routine." With the skillful mind God gave him and the grace that comes from hard, hard times, Jon pours forth his story and his struggles, creating records that will one day comfort me as much as anything can. At the time he is writing them, they are his alone, but in the future, after the rifle under the elm tree has done its work, they will feed my need to understand him.

Jon writes out pages of resentments; philosophically examines expectations, anger, acceptance and forgiveness; and details the traits he needs to cultivate to get well – "honesty, hope, faith, courage, integrity, willingness, humility, love, forgiveness, discipline, spiritual awareness, and service to my family and community." He scrutinizes pain as a motivator: "It hurt too bad to be sick [with addiction]. It hurts worse to get well. I'm reaching deep and finding strength...more deep, inner strength." He writes of regrets, including the worry his behavior has caused to Elliott and me, the loss of friendships and respect, and most of all the "enormous" longing about his distance from Eddie. In this list, he includes a lament I did not know about – "over never meeting two unborn children." He realizes that, while using drugs, he would think and talk about dreams, hopes, and plans. However, he writes, "they would never materialize...Now, I hope, and this one is a big one for me...to actually go after some of those things I always talked about and live them."

Along with regrets, Jon has a lot of anger, mostly directed at himself. He writes he is "angry that I'm an addict...that I'm powerless over drugs... that people in my life have little understanding of how hard I fight this addiction or how it really affects me...that people think I'm weak...that I have to start over again...that I couldn't get this right on my own...that I have more failures than successes...that opiates are so alluring...that I ever picked up a needle...that this progress is so slow... that I spent so much money and wasted so much time." He doesn't want to be a slave to compulsions – addiction as possession.

Returning again and again to the insidious summons of addiction and its siren song, Jon writes that, even after enduring withdrawal, "low energy, insomnia, depression, despair, sadness, suicidal thoughts...on and on for a year or two...We [addicts] heal but it's still far from over... It always comes sneaking up around you. Coming out of the walls. The streets. Everywhere you happen to run. Luring you in like an old friend or a pretty girl."

In Morning Hill, Jon recognizes clearly, perhaps for the first time, the harsh truth that to be addicted is to be constantly at war with oneself. As Joe Herzanek says, "Once addiction has gained access to a life, it will refuse to leave without a fight...When pushed away, it will patiently wait for the opportunity to strike its victim again when his or her guard is down. Addiction is never satisfied. After it has destroyed health, devastated families, ended careers, and put children in foster homes, it still wants more."[86] Jon confronts his bifurcation – the conundrum of hating drugs and realizing they bring destruction, yet returning to them again and again. He writes he "can't believe how powerful the pull is [to drugs]. I know better. I want to be clean. My conscious mind hates that dirty little chemical so much. It has taken so much from me. It wants to kill me. So it's truly baffling that I'm so drawn to it. Pandora's box. Golem [sic] and the ring. The vampire's need to feed."

Jon wrestles with the concept of "a power greater than myself. I don't know if I'm humble enough yet to start processing this step. I am all for spirituality...and would love to reconnect with it. I want nothing more than to get this right. I hope that whatever God may be can get past my reluctance...I'm getting closer God. This is my honesty offered up for you." He writes of his "spiritual confusion," and asks himself whether addiction could be "even in some part the work of a larger dark force? Evil? The Devil?" Other addicted people have asked this same question. In any case, Jon concludes, "this [addiction] is an unwinnable war. You must surrender and make peace."

The next week, he hears two lectures that truly grab his attention and open his mind in new and important ways. One lecture offers a very simplistic, yet riveting, version of the newly emerging view of addiction as a brain disease. It is a nascent theory in the early twenty-first century, and most people outside of specialized scientific circles have not heard about it. We have not. The speaker explains that various regions of the brain are responsible for different functions. He refers to the area around the base of the skull as the "lizard brain" that controls automatic functions such as respiration, heartbeat, and basic survival instincts. The frontal lobe of the brain or frontal cortex, just behind the forehead, is responsible for decision-making, thought, planning, and control. Addiction, says the speaker, lodges in the lizard brain (dorsal area) where impulses become automatic. The lizard brain doesn't think – it reacts. Addiction then essentially moves through the brain, including through the hippocampus and amygdala where memories are imprinted. Promptings coming from the lizard and memory areas are compulsive and extremely hard for the frontal cortex to control. In the addicted brain, synapses (i.e., the brain's pathways) don't connect the way they should. Instead, neurotransmitters send messages rocketing to impulsive regions. These new neural pathways drive the addicted person to seek drugs even in the face of obvious negative consequences that ought to make him/her think ahead and stop.

Not quite an elegant explanation, but it certainly contains some of the kernels of truth we later will come to understand as the brain disease model of addiction. Jon excitedly calls to tell me. "I thought I was just stacking up clean time here...but I actually learned something...This is a revelation for me. And it makes so much sense," he gushes. The disease concept gives him hope and a measure of returning pride. It explains some of the frightening collapse of reason he sees in himself. If addiction is an actual disease, he reasons, then he doesn't have to be so ashamed that he can't manage it by himself. "I always wondered why I was so at war with myself," he writes. "How can I be so self-seeking yet so self-destructive?...It's crystal clear...It's simple animal hunger-drive-need" for the drug. When addiction has progressed deep into the "lizard brain," it "becomes a subconscious drive almost akin to the need for oxygen," he writes. "This sparks a war between the conscious mind – knowing better – and the animal brain – need at any cost." However, the disease model also imparts fear. If his brain has been changed physically, can he recover?

A film by Father Joseph Martin, renowned speaker, recovered alcoholic, and founder of the Ashley Treatment Center in Maryland, also fascinates Jon. Father Martin is known for his signature welcome to each alcoholic/addicted person coming to his treatment facility: "The nightmare is over." He explains in the film that an alcoholic can't *not* drink to excess, and alcoholism is a sickness. The alcoholic who is sick and exhibiting the symptoms of his disease by drinking to excess is really no different, says Father Martin in his famous "Chalk Talk" lectures, than a cancer patient exhibiting the symptoms of pallor, hair loss, weak muscles, or bleeding. Jon is inspired by Father's blunt statement: "Alcoholics can get well."

As Jon listens attentively, he scribbles rapidly in his journal about his own situation. He is painfully realistic, but also inspired and confident. "Opiates are one hundred percent addictive if used for long enough to all human beings on the earth," he writes. "And when it comes to opiates, I got it bad...about as bad as it can possibly get. It's almost unbelievable how I stayed alive for so long. It's almost impossible that it won't kill me one day. I have, according to my best data, a very slim chance... Very grim. What I mean by that is that with my opiate use history, the amounts, and the duration I have about a two percent chance that I'll stay clean the rest of my life...They say that out of fifty people like me, one will make this work. Does that discourage me? No. Not in the least. Does it scare me? Sure. Absolutely. Yes. It's terrifying...[but] courage is not the lack of fear. It's going forward in the face of fear...Do I think I am stronger, wiser or more resilient than fifty of my peers? Oh you bet I am. Is that an arrogant thing to say? Maybe, but I'm not an arrogant person...I'm a survivor. I am doing this thing. I don't care if [the statistics are] one in a million. It's gonna be me. I have an enormous amount of drive for this. Yea I want this more than fifty others."

THIRTEEN
PROGRESS AND UNDERSTANDING

In Jon's second weekend in treatment, Lara visits and raises his spirits even further. He is especially glad the speaker they hear together during family time speaks of addicted people as strong fighters, not weaklings. Jon and Lara are in love, and for the first time since the dismal past winter and spring, they have hope for a healthy future together. He still has withdrawal symptoms, which convince him that staying in treatment is the right choice – even though he would like to leave and be near Lara every day. "I'm really tearing after my addiction," he writes. "I want to break its back. Grip is what I'm working on. Gripping the uncomfortable fact that this will be a lifelong struggle. That people don't understand what these drugs do to us." He then paints a harrowing picture of the compulsion of drug-seeking. Once he was on a "mission" to score drugs, he writes, "It was like I was riding in the back seat" with "my parasite" at the wheel. "My parasite didn't fail missions. It would hijack my intelligence, my people skills, my evasive maneuvering. All my skill sets...[my parasite] used them to get it to what it needed in spite of me. Sometimes it seemed like I had no control."

On his fifteenth day in Morning Hill, Jon moves to another room in an area known as the Second Annex. He's doing well and getting some seniority. He likes the new place because only two men share a room, the showers are nicer, and, best of all, there is a phone just for the annex residents. His first thought is that he can talk more often with Lara.

Jon loves his primary counselor Amos, who spends hours with him: "He's so much like me and he cares. I thanked him for his time and...he said 'You're worth it.'" Amos is perceptive. He sees Jon's innate intelligence, charm, and sweet guile, and warns that these traits can be dangerous. He cautions Jon that his intellect and charisma could combine to sabotage his recovery. Amos recognizes Jon likes the sound of his own voice and enjoys telling entertaining stories, which sometimes tend to glamorize his life on drugs like some kind of "drugstore cowboy" movie. Amos sees the two-sided blessing/curse of Jon's endearing sociability. He's a people person and people are drawn to him. He's a life-of-the-party kind of guy. He's also open to the suggestibility of social groups, where prudent judgment doesn't always prevail.

Amos tells Jon to treasure each day and make something good come of it, because he is exchanging a day of his life for it. Amos says recovery is the progressive discovery of ignorance, denial, and disease. Recovery, he teaches, exists in the here and now. Jon thoroughly absorbs these bits of wisdom, writing that he notices that "when I fume about the past or worry about the future, I find my parasite peeking from the corners... [but] my monster can't [mess] with the moment."

Amos encourages Jon to write a letter to "Ron" – his monster and Demon. Amos hopes it will be empowering, allowing Jon to face and take on his adversary in personal terms. It is at least cathartic. It is also so powerful and raw that, when I read it after his death, I double over and hold my sides. The letter has three distinct parts. First, Jon acknowledges to Ron that he had been a great friend and running buddy at first: "Together we could take on anything. You gave me such an edge. I could work longer, sleep better, be happier and more productive...I used to stash you away for later just to get that wonderful feeling of looking forward to you. I loved you so much, your smell, your taste, the way we were...You always approached me with a pretty face. Bringing gifts. Grinning." Next, however, Jon continues: "If only I had known the price you would ask...You wanted everything. You took from me relationships. Jobs. Lots of money. The respect of my friends and family. So much wasted and lost time...but you continued to demand more. You wanted everything. You want me alone...guilty, ashamed. And in pain. You want me homeless, helpless and lost. You want me dead." In the third part of his letter, Jon takes charge, lashing out at his enemy, cursing: "You and your empty promises...I hate you so much you're poison…You're ugly. You're rotten to the core. You're an agent of the devil…I'm done."

Amos's advice to Jon to speak directly to Ron and restore his own sense of power begins to pay off. It is the end of July, and Jon feels "hope emerging, peace of mind growing and tomorrow starting to become tangible…Today I had a belly laugh that shook my whole body…I lay in the green grass with the sun on my face. Most importantly, I talked with Eddie." As he awakens to the prospect of a new future, guilt seizes him because his drug use has brought him close to death many times: "Suicide…I have been so close. More than once…Now that I'm beginning to feel alive, I can't believe I ever wanted to be dead…Where I've been at times was so dark – so far away – adrift on a sea of sorrow. Almost no thought for my family at all when I was ready to die. Only careful planning to make it look like an accident. For their sake. Yea. For their sake. A final lie, right? So they wouldn't have to face the shame. Just the grief so they wouldn't have to deal with what really happened."

It is time for all of us to write our family impact letters to Jon, a requirement of the treatment center. We must tell him how his behavior has affected our lives, how it has changed us, aged us, cost us, constricted us, whipped and stripped us, and made us feel. He is worried we are going to "dump all over" him, and rhetorically asks his journal: "How can it be constructive to blame me, list off their resentments, tell me how badly I made them feel. How I made them worry…I already know all that. I'm regretful and guilt-stricken so I'm not looking forward to any of that." However, the wise counselors know blame isn't the point. Rather, the point is to make addicted people drop the myth that their actions have been their own business and have hurt no one else.

For the first time, I decide to be honest with Jon and tell him how his addiction has collided with my life. "Your addiction," I write, "has made me feel like I am living on some tipsy piece of ground that is shifting around me all the time…I am always off balance. I don't know if you're going to be high, somewhat 'normal,' or down and sick. I don't even know if you're going to show up when you say you will. I live at an absurd intersection of compassion and disgust, hope and despair, wanting to help and wanting to just give up, thinking I maybe understand and then realizing I don't understand in the least, anger that you trash yourself and sadness that you would, relating to the Jon I know and tiptoeing around a monster Jon that I don't know, rage at the losses for Eddie and us, and disbelief that we are even in this situation."

I tell Jon I feel old and worn beyond my years. I write that Evan and I, "have been savagely torn and ripped by your addiction – Evan calls it 'deep damage.' When we have a new incident with you, a new crisis, a disappointment or horrible realization about a phone call or a lie, a disconnected piece of time when you couldn't be found or a new medical bill in the mail, we just feel like we don't have any legs under us. We feel wobbly and completely blown away. I literally feel like I have been 'tasered' – there is a deep, rippling electric shock that goes through me and gut-punches my heart and actually makes me shake...I can barely breathe and often can't talk for hours. I get that (by now familiar) 'thousand-yard stare.' I feel like I have lived 1,000 nightmares and have a window blown straight through me so that my raw insides are there for everyone to see. Your behavior, and the fear and damage it has caused, has changed me forever." I tell him about my lost friendships and harm to my work, marriage, and other relationships in the family. "I cannot imagine my life without you," I state, "so I kept desperately pushing away the thought that you might not survive. It warped almost everything else in my life...you have NO IDEA the toll your addiction has taken."

I say I'm not telling him these things to make him feel worse, because I want him to celebrate the clean future he is building. However, I want him to take that future *very seriously*. I give him some motherly advice only a parent long familiar with addiction could give: "Watch the small stuff – the tiny, slippery slope places, people, conversations, thoughts, etc. NEVER even have a beer or a sip, never walk into a bar, never take a job in or near a bar, never stop going to AA, never talk to the 'bad old' people, never allow yourself to daydream about being high, never carry a lot of cash, never hook up a deal for someone else, never joke about the things you did or glamorize them, never lie about where you go, never stop being grateful for each sober day, and never think the enemy is gone." I tell him I love him beyond any scope he can ever imagine, and I tell him the future is his to grab and build.

The next weekend, it is my turn to visit Jon. On Sunday morning, I bound into my car eagerly and early, and drive the 210 miles to Seattle. I pace around the parking lot until I can see him at noon. When I first glimpse him, we hug deeply and both of us cry. It is a lovely day, and we walk around the grounds and lounge in the grass and talk. He still has bouts when he is dopesick and "jonesing [feeling withdrawal symptoms] hard." That morning, he has "major cravings. Major. Major...This thing still has me [captive]." He doesn't know what triggers these episodes, but says "time takes forever to tick by, waiting out these cravings... All the while, the parasite [is] whispering that he can fix it all." Jon is glad I bring him socks, body wash, paper, and other supplies. His face looks much better and hurts less. It seems it really is healing by itself, although by all logic, it should not. I still believe the doctor has told Jon no further treatment is needed. He is quiet and philosophical, perhaps because he is soberly facing the strength of his enemy and the deep hole he has dug in his life. He says my letter shook him deeply. He tries to explain the brutish nature of addiction to me, but soon gives up. No one can understand it unless he or she has been there, he says. I touch his hand, rub his shoulder, wait quietly in case he is able to tell me more. I try to be simply open and available, but I suppose my face betrays my puzzlement. All of us on the outside of this disease are baffled by the compelling path to self-destruction. "Why don't you just stop?" we wonder...but we have no idea.

In the afternoon, we learn Jon's counselors have arranged an interview for him for that evening at a group sober house in another neighborhood. It is a place he can live after completing the treatment program if he is accepted. The interview is at eight p.m., and he needs a ride and an escort to go there. He asks if I will take him. I know I will be tired, still having to drive home across the state afterward, but I instantly agree. We have dinner with his group in the treatment center. Then a counselor makes a copy of my driver's license and I take Jon. He navigates while I drive through the old streets in tree-lined neighborhoods. We arrive at an unassuming house with a big front porch, across from the grounds of a Catholic school and just a few blocks from a small lake. I wait outside during the interview; then we return to the treatment center, and I start for home about 9:30 p.m. I know it will be at least 1:30 a.m. before I find my bed and grab no more than five hours of sleep before rising for work. However, I am warm. He is my son, and together we did something wholesome and right. There was no confusion in this interaction, no chance for lies. About 11:30 p.m., my phone rings in the car. It is Lara, telling me Jon has been accepted into the sober house and will be in touch with me tomorrow as to where to send the deposit. I am so jubilant I'm yelling and cheering all by myself in the dark car. I'm also crying. We did it! Things are moving ahead. I squirm in my seat and hunch forward. It seems we have a future.

Jon's last ten days in Morning Hill pass quickly. In a lecture, he hears a slogan he particularly likes: "If you find a path with no obstacles, it probably doesn't lead anywhere." He writes profusely in his journals, analyzing himself, old friends, other addicted people and their chances for recovery, reflecting on his life, and hoping and worrying about his future. "YEA!!" he writes. "Seattle, WA...I'm excited to be stuck here... Fun, fun city. I can walk a lot of places and I can get anywhere by bus. So very, very cool." He is anxious, however, because he has "very few clothes. I have no money. I need bedding and most of all I need a job." He writes about willpower, insisting addicted people have a great deal of it as evidenced by the fact that they quit drugs over and over, go through the sickness, pain, and depression of withdrawals, and sometimes last throughout many months or even years of low energy, mood disruptions, and cravings. Then, however, they often relapse. The problem, he says, isn't willpower, it's staying power. Recovery from opiate addictions can take weeks to months to years.

Observing the people around him in treatment, Jon notes younger and younger people are developing hard-core addictions to pain killers, notably OxyContin. Privately, he names them "Oxy-tots," and he worries intensely about them. "Cute name," he writes, "deadly scenario." He is witnessing the front lines of a new plague. Presciently, he identifies it. "Wow. All these kids comin' in high. Just

kids, nineteen to twenty-three-year-olds...I can't believe their habits!...
They smoke pills! And lots and lots of them. This is truly a new drug
epidemic. Just regular pot-smokin' high school kids getting turned
on to O.C [OxyContin]...The suburbs of America are absolutely rife
with OxyContin. It's only a matter of time before "Generation Y" is
decimated by heroin overdoses...Middle class America has finally been
infiltrated by heroin through the open door of OxyContin." He marvels
at the high tolerances and expenses the young addicted patients report:
"They were up to five or more eighties a day and when they could afford
it more than ten!!...They all say it...What are they robbing banks every
three or four days?" Heroin, he says, is "the same thing as Oxy. No
different. But it's way cheaper. Not only that but it's getting stronger
and cheaper...we're gonna see a whole new emergence – Generation
Dopesick. And all thanks to OxyContin." That year, sales of Oxycontin
reach three and one-tenth billion dollars.[87]

As Jon nears release, another presentation on the idea of addiction
as a disease, possibly genetically based, rivets his attention. "After going
through withdrawals and getting better," he asks himself, "why do I go
back? I have carried the burden of addiction for a long time as well as
the burden of sole responsibility." However, he returns to the idea that
if addiction is a disease, "I may be able to let some of that [burden of
sole responsibility] go...This thing may be a disease. Whoa. Maybe. Still
a big maybe. I'm willing to kick it around...I'm also willing to believe
it's a genetic trait...I actually may have been born this way...Does that
explain why I can't beat this thing through willpower and 'knowing
better'? Here's a big one: Does that mean, even in some small way, that
this thing isn't as shameful as I've always viewed it?" He thinks and talks
a lot about shame, calling it "a perpetual condition of my sad...state."

Another speaker bores straight into the topic of the cunning nature
of addiction and the mind-games that occur in the head of an addicted
person before a relapse. Jon writes this subject is "very real to me...I
never wanted to be a junkie. I fought this as hard as I could at times.
At other times I became hopeless and almost gave up. But even still,
I resisted...We think we can control it...we prove it to ourselves [by
quitting for a while]...But our addiction is tricking us...The parasite is a

liar and [he's] sneaky...[We think] I got this...After I feel nice and safe using drugs 'responsibly,' the parasite is...waiting to pounce. It can flip the tables...without me even knowing it. The power has shifted to the parasite's advantage. Try to quit now and it'll [mess]...you up...This is how it has gone for me. Time and again." Later, he will paraphrase these thoughts for me by saying that "when I'm clean and sailing along thinking I have a future, this little [devil] is in the next room doing push-ups, just waiting to body-slam me."

The mood swings of PAWS continue to plague Jon, along with the PTSD of a survivor who cannot fathom deliverance. He writes he is anxious, depressed, nervous, and fearful. He has insomnia, agitation, and "aggression is definitely part of this for me...[and] impatience... And I'm emotional. I feel inside out sometimes. I feel stripped naked. I feel vulnerable and that makes me want to bite. Lash out. But I won't. [because]...I know why this is happening...PAWS is so aggravating...I'm somewhat fit and healthy...but...I'm a veteran doper. I'm a 10-year, several-tour survivor. I'm shocked I'm alive...My time out there and the weight of my addiction was huge...and [there is] all the other... [wild things] I've done...I should be paralyzed or dead...I've had so many broken bones, deep cuts, stitches, bruises, fistfights, adrenaline chasing – cliff jumping, big air snowboarding, paragliding, collisions, car accidents, dirt bikes, guns, homemade explosives, etc. etc. etc...But here I sit." Shivering through all the memories, Jon thanks God: "I know you're here. I'm pretty sure even through all my confusion and reluctance toward you that someone or something had my back."

On Jon's last weekend in Morning Hill, Lara visits again. She tells him she will wait as long as it takes for him to heal, because there is so much they want to do together in life – but without the lies and deceit of his drug use. Although both are somewhat rebellious personalities, their love is pure and sweet. They bring out the best in each other. Jon loves her, and he loves Eddie to the ends of the earth and beyond. For Lara, Eddie, and the rest of us, Jon writes, he will climb out of the "pit of darkness" of drugs. "I know it all sounds corny," he writes, "but it's real...It's a good analogy...[the pit] whose depths are unknown, whose depravity is unimaginable, whose bottom is death...Ascending past horrible specters known only to those who have passed through this desperate and tormented place...the climb is hard fought and daunting. Every step is treacherous...The parasite fights us from within as the torments of the pit slice and tear at us from all sides...It sounds un-doable to some and maybe it is. But it is possible. The alternative is death – either by your own hand or by letting go and plummeting to the bottom."

During Jon's last week in Morning Hill, he reflects that he has been doing drugs for seventeen of his thirty-two years, and doing opiates for ten years. He estimates that he's been "hopelessly addicted" to opiates for six to seven years. It is "absolutely true," he writes, that "drugs are a road to ruin...I have been certain of this for years. The fact that I have continued to let my guard down and gotten pummeled by this thing makes me confused...I must have a disease. I feel sick from all this... It's scary. I'm...[unbelievably] scared. But then, I should be." He passes the hallmark of fifty days drug-free and sober, remarking that "this is probably the longest I've ever been clean and sober in my life, since the first time I tried any drug...This is certainly a milestone." He has drug cravings, but "they are less frequent and noticeably less intense. They still creep out of nowhere and catch me off guard. I'm still on shaky ground because I notice my moods swinging like a pendulum." However, he writes, "I really value this new path."

He vows to volunteer at a soup kitchen or shelter when he gets out. He has developed a strong sense of community with other addicted people and wants to help. He also says he will do community service for "selfish reasons" – he does not trust himself. "I know I could go a little while away from drugs, no problem. But the day may very well come that everything lines up just wrong to set up a relapse. There is one thing for sure – relapse is not part of my recovery plan. Not this time...I've been there and it just set off a chain reaction that lands you right back in" the world of hurt. He confesses that he is very "nervous about leaving the safety of this place. I am. I don't know what to expect. I don't know how I'll react. Could be that the parasite is waiting to attack. I feel like I may be walking into an ambush...The parasite is incredibly sneaky. I'm on terror red alert. I know that little [devil] is lurking in dark alleys waiting for the perfect opportunity to blindside me. But at least for today my guard is up. I'm well armed. I'm well trained. And I'm expecting that little punk." I wish now I had known how frightened he was. I wish I had known that, while inpatient treatment is hard, the recovery journey afterward is even harder for addicted people.

On the final day, his group surrounds him and gives him kudos for his progress and offers advice about how to stay sober. Amos tells him the stakes are deadly serious: "You will have to figure out how not to die of your disease." He tells Jon there are things he will have to give up. He will need to draw a line in the sand and just stop. Most of all, he will have to put his recovery first, before anything else in his life: "Priority #1." Amos also advises Jon he doesn't have to know all the answers as he leaves treatment. He just needs to keep seeking answers, AA and NA meetings, sober friends, and constructive activities. Jon admits privately he is going to miss Morning Hill: "Where else can you be drawn together in such a close collision with a room full of strangers and within weeks know each other so well, and feel cared about like we do? Everyone should be so lucky...I really will miss all these people...What a wonderful and positive place." He feels "comfortable" there, "peaceful and calm...[it] sounds cheesy, but I feel loved." Reflecting in his room, he nearly misses one of his last meetings and can't wait to rejoin the group. "I was so glad to be heading back toward a room full of junkies, tweakers, burnouts and drunks...misfits. And I feel really good" around them. "Thank you all," he whispers to himself. "I love you."

Jon writes that "I honestly didn't think I'd learn that much here [Morning Hill]. But I did...I learned a lot about this parasite of mine. I added many important tools to my arsenal...I'm finding more and more that battling this thing is no simple type of warfare. This is chess, not checkers. Every weapon, every technique, every angle, every tactic is vital and without all of them – I'm in check." Looking back, getting some perspective, Jon concludes that "drugs took my soul...It left me little by little. By now, after this long, after such huge quantities, and after pushing heroin during the end game, my soul is missing. It's growing back, but it's little by little...for so long, opiates were my soul." He feels old, worn down, threadbare, and wise in ways he wishes he did not know. "God help me," he writes. "I don't think I have another run in me. Another dopesick. Another move. Another self-induced loss. Another broken heart. I am done. Sobriety hurts right now...but I know I can do this and I'm in this fight."

Constantly, he goes back to the question of whether addiction is a disease, calling this dilemma "the most complex intellectual puzzle in a long time...The frontal cortex, Morality. Reason. Personality. Emotions. And the evolutionary pinnacle – spirituality." His gifted mind swirls with these issues of the divided self, at the same time the practical tasks of building a new life in sobriety consume him. He knows he has always eschewed AA and NA meetings and the famous Twelve Steps. He's impatient with some of the people he terms "book thumpers" in these meetings who speak "psychobabble," pontificate, and simply repeat slogans. Yet, he admits the AA and NA meeting rooms "are full of vibrant, intelligent, energetic, positive success stories. Plus...these Steps lay out a spiritual path. A way to look the world straight in the eye. Head held high. A way to a closeness with the spirit that I may never have known. This is a path to a righteous and fulfilling life. I don't want to miss out on that." He concludes: "I feel good today. I'm ready to go out there and begin the work of recovery...I want to get down to business."

FOURTEEN
REAL LIFE

The next morning, I drive to Seattle with new bedding, a bus pass, food, and some cash. We meet at the sober house where Jon has already arrived, walked around the neighborhood and its little lake, and bought a lunch of wraps. "Wow that food is delicious," he tells me. It is Friday the thirteenth of August 2010, an absolutely beautiful day. Seattle is experiencing its hottest week of the year, showing off as the Queen City it is when skies are as blue as the lakes, bicyclists seem to be everywhere, and people in colorful outfits bustle about a prosperous, exuberant city. There is very little air conditioning in Seattle except in high-rises, so most windows and doors are open in Jon's new neighborhood. Together, we pull open the packages of new, chocolate brown sheets, pillowcases, quilts, and towels, snapping them in the air with sharp cracks as we spread them out. Soon, his half of his room looks cozy and neat. Watching him, I sense some anxiety. Later, I wish I had taken it more seriously. It is one of my many regrets that I didn't know a four-week stint in a treatment center is rarely enough for a person with advanced addiction. That night, he will confess to his journal that he "should have enjoyed…this day…but I'm jumpy. I'm just nervous…I can't explain it. I just feel generally uneasy. Not scared. Just uneasy." He thinks it is caused by all his moving around. "Now I'm once again in a place where I don't know anyone. Starting over."

Late in the afternoon, we drive out to Jeff's place in the suburbs. Although Jeff has owned this condominium for five years, Jon has never been invited there nor been allowed to know the address. We all feared he would burden Jeff, freeload, or even bring addicted friends who might cause trouble. Now, we show belief in him, and the three of us go to dinner at a bistro in a fashionably remodeled old brick building.

Jeff and I order sodas, not wanting to drink alcohol in front of Jon. When he sees our drinks are ready, he sprints to the bar to scoop up the three large glasses in his long, practiced hands. We talk animatedly, and afterward I ask my sons to stand together for photos in the parking lot as the brilliant setting sun glints behind them. They are so handsome they literally turn heads, both looking fit, slender, and sturdy. The best of these photos is still framed in my home office. That night, Jon tells his journal the food that night was "super good. The conversation was better...I had a great meal and a really good time with my family."

After dinner, he asks to be dropped off at Morning Hill to attend an evening AA meeting there, knowing he can get a ride to his new house from others attending the meeting. Sitting among the twitching, sweating, scratching, antsy group, some of them falling out, he feels at home. He confesses to his journal, "I was missing those psychopaths. I know they miss me too. What can I say people? Treatment won't be the same without me." The stories of the addicted people in treatment are individual, but in a sense, they are all similar. The cost of drug use became higher than each was willing or able to pay. The road back was very hard and was accomplished only with immersion in the recovery community. Ties made in the sober groups are not just friendly and understanding – they are fundamental, requisite, and organic. Connection doesn't just run through these groups – it is their engine.

As Jon settles down for his first night of sleep in the new house, his anxiety seems to subside. "This house," he writes, "is nice...and the people are cool and friendly and funny. The location is better than anyone could ask for. What a score." The next day, he gets his hair cut and takes two long walks into Seattle's U District to find some healthy food and look for Help Wanted signs. He writes that the men in his sober house "are like looking in a mirror sometimes. Super fun to be around." Lara is traveling to visit him the next day and he looks forward to it intensely. He describes their simple plans: "We're gonna have so much fun," he writes. "We're gonna blow up a raft and paddle to an island in the lake. Then explore the town a little...I'm so happy!" Feeling like "a kid at Christmas," he wakes early the next morning, but Lara calls to tell him that her car is overheating. Of course, once I am informed of the problem, I tell Lara to borrow my car, and she continues on her way to Seattle and Jon.

They revel in their beautiful day together. They take her small, tippy raft out into Green Lake, swim, and then drive to the U District where he shows her his old neighborhood and house. After a meeting at the sober house, they drive out to Alki Point in West Seattle, visiting the lovely waterfront restaurant where Jeff, Jon, and I dined on a memorable night nine years earlier. They can afford only an appetizer, and then they walk around West Seattle Beach amidst the crowds on this gorgeous evening. "Everyone's out," Jon writes later. "Cars were shimmering in the streetlights...We sat on the dock and watched the light fade as the city became a sparkling light show...We decided to finish off the night with a visit to Seattle Center...We walk right up to the Space Needle and touch it...Almost curfew...we get home just in time." The next day, they walk around Seattle's downtown waterfront, reveling in the "sights, smells, the heat. Another absolutely stunningly beautiful day in Seattle. The Emerald City." Lara stays another night, then drives back to Richland early to return to her job. She works hard; Jon admires her. So do I.

After Lara's visit, Jon is quickly bored at the sober house, and writes of his fears: "I feel myself slippin'...I'm being tested by the biggest and most common trigger: Boredom...My parasite likes me bored. This is its playground. I'm staying extremely vigilant. But it's a sneaky [devil]...I've been thinking about drinking lately...So I see what's on T.V. and plan to hit a meeting. Keep starving little parasite. I'm bigger than you now. And keeping it that way." The Demon is close, but he's low-key – almost subtle, but not quite. He knows how to play his hand. He knows how to wait. Jon begins his outpatient, follow-up treatment sessions and finds several AA and NA meetings in neighborhoods he can reach by bus or on foot. One night, after only a week in the sober house, he takes a bus to Morning Hill for an evening meeting, but his ride back leaves without him. He has to catch a roundabout series of buses to get back and arrives an hour after curfew. The senior guys in the house are not happy and they drug-test him on the spot, but he passes with no problems. He lands four days of work painting the interior of a nearby house and loves it. He's glad to have the company of music and has a "solo dance party" while painting. He writes that "dancing felt good. Working hard felt good. But being lonely [is really bad]...I've really been needing a meeting. Bad thoughts spinnin'. Bouncing around my skull."

Back in Richland, Kathy and Clark's wedding is coming soon, with Lara as the maid of honor. At a meeting of the sober house group, Jon asks permission to attend the wedding, although normally new residents can't be away overnight during their first month. The guys vote to let him go, but just for thirty hours, provided he takes a drug test as soon as he returns. I buy him a plane ticket. When Evan finds out, he is angry with me and says I'm putting Jon in harm's way. "What if Jon drinks alcohol and relapses at the wedding reception," Evan asks me. "Won't I feel guilty?" Yes, of course, I will. I get a chill and call Jon. He reassures me drinking is not tempting for him, and teases me by saying he is looking forward to the "fun" of watching drunk people act foolishly! He continues joking by saying, "It's not like they'll have an OxyContin and heroin open bar!" He tells me not to listen to his words, but to "watch his footwork," meaning he knows I will have much more reason to believe him if/as/when he walks his talk. Privately, he worries he hasn't really been able to reassure me. He is painfully aware, he writes, I have "no reason to believe" him. He writes that his real "concerns are deeper in the future."

On and off, like an erratic, unbalanced see-saw, his body and his emotions gyrate during his first few weeks in the sober house. He is ravenously hungry and enjoys stopping at all-you-can-eat sushi bars as he walks the nearby Seattle neighborhoods. Sometimes, he can't believe how much he eats. "My body is still a little bashed up from all those drugs...from time to time I feel dopesick. Sometimes, out of nowhere, I want to off me...Suicidal thoughts? What?...Maybe [I'm] just reeling and busted up." His long sojourn in the drug world has been time in agony, he writes. No wonder he has PTSD. Neither of us knows it is typical for people in early recovery to have unpredictable and rapidly changing emotions that surprise them. Their brain chemistry is adjusting to major changes, as they have blunted their feelings with drugs in the past.

On the day of the wedding, he is too excited to sleep so he rises early and travels the bus and light rail system to SeaTac Airport. He takes his time in the airport, enjoying all the sights, people, freedom. From his window seat on the airplane, he loves watching the sun gleaming on the wings, the specks of clouds, the familiar mountain peaks, and "mighty" Columbia River. Although he has been away from Richland just over two months, he says it feels like two years. That evening, the late summer air is lovely, and lights twinkle in the trees as darkness falls. The wedding is sweet and simple. I stay just long enough to be polite, as I don't want to appear to be hovering. Jon writes of his feelings later: "Everyone was drinking hard. I didn't think it would bother me but it did." It wasn't that he wanted to drink, but, "what I didn't like at all was being different. Being less. Being defective. I felt like everyone I came across thought...I was a broken defective drunk with no self-control... and they should be wary of my behavior...Mostly just standing out as different REALLY [HURT]...I felt overwhelming contempt for any glance, any whisper, any false sincerity...I know people were trying to be polite and their intentions were, for the most part, true and good and coming from the right place. I held my head up and tried to remember that but inside I was burning."

Jon and Lara have a sweet night together. The next day, I come upon them by chance in a store a few hours before Jon's airplane is to leave. They are walking very close to each other, downcast, sad to think of being apart, but determined to wait for a time when addiction and the Demon will leave them free to be together. Later, walking by the deep blue, late summer Columbia River, I watch Jon's airplane fly overhead. I gaze as it hurries west, becoming less of a shape than a speck, and then it simply fades and disappears. Like many things involving Jon, it is beyond my reach.

Back in Seattle, Jon fills pages of his journal trying to explain his addiction in terms he wishes all of us who love him could understand. It is a heart cry, a lament, a tragedy, a soul-wrenching ache. He has seen the power of his disease and stood at the edge of its awful abyss. "I feel like I'm at the bottom of a pile of disgust, contempt, shame and guilt that I don't even own...I wish she [Lara] would understand that this has been a war raging in me for over a decade. I never wanted it.

I always fought back. I'm a good person. I'll never expect anyone to understand the power of the grip of this dark force. What it does to a human soul. A kind soul. A strong and righteous person possessed and twisted against their will, against their morals. Against their love and compassion. The disconnect from the energy, the positivity, the light. How terrifying it all is."

He writes chillingly of the Demon: "The Devil is very real and… scary…It doesn't release you because you know better. It doesn't want you to hold onto your values or your humanity. I fought…with everything I had. I made every sacrifice to reconnect with whatever God is…But… the Devil always found me….I can't explain it because this enemy of mine is smarter, stronger and more cunning than me…This dark and evil force is all around me and it wants all of me…I don't expect Lara to understand…that my plight has nothing to do with her…I was gripped by this [compulsion] long before we met. Long before I met Eddie. It has nothing to do with how much I love and care for either of them…I never had a drop of spite in my heart when I hurt [Lara]…Look at what I'm doing…Do you think this is easy?…[But] I'm doing it for everyone [my whole family]. I'm doing this so I can be a part of everything and everyone." The battle isn't fair, and the stakes are as high as they could ever be – values, love, parenthood, safety, strength and willpower, staying power, fidelity, trust, and life itself hang in the balance.

Evan, Brett, our dogs, and I spend Labor Day weekend at our cabin in central Washington State. We pick huckleberries and blackberries, which I wash, drain, and package for delicious baking throughout the winter. One day, Evan and Brett go rock-climbing at a nearby set of cliffs, and I am left with a free day. I decide to drive into Seattle to visit Jon. Lara and her mother Alyssa also are visiting him. The drive is beautiful -- up and down a mountain pass and through the flatlands of western Washington in the almost blinding last blaze of summer sun. I arrive at Jon's sober house and the four of us go to lunch in the quaint, tiny, walled garden of a diminutive restaurant. The sun slants at odd angles above the wall and through overhanging vines. It keeps moving throughout our long, lazy lunch. I am soaked in contentment, flooded with gratitude. A simple lunch others might take for granted seems to me an infinite gift. It is so *normal* – but nothing has been normal for me for so long I cannot believe we are sitting here, just talking, laughing, relaxing...is this what regular families do?

A few weeks later, a business trip takes me back to Seattle. I bring a sport watch with variable features for Jon. It has a thick, masculine band and a bright yellow face. I would rather have dinner with him than with my co-workers, so I excuse myself from them and ask him to meet me. I watch as he strides down the street, long legs outdistancing most others on the sidewalk, ample arms swinging, chest full and broad, eyes alert and enjoying the crowds and lights. I give him the watch, in celebration of seventy-five days drug-free and sober. He hangs his head. "How can you be proud of me?" he asks. We hug. Neither of us can speak. Then we walk along and have a great dinner. His mind is so inquisitive, his conversation so wide-ranging and stimulating. I go to sleep grateful.

September moves into October and still, Jon can't find a job. He is enormously upset about having no income and too much time on his hands. "I Really, Really, Really, Really, Really want to get a job," he writes. "I wake up every morning wishing I was getting ready for work. I have resumes all over the city." However, he makes good on his promise to reach out to help others. He finds a neighborhood church that holds a free supper for homeless teenagers and volunteers to mingle with the teen boys to talk, encourage, pray, and offer what wisdom he can. This program is a wonderful fit for Jon. He looks the part of a street-wise guy, although he has no tattoos or piercings. Despite his appearance, his heart is soft, loving and it opens wide when he hears about the home life some of these teens have left and the street life to which they have gravitated. The boys are guarded, he tells me. They won't even tell Jon their real names, but instead adopt street names such as Monkey, Zippo, Skate, and Diver. The homes they have fled, Jon says, are places they *should* have left. They were abusive and cruel. Talk that glamorizes drugs or drug deals, exploits, or scores is not allowed, yet Jon can see many of the boys are high, and he does not condemn them.

He goes to the meals for the teens even on nights when he doesn't feel like it. "I've really internalized the fact that when you know you should do something, especially if you don't want to – do it anyway," he writes. "This is the pathway to rewarding experience. Some of the best meetings I've been to and the best nights at the teen suppers have been the nights I really, really didn't want to go." Later, the program's director will write a recommendation for Jon commending his dedication to clients, service to community, teamwork, attentiveness to the needs of volunteers and staff, and his ability to take on various roles. The recommendation also states Jon is intelligent, dedicated, and a good adult role model for the at-risk youth who come to the program.

To my amazement, and as part of his pledge to be open and honest, Jon invites me to read some of the journals he has kept over the previous summer. Humbled by his confidence, I accept. However, I am in no way prepared for the power of his story, his struggles and near-misses, his despair and agony. My heart twists sideways and downward again and again. It seems to intrude so far into other organs that my sternum aches and my whole digestive tract contracts violently. I read late into the nights. I cannot put away the pages, and even when I do so, I cannot sleep. He is evocative, gritty, real, and headlong. He has a whale of a story to tell, and there is absolutely no doubt that he knows his subject.

I also ask him several blunt questions:

How and when did partying become addiction? He says he wonders himself "how this opiate thing started, where and when that spark struck, when the door was opened and this awful parasite slipped in. I cannot pinpoint it."

Has he become a habitual liar? He hopes not. Honesty "is a keystone piece of this whole thing. It doesn't work without honesty. I'm trying very hard at this. It [lying] does sometimes feel like second nature...[but] I'm really working on it."

How could he put a needle full of poison in his body? "IV drug use scared...me [terribly]," he answers. "Especially when I became comfortable with it...The problem, of course, is when you have gotten there it's already pretty much too late. The road out isn't even visible from there."

Has he overdosed? "I'm sure I've had several [overdoses]," he answers truthfully. "None were what you'd call 'deliberate' although I guess there is some gray area. What's a fatal dose to someone with an inhuman, ungodly tolerance?"

Why didn't he accept treatment and help sooner? He has "no regrets," he says, because his long path through the darkness "could very well be what it took. Could be God's plan...Maybe I needed to learn all this. Maybe it's good for me, maybe, hopefully, it can help other people. Either way, I don't regret my experiences, only the pain it caused you and everyone else who cares about me."

What about Eddie and the effects of his drug use on this beautiful little boy? Jon "still can't write about him much. He's awesome. Solid gold." The regrets about Eddie are too heavy. "I'm only glad he didn't see me going through this again and again." Tomorrow, Jon says, he and Eddie have tomorrow.

In October 2010, Jon steps out into the broad daylight with details of his addiction in a letter to Dori. His letter is powerful, honest, raw. He speaks of sickness, deceit, broken relationships, lost jobs, and despair. "One thing I know for sure," he recounts, is "that I couldn't quit on my own...It's impossible beyond anything that most people could ever understand...I've been trying to win this unwinnable fight all these years and all I had to do was lose, surrender and make peace... When I started being honest, truly letting go and being honest, that's when I knew I had a shot at this [sobriety]."

Then Jon tells his sister the best part -- how it feels to him to come out from addiction and be a real person again: "My feelings came back. Compassion, sympathy, empathy...It was like I didn't know my soul was missing until it started coming back...I laugh harder now, sometimes till it hurts, and more often. I think more clearly...My relationships with the people I love are starting to work again...I'm finding freedom from things I never knew had a grip on me. I know four months [of sobriety] isn't all that long but I'm proud of it. I don't have [any possessions of my own] and I live with NINE other guys...But I'm so much happier and actually on my way. Now and only now do I have a shot at making something of this life and I'm so grateful I can't put it into words."

I can't stop visiting Seattle as I am so excited to be able to enjoy two healthy sons, so I plan another trip the last weekend of October. Jon writes that he, "can't wait to see Mom...we usually have a really good time." He plans for us to shop for a rain jacket for him, hike in a park, and climb to the top of the historic stone water tower in Volunteer Park. Built in 1906, the tower is seventy-five feet tall and sits at an elevation of 520 feet on Seattle's Capitol Hill. Jon and I climb the 107 winding, narrow stairs and are rewarded with a stunning, 360-degree view of the entire Seattle area. He knows the city well and points out all its lakes, surrounding mountain peaks, neighborhoods, and bridges. I marvel at his voracious mind. For dinner, we find a charming restaurant with twinkling lights and tell Jeff and his girlfriend to meet us. We all have a delightful dinner. Jon writes in his journal, "It was really nice to see Mom relaxing and having a good time."

November passes and he asks me if he can enroll in community college in the winter to work toward certification as a Chemical Dependency Professional (CDP).[11] I am more than on board – I am thrilled, as is Elliott when I talk to him. We tell Jon to go ahead and apply. We will handle the expenses together. He works piecemeal jobs for a few days here and there, while he searches for real employment. Seattle turns cold and rainy, and I buy him a huge snow jacket, which he appreciates because he still walks everywhere. His old crate of an SUV is home in Richland, where we insist it stay. He takes a bus to meet us at our cabin to celebrate Thanksgiving. Jon loves it: "Snow everywhere. Cold. And all of us [family members except Dori] and Lara together by a crackling fire. Feasting and enjoying each others' company." In Seattle, Jon helps many other addicted people, and his advice begins to be sought in the local recovery community.

---

[11] Today, this is called a Substance Use Disorder Professional (SUDP).

FIFTEEN

HOW GOOD LIFE CAN BE

In January 2011, I again visit Seattle and Jon greets me with one of his best bear hugs. After a day, he drives back to Richland with me. Halfway back, we veer off and take a road through a beautiful canyon that follows the twisting Yakima River. I have never taken this road, but I'm not surprised Jon has found it. His curiosity and desire to explore have been integral parts of him all his life. We see eagles perched high in trees, scanning the river with their piercing eyes, looking for food. Traveling with Jon always means having a non-stop, fascinating conversation ranging over a myriad of topics. Evan always marvels at Jon's breadth of knowledge on a variety of things – music, science, the environment, the economy, history, machines, and many other subjects.

Arriving back in Richland, Jon wants to go straight to Lara's house. He has offered to fix engine problems in her old car. Together, they work on it and finally get it running. They take a day trip to Palouse Falls, a 198-foot-high water fall that that drops from a basalt cliff into the Palouse River about eighty miles northeast of Richland. The scene is spectacular. The water is, in Jon's words, "absolutely rippin from all the snowmelt...[it was] thundering a powerful roar...we had to get close." Lara tells me later they got perilously close to the edge, in an area where hikers have fallen to their deaths. With Jon's affinity for risks, I am not surprised. Then he hurries back to Seattle where he begins community college, taking Sociology as a first step to becoming a CDP. He hasn't been in school in fifteen years, and we are joyous. He puts his beautiful mind to work.

He passes the milestone of 200 days drug-free, and marvels that he hasn't "cheated...not one pill, not one sip of beer. Nothin. And I can say it's not so bad." At the sober house, the old furnace breaks in a deep cold spell. When repair calls go unanswered, Jon takes it apart and fixes it with no instructions. His greatest frustration is the lack of a job. "I feel so worthless," he writes. "I feel like what's the point of being clean if I'm not producing anything...It's stressful and very depressing."

In February, Eddie flies to Washington State for a visit. All of us are very excited, as we haven't seen him in eight months. I go to Seattle, pick them both up, and drive to our cabin for two days. We then drive back to Richland, where Eddie and Jon stay nearly a week. Jon has arranged to receive and complete his schoolwork remotely, after telling his professors of the importance of his son's visit. We play with dogs, Legos, and sidewalk chalk, see movies, and have sleepovers with Miles. Jon reads bedtime stories to the boys, and we serve their favorite pizzas, chicken nuggets, ice cream, and my "special" toast with cinnamon sugar.

We allow Jon to take his car back to Seattle for the first time in eight months. Soon afterward, he learns he has landed a job as a server at a gorgeous waterfront restaurant. He is ecstatic. "This place is beautiful," he writes. "It's an enormous restaurant that can probably hold close to 500 people. It's...ON the water at Shilshole Bay right next to the entrance to the Ship Canal. It's got all these tiers and levels with enormous windows. It's in a perfect spot to catch the sun setting behind the Olympics [Mountains] out across all that water." He begins training on March 1, 2011.

Throughout the spring, Jon does extremely well. He earns an A in his Sociology class and begins the spring quarter, taking Law and Ethics in Chemical Dependency. He writes a paper he calls "Do No Harm," in which he states, "There is no one way to recovery...everyone's struggle is different...There is no one prescription for addiction." As an addicted person himself, he realizes, "The thought of not doing drugs can be a foreign and even terrifying prospect to an addict, and the journey is often very uncomfortable and hard-fought. Most clients are vulnerable and scared." He concludes by stating each addicted person who might become his future client "is worth all my best efforts... It's difficult for me to imagine a more valuable objective or a more worthwhile undertaking than helping people retrieve their loved ones from the brink of such misery and such tragic waste." He receives an A on the paper.

In mid-April, I visit Seattle to shop for birthday gifts for and with Jeff. I have kept this tradition with my oldest son for nearly fifteen years, ever since he went to Seattle as a freshman at the University of Washington. This year, the trip is extra-special, as we scoop up Jon and head to our favorite shopping mall. We race from store to store, marveling at the selection, bargains, and resplendent displays. Jon needs everything, so I tell him to pick out some things. Shyly, he tries on some items, preening sideways in the store mirrors. He seems proud of his healthy and dignified look, a feeling he hasn't experienced in a long time. Jeff chooses his gifts carefully, with long deliberation, as is his wont. I'm not really looking for myself, but I find a green sweater that fits me well at a discount price. I don't really need it, but decide to buy it just as a reminder of this wonderful day with my sons. Later that evening, we have dinner at a fun, upscale pub in Seattle. Sitting side-by-side across from me, Jeff and Jon are striking in their vibrant good looks – Jeff's features chiseled, Jon's more rough-hewn. The female server flirts with them outrageously. I am enchanted. I feel restored. I am the most blessed mother in the world. Years later, I will keep the green sweater in the bottom of one of my dresser drawers. Looking at it will be hard.

Later in April, Jon passes the mark of 300 days drug-free and sober, a new record he hasn't achieved since the age of thirteen. He finishes building a cart with pedals for Eddie, and calls it "a reminder of what sobriety is doing for me. Without the constant storm clouds of drug addiction, projects actually get done." His job is going well and he visits Richland twice. He enthuses about the "clear [mountain] peaks showing off their heavy snow cover...miles and miles of...blossoming orchards... the rust red basaltic rocks, the steep never-ending hillsides shin[ing] olive green between the shadows." He takes the scenic canyon route and must stop twice as families of bighorn sheep cross the road. He has always loved nature and now his mind is clear enough, and his heart full enough, to thoroughly appreciate it. On his visits, he and Lara venture out on the Yakima River in our old red canoe, which I have now told him belongs to him. The Columbia is flowing bright blue and gorgeous, but too high with spring run-off to chance it in the canoe. Jon and Lara explore campsites for the summer, and one time they are dumped into the Yakima River when a surge of fast water catches them off guard. They get soaked and cold, but go back on the river the next day.

As an early Mother's Day gift, they take me on a hike across a desert plateau on the north side of the Columbia where the river turns sharply to rush toward Richland and eventually meet the sea. The Wahluke Slope is magnificent in its stark beauty. It sports virtually every shade of tan, beige, almond, khaki, ecru, taupe, sepia, bronze, mocha, ochre, and buff in God's design, interspersed with rocky outcroppings of hard black basalt. We walk miles across the windswept slope to reach the steep, ashy cliffs that fall away toward the river. Kathy and Clark's yellow Labrador retriever and our wonderful dog Mountain accompany us. The dogs are sturdy and scramble down the cliffs to drink deeply in the cobalt river. We watch them jump and play while we eat our picnic lunch. On the drive home, Lara sits in the front seat next to Jon and I sit behind them. This new configuration seems exactly right – the young people taking over the driving, talking about their plans, and me getting older and treated to a ride.

They are planning to get an apartment together in Seattle around June 1, as long as Jon continues to be drug-free and sober. Lara has been working extra shifts as a server to save money for furniture and the security deposit. Jon has now taken over his own rent and child support payments, but has essentially nothing left to put into savings. He is planning for Eddie to come and stay most of the summer with him, but worries that somehow the visit won't happen. "I am filled with stress and worry, sadness and despair," he writes. "Standing up for my rights as a father is and has proven to be a significant struggle. But I do it. I continue to fight. Because it's Eddie. Plain and simple."

Jon visits Richland in late May to inventory the belongings he and Lara have for their new place. He still has possessions in a storage unit I have been maintaining, and Lara has saved diligently. They stop to see me, flushed with exuberance. They are so happy, so young, so in love. I realize I haven't seen Jon smile like that, or look so fresh and wholesome, in nearly twenty years. My heart is bursting too, and for once it's in a good way. They are short a few hundred dollars for a sofa they have found, so I write a check. With big hugs all around, they race out the door.

A few weeks later, they move into a small apartment a few doors off busy Aurora Avenue in north Seattle. Jon has earned an A in his class at school, but decides not to take a summer class because Eddie's visit is confirmed for six weeks. Soon, Evan and I visit Seattle, gathering Jeff, his girlfriend, Lara, and Evan's daughter June who is in the area visiting her mother, and go to dinner at Jon's restaurant. It is an enchanting early summer night of the kind on which Seattle sparkles and glows. Jon has reserved us an ideal deck table overlooking Puget Sound, which is filled with yachts, sailboats, and the grimy working boats that give Seattle's harbors their historic authenticity. He is impeccable in his white apron and striking grin, deftly moving among the tables, his long arms giving and gathering all manner of sustenance, dishes, and glassware. Often, the eyes of customers linger on him as he moves about. He is capable and stunning, friendly but professional – the young man every parent and young lady would like to have, and every young man would like to be. At our table, we laugh with a level of joy we rarely experience, and Jon joins us for a few moments when he can.

A week later, Eddie arrives for his summer visit. Jon and Lara have arranged their schedules so that she works days and he works evenings, so Eddie will never be alone. This summer will be the longest time Jon has seen his son since moving away from Wisconsin five summers earlier. Jon has been in recovery almost a full year. He has outfitted a large fish tank and stocked it with colorful creatures that fascinate Eddie. He has programmed a constantly changing photo display onto the television, so the screen flips through photos of Eddie from his babyhood onward. The small apartment is stocked with Legos, Eddie's favorite toy, as well puzzles, adventure books, sidewalk chalk and digital video discs (DVDs) for children. Eddie has the one bedroom in the apartment, while Jon and Lara sleep on the ample, L-shaped sofa. Although quarters would be called cramped by the standards of many, to Jon, Lara, and Eddie, they are snug and blissful.

The third week of July, Jon, Lara, and Eddie join us for two nights and days at the Washington coast island resort where we have gone for many years. Eddie is almost nine years old and intensely interested in nature – the foliage, the big Dungeness crabs and shrimp that we catch, the deer that feed on island grasses, the seals our boat passes lounging on rocks, dolphins that surface occasionally, and eagles that soar and hunt from high trees on the island. Jon takes him rafting to a nearby outcropping of rock at low tide. With me, Eddie explores tiny crabs and other sand creatures while Jon and Lara hold hands and walk. Lara tells me shyly that she and Jon have plans. If he can stay in recovery a full year after leaving the treatment center – a time period almost finished – she will agree to marry him and have a baby. I am suffused with joy and a calm sense of well-being. We have made it through the worst of times, I think. We have tamed the Demon or at least driven him past the outer boundaries of our world.

About a week later, back in Richland, I drive to Seattle with Kathy and Clark's son Miles to have one last summer visit with Eddie. Jon is working both nights, but Lara and I take the boys to waterborne bumper cars, a huge outdoor trampoline, a special dinosaur exhibit at the zoo, and then to pancake houses for dinners. The boys participate enthusiastically in all the silly fun we offer. They bump their cars ferociously, beg for more turns on the trampoline, stare with fascination as the animated model dinosaurs roar, and burp and giggle loudly at dinner.

On Saturday morning, all of us drive to West Seattle's Alki Point Beach. Located across Elliott Bay from downtown Seattle, the neighborhoods of Alki Point range from funky and colorful to elegant. They have something of the flavor of Golden Gate Park in San Francisco. Rollerbladers and joggers clog the sidewalk that runs just above the beach looking back at Seattle's stunning skyline. Couples and families stroll the beach, eating ice cream or savoring cups of Seattle's dark, rich coffees. Jon is an expert at tide pools and quickly rolls up his sleeves and pants to wade in. Easily, he pushes over rocks to reveal small sea creatures scurrying from visibility or multi-colored starfish. The boys squeal with delight as Jon shows them how to grasp tiny crabs from the back of their bodies to avoid the claws. We use a pail in my car as a crab shelter. We line it with seaweed, sand, and seawater, letting the boys keep a few crabs for a short time before releasing them. As the day warms, the boys venture more and more boldly into the water. Soon they just plunge in, emerging cold but laughing. We let them select a "beach casual" pizza restaurant for lunch, and we sit outside in the sun. Jon and Lara look like a golden pair. Sitting across from them, watching them parent the boys, glancing at each other for a quick kiss now and then, I am content. This day is so precious, so much the epitome of a life I had hoped for, but thought, for a long time, was lost to us. I rest with the sun on my back and literally feast on the sight of these four vibrant young people. It is the last time I will see Jon sober in many months.

The last night of my visit, the boys are still bouncing around the apartment as Jon walks in from his shift at the restaurant. He loosens his tie as he surveys the loud, happy scene in front of him. "I wish things could just stay like this forever," he says. "I love this life."

The next morning, I collect Miles and drive back to Richland. Jon, Lara, and Eddie are getting ready to drive to California to visit Elliott and Dori. Dori has fallen in love and become engaged to a young soldier named Derek. Jon wants to meet him and show the sights of the beautiful Bay Area to Lara and Eddie. I am afraid of the 800 miles that lie ahead of them in Jon's old SUV. However, they are beside themselves with enthusiasm – the mountains, the Redwoods, the beaches, the coast, the cozy campfires they will build, falling asleep in clear, fragrant air. Their trip down the coast is blissful. One morning, as Jon is folding up their tent, he turns and sees a ray of sunlight falling on Lara's blond hair. He breathes deeply. "Life is absolutely perfect," he thinks to himself (and later writes in a journal). He has her and Eddie, a job, and his own health. However, as often happens when life seems perfect in this world, Satan is very near. He is watching Jon with his viscous, unblinking eyes, and wants him back.

At the same time that he slouches in the corner watching Jon, the ugly Demon strikes hard at Derek. In recovery from addiction for several months and looking forward to life, Derek experiences an old craving, drinks alcohol one evening, swallows some pills, and dies of an overdose in the night. "Oh No, Oh No, Oh No," I repeat numbly when they call to tell me. I sit down abruptly on my kitchen floor, then stand up, then repeat the words several more times. Everyone is deeply and irrevocably shocked! The day after it happens, Jon's resolve falters and he finds and swallows a pain pill. Later, when we learn about addiction science, we will realize stress often correlates with relapse in addicted people, as increased levels of the stress hormone cortisol trigger a cascade of responses in the brain. According to Dr. Robert Lustig, Professor of Endocrinology at the University of California, San Francisco, when the brain is "under fire by cortisol, your rational decision-making ability is toast. You can't differentiate between immediate or delayed gratification."[88]

Lara immediately notices Jon's demeanor and glares at him with scorn and refuses to speak to him that night. After two more very uncomfortable days, they drive back to Seattle in a frozen silence. Both are kind to Eddie and it's doubtful he notices the tension between Jon and Lara, but he may. A few days later, he returns to Wisconsin. Lara's anger at Jon is driven by her fear. She thought drugs were behind them. She thought she could count on him. She thought they could have a future. She thought their love came with a bond of trust. She decides to leave Seattle to visit her family and friends in Montana. She writes to Jon that she misses him, but when old friends offer her temporary work in northern California, she decides to extend her break from Jon and go with them. She tells Jon she doesn't know when she will be back. I do not know anything has happened in their relationship.

Jon age 24, with baby Eddie

Jon, age 25, with Eddie

Jon age 26, with Eddie

Jon, age 29, with Eddie

Jon, age 30, in Sausalito

Jon, age 30, on California Beach

Jon, age 31, clowning with Eddie

Jon, age 31, Legos with Eddie

Jon, age 31, puzzles with Eddie

Jon, age 31, with Lara

Jon, age 32, building a cart for Eddie

Eddie with special carving in sand

Jon, age 32, with Eddie

Jon, age 32, with Mom, Eddie and Miles

Jon, right. age 32, with Jeff

Jon, age 33, with Lara, Eddie and Miles

SIXTEEN

DARKNESS DESCENDS

At my work, we are pursuing a very important contract, working twelve-hour days with firm deadlines each day. It is an intense time when our team meets each morning, determines assignments, and must submit them electronically before we can leave in the evening. There is no such thing as being late or not delivering. I'm also teaching a night class once a week at a college an hour from home, eating dinner on my lap, and starting each day before dawn.

In mid- October 2011, just as the huge push is ending at my work, Lara texts me asking me to call her. I still don't know she had left Seattle and Jon in August, or that she had decided, four weeks later, she loved him so much she returned and gave him another chance. When her message arrives, I gladly call her. "Jon has something to tell you," she says ominously. "He sure had me fooled." I am standing in the hallway at work, waiting for the elevator. Yet instantly, I feel as if I have crashed through all the floors of the building and into a crater in the ground. Her words can mean only one thing. My heart wrenches down and sideways so hard it seems certain to tear out through my skin. Dumbfounded, stunned, astonished, broken, and sickened – all in one instant. Lara puts Jon on the phone. He tells me he "slipped" but has a plan to fix it. He has been using heroin. He just needs a few Suboxone pills. He asks if I know of a doctor who can prescribe them. Anxious to help, I agree to try. I don't stop to ask whether I should jump in.

As I have done so many times before, I hastily pack a bag and drive to Seattle the next morning. This trip will be the first time I have seen my son when I knew he was using heroin. No doubt Jon has been "on heroin" other times in the past when I have seen him, but I didn't know it. I feel trepidation, but he has asked for help and so I gird myself. At his request, we meet away from the apartment, just Jon and I, and he tells me he wasn't sure I would come. He says he is "on a run," but wants to quit. His eyes are pinned. We drive to the apartment, where Lara's eyes are the opposite of his – they are wide and mournful. Suboxone is still very tightly controlled, and only a few doctors are licensed to dispense it. We start a computer search for providers in Seattle, hastily scribble down names and phone numbers, and divide up the list. I haven't even sat down or taken off my jacket, but we are all making calls. Many doctors are booked ahead for many days or weeks. Many are not taking new patients. Finally, very late in the afternoon, we talk to an office that will see Jon that day. It is open until seven p.m. and located in an unsavory part of Seattle. Nevertheless, having no options, Jon and I hop into my car, and he starts driving. It is rush hour and our advance is achingly slow. Lara calls twice to ask about our progress.

Finally, we arrive at a run-down little building, but the nurse and doctor are licensed. (I have checked online en route.) The exam is reasonably thorough and Jon answers the doctor's questions truthfully. It is then I learn that after his slip by taking a pill in California, and the departure of Lara, his downward spiral started. He found heroin by approaching prostitutes on Aurora Avenue. He knew many of them would be addicted and could connect him with dealers. The dealers, he says ruefully, often made him wait agonizingly long periods of time in dark parking lots, sick and anxious. "These people are not into customer service," he says with sardonic understatement. I almost don't have the time or energy for my heart to wrench and pound. I am so weary.

We leave the doctor's office with a prescription for ten Suboxone pills, which we fill on the way back to the apartment. Jon says that number will be plenty. In fact, he will need only half the number, as he will use his special "Jonny method" for getting clean. He'll take a Suboxone, stretch out the time intervals between the next four, and transition to Neurontin[89] (a brand name for generic gabapentin), which enhances the neurotransmitter gamma amino butyric acid (GABA) and takes the edge off withdrawal by inducing relaxation and inhibiting synaptic firing. Originally prescribed for nerve pain, Neurontin mimics GABA itself and acts as a mild sedative. Jon has done this transition before and has a previous prescription for Neurontin. Back at the apartment, Lara and Jon decide Lara will keep half the Suboxone pills, doling them out at intervals, and I will take the remainder back to Richland. This is a terrible plan, but we don't realize it. I leave in the morning. Jon has his plan, as well as a new appointment with a dental surgeon to look at what he believes is an abscessed wisdom tooth. The tooth has been aching, but he has no health insurance. Of course I have agreed to pay.

A few days later, Jon and Lara call me. Jon needs me to send the rest of the Suboxone, as the step-down plan is proving harder than he anticipated. Jon's long years of drug use have conditioned his body and brain, so each withdrawal becomes harder than the one before it. It is a progressive disease, as the Demon well knows. As a parasite will, the vile creature wrestles with Jon, fighting to survive. The bloodsucker owes his life to Jon, but swears loyalty only to itself. Jon is fighting too. Lara and I, in our own ways, also are fighting. We know Jon wants to recover, and so we are willing, trying, hoping, praying. There is so much at stake. He uses all ten of the Suboxone pills, holding tenuously to recovery. Once again, none of us knows that continuing Suboxone for an indefinite period while other recovery skills were built could have made a key difference.

Jon's oral surgery takes place in the third week of October, and he and Lara ask me to visit soon afterward. Perhaps they just want a reassuring presence. Both seem to think I have more power than I do. However, maybe my value simply is to be with them, testifying by my very presence that I believe they will make it. Once again, I drive to Seattle. As always, Jon is upbeat and as talkative as possible with his sore, swollen mouth. We drive to a nearby restaurant. The server brings wonderful, crunchy Seattle sourdough bread as we survey the menu. I am looking directly as Jon, who is telling a funny story about his work. He bites down on a piece of bread and his whole face changes in a milli-second, contorting in pain as his hand flies to his lower jaw. Something is terribly wrong, but he insists that we stay through dinner. He consumes only soup and water. Most of the night he is wakeful. I hear him going back and forth to the bathroom.

In the morning, we go to the dental office, where it is confirmed that his lower jaw has broken. The surgeon had scraped deep into the jaw to remove all of the infection from the abscess, leaving the jaw temporarily thin and vulnerable. Yet, he did not warn Jon to ingest only liquids. Jon is angry, and afraid. How will he keep his job? The next place we stop is his workplace, where we show them his swollen face and I assure them the problem is medical. His jaw doesn't have to be wired shut, but still he cannot talk easily and should rest. The management agrees to give him ten days off.

November goes badly for Jon. After vowing not to access the pain medication the dentist has prescribed, he picks it up at a pharmacy and sinks into opiate oblivion. Just like that, the match is lit, the ship is burned, the tie is cut, and insatiable craving exerts its chokehold. When the medication runs out, he turns to heroin. The Demon writhes and howls with pleasure. He knew it was worth his while to keep his hooded eyes on Jon.

Jon's jaw heals to the extent that he returns to work. He functions in basic ways, and all I know is he has returned to the doctor we found and obtained more Suboxone. I text him often, urging him to go back into treatment or at least into a ten-day detoxification center. I tell him how much he is loved, how I believe in his strength, how there is no shame in taking a step back. I tell him I dream about Derek, and dread he may share the same fate. He writes back with impossible assurances. He says he can't stand the image of me thinking about death. He is a practiced hand at drug-using, he says, and knows how to be "careful... Thank God for you Mom. I'm going back in this fight with everything I've got...I love you." However, there is no being careful in drug use. There are only brain-based compulsions that block out reason, haphazard street concoctions, vicious suppliers, dirty needles or the "cotton fever" that comes from cleaning them, and every other manner of summons to death.

Just before Thanksgiving, Jon moves back into the sober house where he had lived successfully and soberly for nine months. He thinks being in that place will bolster his intentions to get and stay sober. He writes he is "riding out the danger...Have no intention of blowing this. I remember now how tricky this first few weeks can be. My guard is up." He begins attending AA meetings every day and spending "all spare time" with house members. However, when the house members learn he is taking Suboxone, they discharge him. They know this medication can be abused and they take no chances. (Once again, the "no medications" policies of many treatment centers and sober houses remain in effect during Jon's time of need.) Once again, I suggest a treatment center or a detox. He assures me: "I'm still in this fight and completely committed to overcoming this relapse...It's no walk in the park but I've done this a few times."

Worry tugs at my nerves, bringing indigestion and headaches. I develop multiple personalities to deal with my fractured life. I am competent and cheerful at work, but often close my door for frantic conversations, or huddle in hallways, bathrooms, and parking lots searching for treatment options. Sometimes in meetings, I pretend to choke on a snack so I can leave the room when I cry unexpectedly. Pretense is de rigueur for the parent of an addicted person. I pray constantly for calls or texts from or about Jon, and my wallet is always filled with scraps of paper bearing phone numbers with no names, portions of license plates, and partial or approximate addresses. I live in my own private holocaust, silent but searing.

In mid-December, Lara again finds heroin paraphernalia. She confronts Jon and calls me. I'm angry! I don't understand! Why does he do this to himself? Why does he lie and hide and take poison and pay money to repugnant people? Fundamentally, I don't understand that addiction is a real disease. As yet, I don't know crucial parts of his brain literally have re-wired themselves. Physical changes carved in neural pathways mean he does not think straight in actual terms. The person I see when I look at Jon is not the same person he was before the Demon infected him, although he looks remarkably the same on the outside. Two people – or beings – inhabit my son's body.

I unload my anger to Lara, but not to Jon. "I'm so mad at him I could push him into the river," I write to her. "I am refraining from sending him a really awful message – waiting until I calm down." The reassurances I am getting from him, I tell her, are "just garbage." I invite her to come and stay at our house, without him, if she wants: "YOU matter and should not have to be jerked around by his horrendously unfair behavior." We have promised Eddie a trip to Seattle at Christmas, but with Jon in active relapse, we don't make any travel arrangements. Hopefully, Eddie regards the disappointment as just a vagary of the adults. Hopefully, this nine-year-old boy does not think the cause is something he did. All we can do is pray.

I hold back my fury and try to encourage Jon when I talk to him. Innately, I know shame and guilt are poor motivators for any positive change. I again urge treatment. He tells me "we're nowhere near that state of emergency...But if does [come to that] we'll talk. And talk new town, new state maybe." I tell him bluntly, "You know location isn't the answer. You have found drugs everywhere you've gone." Intellectually, Jon well understands relapse, but emotionally, physically, and biochemically he cannot resist it. Maia Szalavitz understands. She recalls that when she was in her active addiction, "desire for immediate relief obliterated any consideration of long-term consequences – even deadly ones."[90] William Moyers also recognizes the compulsion: "When want became need...that need became so deep and strong that I was powerless before it...I didn't understand what was happening to me."[91] Dr Grisel affirms that in active addiction, "there is nothing we would not do, no sacrifice too great, to be able to use."[92]

A week before Christmas, Jon is heartbreakingly sad and contrite. "I can't begin to describe how awful it is to be in this situation," he writes to me. "The overwhelming guilt. The crushing shame. I let everyone down. I feel like a real dirtbag and on top of all that I have this slippery and hazardous path to navigate just to get back to square one." We do not know he has overdosed in the bathroom of the apartment that week. We will learn later he had injected himself with heroin and lost consciousness on the floor. He thought to himself, "I'm dead," but later awoke. The next day, he obtains methadone.

Although we don't know the full extent of Jon's drug use, Lara calls me to say she "can't leave him alone to get worse during the holidays...I feel like there is a magnet holding me here." I write to her, "Follow your heart – but don't enable. Only you can find the balance that is right for you. You both have my unconditional support. Jon's actions do not have my support, but Jon the person does…I pray for you both." Lara does not tell me Jon has begun to talk about suicide with a gun. He tells her the mechanics of shooting oneself would be "easy," but it would take "incredible balls." He brings up the subject more than once. I have no idea of the extent of his desperation.

As New Year's approaches, Evan and I decide to travel to our cabin alone. We drive, mostly in silence. We shovel snow from the cabin steps and porch, and start fires. We pull out the ancient television and DVD player and coax it into showing us obsolete, intensely silly comedy videos. We spread out our dogs' pillows and their cabin toys. We perform our actions by rote, almost like sleepwalkers. Our phones remain off throughout December 31. We skip our New Year's Eve tradition of recounting the best and worst things of the outgoing year and our hopes for the coming year. So many things around us have turned to ashes that we are just silent. I'm heartbroken, wrecked, distracted, and restless, but unable to sleep and guilty about the toll on my other relationships. I wonder if drowning feels like this. I know I can't help Jon and I can't let go. Although I expend a lot of energy, I accomplish nothing. Thus, I learn the hard truths parents of addicted people always learn: Drugs are immensely powerful, most addicted people won't give them up without horrific fights, and you can't talk them out of it. As 2011 comes to its grievous close, sales of OxyContin continue at their breakneck pace, bringing in another three billion dollars for Purdue Pharma, and drug overdose deaths in the United States top 41,000 people.[93]

SEVENTEEN
LABYRINTH

January 1, 2012, dawns clear and cold. We don't feel like skiing in the crowds and really don't feel like doing anything. Depression has made everything feel hollow and useless. On the way home, we turn on our cell phones with trepidation. Lara calls from Seattle. Jon has pawned both his and her snowboards and sold their most valuable Christmas gifts, including a high-definition DVD player. The sub-woofers also are gone from his SUV. Lamely, he tells Lara these items have been stolen. We realize Jon needed drugs more than he needed Lara, us, truth, or sanity. Clearly, he has reached the point Joe Herzanek describes so well: "Once addiction has control of a person, craving can far outweigh good decision-making and the 'almost unthinkable becomes rationalized' – choices are limited – the person MUST satisfy their need/craving for drugs."[94] Riding through the white landscape, my world doesn't seem like it could be real. How could things have gotten so bad? I ask over and over: *How could this have happened?*

A few days later, Jon calls and again assures me he can handle his problem on his own. He can reel in the relapse and intends to do so. However, as the Demon knows so well, each relapse is harder to conquer than the one before it. The addicted brain transmits thought to desire to action literally faster than the addicted person can stop to think. The signals are powerful, insistent, relentless. The addicted person with multiple relapses under his belt is drowning. In Jon's next call, he speaks haltingly – extremely slowly – pausing often. He tells me he thought he could get past his relapse by himself. "But," he concludes, "I...can't." For this proud, determined man, who loved to project such a carefree and competent image, I can scarcely imagine the incredible courage it takes for him to say these words. "Go into treatment," I tell him! Of course, we will pay. I know Elliott will join me. I tell Jon to make arrangements with a treatment center as soon as possible. Using his own (almost certainly illegal) methods, he obtains more methadone and Suboxone and tries to wean himself off heroin before he enters treatment.

He chooses to return to Silver Star Recovery Center, the place where he was first treated more than half of his lifetime ago. The normal treatment stay there has been shortened to three weeks in the ensuing years, a week shorter than the program he attended at Morning Hill. Both sessions are far too truncated. Almost universally, addiction experts agree longer stays in treatment bring better results. As in most diseases, treatment that is stopped just when promising results begin can bring unintended and brutal rebounds. We urge Jon to choose Morning Hill, where he did so well in 2010, but he is adamant. He wants to get in, get clean, and get out. We insist he cannot have his SUV at Silver Star. It would be too easy to get discouraged and leave on a whim.

On January 22, Jon takes a bus from Seattle to Silver Star. He has five dollars to his name, which he had to borrow from Lara. "I've been trying with no success to kick opiates at home," he writes. "I have made a dismal failure of that…These attempts have been made with honest intentions and steadfast determination, willpower. For all the right reasons…All of that…[but] I never imagined I would be neck deep in… again." He is baffled, depressed, sick, and afraid. "If I try to pinpoint where exactly it was that I went wrong I come up with nothing…I always knew there was potential again. I just never expected to feel the cold sting of acute withdrawal. The all-consuming need. The full, overpowering force of addiction gripping me, pinning me down, and devouring my life ever again."

I have brought Dori back from California to Richland to help her deal with her grief over losing Derek. All of us are relieved Jon is back in treatment. He finds it somewhat comfortable, although no walk in the park. "The people are nice," he writes. "The staff is helpful. The patients are friendly…This time feels different somehow. I'm …every bit as determined to succeed. His main worry concerns Lara. He knows he has "hurt her badly. I have reinforced all her fears. I have made her worst nightmare come true…If she leaves me I won't blame her. I'm sure that everyone in her life has told her to run – FAR. I can't disagree with that advice…Nobody as sweet as her deserves an uncertain future. A ticking time bomb. A potential hazard with the capacity for such destruction and pain."

Once again, he tries to understand the confounding nature of his affliction. "Everyone, including myself, just flat out expected me to stay clean forever. Why wouldn't I? Why…couldn't I? I do know one thing for sure. There is a real evil. A real darkness. A force. A cancer. It's misery, pain, anguish, guilt, regret, deep sadness and hatred. It's pure evil. Some call it the Devil…And it wants me back." He's learning the hard way, experiencing in the most grating terms Saint Peter's clarion declaration: "Your enemy the devil prowls around like a lion looking for someone to devour."[95] But why Jon? Why my poor, star-crossed son?

On Jon's third day in Silver Star, his withdrawal sickness hits full force. "It's here. All over me. Welling up from fissures in my bones. Crawling just under my skin like army ants lifting every follicle on my body, standing every hair on end. It's chills trickling up my spine like ice water. …Most people have no idea what this is and they are very lucky. It's not like sickness that comes with a violent flu or food poisoning. It's so much worse. The symptoms are similar: chills, aches, nausea, cramps, diarrhea, sweating – all that but exaggerated to an unimaginable extreme. And then the mental anguish, emotional suffering, torment, hallucinations, …despair, hopelessness and overwhelming exhaustion. But there is no sleep…seconds tick by like hours; hours feel like days." Using the methadone and Suboxone ahead of time, he knows from experience, will make his withdrawal longer and slower than it would be otherwise. "It's not going to be as bad, but it will…[last] longer," he writes. "Most likely the duration of my time here." However, he is philosophical: "Oh well, though, this is what I signed up for when I started slipping up, when I started getting high again. It's a simple and unavoidable law of physics: for every action there is an equal and opposite reaction. Or, what goes up must come down."

Jon's self-hatred and shame, the baggage of every addicted person, crest with the wave of dope sickness during the first week. He feels like a "dirtbag," he writes. "I'm ashamed of everything that led me up to this. Feel awful. I don't know how to ask forgiveness." He worries about my thoughts and those of Elliott and Evan, but he worries most about Lara's opinion of him. "I must rate pretty low on the prospects chart. I...realize how dangerous and unreliable I am to Lara. I'm a rotted apple core. Something nobody would want to touch...I don't know how Lara could...want to put any stock in a future with a potential junkie...I knew I wouldn't get out of this without it costing me something. I've just been hoping it wouldn't cost me her. I actually cried about it in front of eight other men...Didn't know I was capable of that."

Like most addicted people, even Jon doesn't understand the special kind of derangement that causes him to succumb to drugs when they cost him so much. William Moyers says the obsession can't be explained "to anyone who hasn't experienced it...[science] doesn't get close to describing the desperate hunger, the consuming thirst, the unbearable craving, the furious yearning, the excruciating need that grabs you and shakes you and won't let go...a howling internal torment that overrides the need for food, for water, for sleep, for love."[96] Many other addicted people have tried to fathom the inexorable pull of drugs, and give voice to it so others can comprehend it. Most fail at this task. Because the disease manifests as simply bad behavior, it seems willful and hostile to people not afflicted. "Normies" (as non-addicted people sometimes are called) don't hear the insistent, repetitive, drumming voice that propels addicted people to seek drugs at all costs, and drowns out reason, loyalty, honesty, and what most of us would call sanity.

Jon waits anxiously for the end of the "black-out period" most treatment centers impose during the first few days of inpatient stays. It keeps the addicted people from active family interference and allows the staff and patients to focus on, and get to know, each other. At Silver Star, the black-out period lasts five days. Then he can call Lara and "get a feel" for her plans. "I know her family is calling her home to Montana. I know they all tell her to kick me to the curb...I can't and don't blame her. I want her in my life. She is my rock. My anchor. What will become of me left to my own devices? Alone and tempted. With nothing but my twisted thoughts driving me back down that dirty road to ruin." The Demon, filthy and fetid, purrs inside him, biding his time, guarding his captive. Dismay, self-loathing and condemnation, and finally panic take hold of Jon. His words spill quickly onto the page of his makeshift journal: "Please don't leave me Lara. But I don't want to destroy you either. I have a demon in me. Listen to your heart Peanut. Do what you gotta do."

January 25, is crisp and cold in Richland. I am walking, trying as always to clear my mind and excise my stress, watching as the clouds of steamy breath coming from my lungs momentarily blur the glinting sun. My mind whirrs and gyrates when Lara calls to tell me she is planning to leave Jon and leave Seattle. She simply can't take the ruination, lies, and chaos of life with his addiction. I tell her Evan and I don't blame her, and we are sorry. She is a very good person and deserves better. She has quit her job in Seattle and is staying at Kathy and Clark's house in Richland. She is trying to sub-let the apartment in Seattle until the end of the lease in June. She asks me to help her sort and clean it out if she can arrange for new tenants, and I agree readily. I compliment her stability and resourcefulness. As I am walking, I pull my fingers out of my thick mittens to call Elliott. I tell him of Lara's decision, and he immediately agrees we cannot allow Jon to go back and try to live in the Seattle apartment without her. There is a one hundred percent chance that he will fail – it is a matter of life and death. Because Jon has no assets with which to pay the rent, we decide to force the situation and tell him he will have to live in a sober group home after completing treatment. We will wait to give him that information until after Lara talks to him.

Two days later, Lara informs Jon she is leaving. He is extremely sad, but amazingly philosophical. "I can't say I blame her," he writes just after receiving the news. "I lied to her all the time. Using drugs really scared her...I can't say I was expecting a different outcome...As much as I accept this and understand and all that, it's still pretty painful... [I was] cheating on her with the Devil...Lara has to get out for her own health and happiness and if I care about her at all I will let her... This will be very hard on her." His self-hatred surfaces immediately: "I'm untrustworthy. I'm dirty. I'm bad," he writes. "I have a terrible disease that's incurable and quite dangerous. I'm in bed with Satan. I have a monster in me, and it has shown its face one too many times." Personalizing his addiction, Jon continues: "I have been cheating on her [Lara]. I've had this mistress [drugs]. And I've been seeing her again... She demands all my time and attention. She wants me all to herself. She loves to see Lara in pain...She loves to see me in pain. She sits and waits for me to be weak and run to her. She is cruel and manipulative and conniving and cunning. She wanted Lara out of the picture from Day One. After all, she considers herself my first true love...She was born thousands of years ago and has stolen many a man's soul and faith."

The next few days are excruciating for Jon. He learns he has been fired from his job at the beautiful restaurant and takes stock of his situation: "I am completely broke. Completely. Not a dollar to my name...I have no life partner anymore. My little family I had built and cherished so much has disintegrated...How does one get broken up with and fired in the same day?...Hopeless and miserable. Everything coming apart." However, he vows to stop feeling sorry for himself and move forward. He floats the idea of moving back to California. Elliott and I instantly agree we won't support such a plan, due to Jon's drug connections there. Since he has no money, we can insist on him living in a sober house in Seattle or Richland.

On Sunday, Evan and I drive to Silver Star with a few items of clothing, chewing gum, and a carton of cigarettes for Jon. I abhor cigarettes and never before have I brought any to him. However, his level of misery seems to warrant our flexibility this time. We leave and then Lara visits him briefly, brightening his spirits somewhat. "She is still very much in love," he writes. "I just don't know if it's fair to take advantage of that...I've got some moral inventory to make. I'm praying again. To God." From memory, as he did in Morning Hill eighteen months previously, he pens all the words to Bob Dylan's cynical song *Not Dark Yet.*

In the meanwhile, Lara moves ahead with the logistics of dispositioning their apartment. She plans to give the beautiful new sofa to Clark's mother, who lives in a Seattle suburb. She also negotiates a move-in date with a couple she has found who will sub-let. I praise her determination and hard work. "This is really hard to do," she writes to me. "I wish it was different." Despite their impending separation, Lara decides to attend the Family Session at Silver Star with Jon. They have some important things to say to each other, to clear out the web of lies, and perhaps soothe part of the raw damage. He finally agrees. However, he warns, some of the truths he will have to reveal are "going to hurt pretty bad."

Lara visits briefly a few days before the Family Session, but they have an argument and Jon explodes in anger. He is beside himself with withdrawal sickness and all the twisted, obsessed longings of his addicted brain. He packs his things and begins walking away from the center. A burly male counselor runs after him and talks him back. Jon's small group is called to a hurried meeting and they surround him and offer support. They convince him to stay, and he agrees mainly because Lara refuses to give him a ride, and when they call me, I refuse also. Jon lashes out, calling me and shouting that he feels out of control. I tell him he needs to stay in treatment, and urge him to think of Eddie being fatherless if he makes more horrendous choices. The Demon writhes and screeches with delight, savoring our desperate shouts and pleas. Facing the monstrous mess this reptile has wrought, we lash out at each other, twisting, feverish, and blind, not knowing whether we help or only hurt. We just want Jon to make the one decision that will let him survive another day. Discord, fear, angst, strife, a family divided against itself...The Demon reaps his grotesque harvest.

Later that night, Jon calls Lara and I to apologize. Two days later, via telephone, he is turned down for a vacancy at the sober house in north Seattle where he did so well during 2010-2011. The house will not take him because he brought in medication there on his last brief stay in late 2011. Once again, the policies against medication hamper him. Once again, he lashes out and his counselor decides to dismiss him. Soon afterward, the counselor will tell me Jon displayed the emotional age of a thirteen-year-old, and his chances for sobriety, given this state of mind, are slim.

Lara picks up Jon and drives him to Seattle in his SUV. She is worried for his safety if he is alone, so she has agreed to stay with him until he finds placement in a sober house. However, she soon finds heroin paraphernalia and observes that his eyes are pinned. Having no choice, she calls a taxi and leaves. Alone, Jon calls me to say his sponsor has dismissed him and he has no money. Lara has given him fifty dollars, but he doesn't have it anymore. He says he had to use it "to pay someone back – may have been dangerous not to."

Discovering he is alone in the apartment with his SUV parked outside, my heart does one of its most violent, classic wrenches. It thuds down and sideways hard as I leap into full panic mode. I know that he *cannot* survive there alone. I urge him to call his father, who has located programs for long-term, relapsing, addicted people in San Francisco, or to call every sober house in the greater Seattle area, or go to any emergency room and say he needs detox. I don't realize that emergency rooms don't help and hospitals don't admit people seeking detox. "You are dancing with Satan and you know it!" I text. "Please...[go to a place] where you can at least not DIE!!!...I want you to LIVE – not die of drugs!!...bottom line. I don't want doubt, smoke, mirrors and distrust... People can't stand any more lies so please just tell the TRUTH!!" Jon denies using heroin, but says he has taken a little methadone. "It worked great," he says. "I haven't felt sick at all." At home, I won't stop texting and calling him. I can't disconnect. There is too much at stake. "I cannot tell what is real and what is not," I text. "With you I never know the whole truth and I feel foolish and exploited. I DON'T WANT to bury you!!!!! I want the man we saw for fourteen months before relapse – what a fantastic man!" The piercing irony is Jon wants that man too, but he is not capable of grasping him. I continue texting him: "I don't have any answers – only pain...WHAT will WORK to keep you safe and whole and honest and real??" Near midnight, Elliott and I talk on the phone. Elliott has talked to Jon and says he "sounded awful."

Although it amazes me, I do sleep that night. It comes from pure exhaustion. The next day, I again implore Jon to call his father. "PLEASE," I beseech him. "We are in it with you. He [Elliott] is taking the lead but we both love you. Don't throw yourself away. Your father will help!!! Leave Seattle...just GO and save your life!" That night, he tells me he has called Elliott and is considering moving to California. He also is considering taking Vivitrol,[97] a timed-release form of the opioid blocker Naltrexone.[98] "Don't wait very long," I plead. I am crying and shaking. "Save yourself!! If you need to go fast, GO! Let me know and I will clean out your apartment. Just LIVE!!" Nonchalant as always, Jon assures me, "I'm working on things. I'll be OK." However, I have glimpsed the Demon's terrible power and I know nothing is okay. The next morning, I am busy entreating Jon again: "You are NOT OK and there is reason to worry – GO to California...get into a long-term program!! Don't worry about ANY details – everything can be worked out as long as you are alive!!" My heart has not stopped twisting and wrenching in various degrees of intensity for two days.

The next day, Elliott makes flight arrangements for Jon. We all pass a sleepless, heart-racing night worrying he will just disappear and not take the flight. In answer to our prayers, he flies to California the next morning. Elliott places him in a private detox facility.

That same day, Lara and I set off for Seattle in the large pickup truck Evan and I have bought for outdoor adventures. Lara looks so tiny in the large front seat. Her hands fidget and flutter on her lap. Usually extremely quiet, she is more talkative than usual. She is glad to be getting on with cleaning out the apartment. It is hard to hang in limbo between her old life with Jon and the new life she will begin soon at her brother's home in Montana. The Columbia is dark gray when we cross it, making its way somberly and deliberately downstream. We open the door to the apartment and find utter chaos. It is clear a very sick person lived here. Absolutely nothing has been picked up or put away. T-shirts are strewn across every room, some half inside-out as if they had been almost ripped off. Dirty dishes and dried food, none of it nutritious, lie all over the little kitchen, along with empty beer and whiskey bottles. The television is on and lights are burning. My heart doesn't wrench this time. Perhaps I am past the almost electric shocks of fear that have tangled me so often. This time, my heart simply falls very low into my intestines and stays there, heavy and nauseated. We get to work immediately.

Lara and I toil quietly and efficiently, keeping our heads down. We fold the clothes in a large pile. I will take them home and wash them in a few days. Lara washes the dishes and packs them, along with Eddie's toys and non-perishable foods, in boxes we have brought. Every now and then, I see a tear run down her cheek as she works. As the AA Big Book says, an "alcoholic [person addicted to a substance] is like a tornado roaring his way through the lives of others. Hearts are broken, sweet relationships are dead. Affections have been uprooted. Selfish and inconsiderate behavior have kept the house in turmoil."[99]

I have decided I will throw or give away most of Jon's furniture pieces, except the beautiful new sofa. I have carried his chairs, lamps, waste baskets, throw rugs, and mattresses in and out of too many storage units, apartments, rented rooms, and my own garage, and I am done. We place some of these items on the sidewalk outside the apartment, and nearby tenants come by and take them. They ask about Jon and we tell them he is ill. I locate a warehouse that will take charitable donations. Lara and I load the truck as full as we can and I drive there, while she continues her deliberate, silent work in the apartment. I return and we load in the sofa for delivery to Clark's mother Donna at her house not far away.

It is February and getting dark by 5:30 p.m. We have had a big day and we are tired. In my truck, I follow Lara, who is driving Jon's SUV, to Donna's house. We unload the sofa, and Donna and one of her friends greet Lara with big hugs. She will spend the night there. They ask me to stay, but I am weary and anxious to get to Jeff's condo, where I will sleep. They seat Lara at the kitchen table in a pool of light. She looks fragile and old beyond her years. They try to cheer her up, joking about the folly of getting close to any man. "They [men] are all foolish," Donna says. "Are you taking notes?" Lara laughs in spite of herself, and as she does, tears spill out of both of her eyes and she half-chokes. I know she is in good hands for the night, and I head out into the darkness to find my own circle of light with Jeff.

Jeff is a very neat person, and his condominium is spotless. It is painted and furnished all in soft beige tones, and he has carefully chosen and installed new baseboards, fixtures, and other amenities. His place is the diametric opposite of Jon's surroundings I have just left. The drapes are closed against the darkness when I arrive, and the lighted indoor space feels very welcoming. We get take-out food and settle in to watch a presidential primary debate on television. Four candidates are sparring, and we cheer when our favorite one makes a telling point, and jeer and boo when an opponent speaks. It is refreshing to protest loudly and foolishly at something over which I have no power, instead of quietly enduring my powerlessness over Jon's life. We go to bed early and I sleep deeply. In the morning, I return to Jon's apartment and resume work with Lara. We sort and pack and make two more trips to the charity's collection warehouse, working quietly in the wan winter light. By day's end, we are finished, having utterly dismantled the little life Jon and Lara had built. Before closing the door, she takes a long look back at the place where her dreams were demolished. She returns to Donna's house for the night, and I return to Jeff's condo.

I realize that, driven almost solely by stress, I have no life of my own. I feel lost and do not recognize myself. I control nothing.

EIGHTEEN
DESPERATE TIMES

In early March 2012, Jon completes his time in the California detox facility and moves into a sober living house for men that Elliott has located in San Francisco. On weekends, Elliott visits him, and they have some fun times exploring the city. Late in the month, Jon flies up to Seattle to meet Eddie, who flies in the same day for a visit. I drive to Seattle to get them both. As I cross the slate gray Columbia, I see that spring run-off from the mountains is just starting. In Seattle, we head to a marina where Jon has been mooring the old red canoe. He straps it to the roof of my truck, and we drive back to Richland. Along the way, we must stop three times for Jon to smoke cigarettes. Smoking seems more important than ever to him. He and Eddie stay at our house for a week, catching minnows in Jon's homemade traps and drawing exaggerated chalk designs all over the driveway. Years later, Eddie will recall the huge Golden Gate bridge Jon drew for him with red sidewalk chalk that week. We swim at our exercise club, play with Miles, read bedtime stories, and Jon and Eddie construct elaborate spaceships and castles with Legos. Soon, it is time for Eddie to fly away so Jon drives him to Seattle's airport. He then drives on to California in his SUV. Jon promises Eddie we will fly him to San Francisco for a summer visit.

Back In California, Jon is dismissed from his sober living house for taking Neurontin. (Once again, he experiences a destructive "no medications" policy that thankfully is changing in many recovery residences today.) He moves into Elliott's house, supposedly on a temporary basis, to help with repairs to Elliott's boat and other caretaking duties until a clear forward path emerges. One of the tasks Elliott assigns to Jon is fixing Dori's car, which has remained at his house in California. Jon begins work on the car in early June, but the task goes incredibly slowly. Strange things begin to happen. He tells Elliott odd currents of electricity permeate his garage and the car's motor responds oddly to his attempts to troubleshoot its problems. Soon, he tells Elliott the fence around his property has unnatural electric properties and next, that the boat's engine has peculiar tendencies. Sometimes, he says, the electricity energizes itself and jumps out at him. Baffled, we discuss the possibility Jon may be having seizures or heat strokes or he may have suffered a severe electric shock. One morning late in the month, I call Jon to ask about progress on Dori's car and he begins to speak very hastily. His sentences run on and on and do not make sense. I can't break in to say anything at all. When I hand the phone to Dori and she hears Jon rambling in rapid nonsense, she speaks to him softly and soothingly while hand-signaling me to contact Elliott. I text him urgently: "Jon in VERY bad state – needs HELP!! Get home right away please!!" Immediately, Elliott drops everything at his work and races the thirty miles to his house.

The summer turns dreadful and then gets even worse. In California, Jon's hallucinations continue and Elliott almost cannot go to work. Jon tells the neighbors Elliott's house and theirs are about to crash down. The next day, he spends an hour trying to straighten the engine in one of Elliott's boats because he says it is "too short and out of position." He threatens to hit Elliott or anyone else who suggests he is having delusions. Elliott takes him to a psychologist and also consults a wonderful local pastor named Don, as well as the sheriff, and counselors from a mental health organization. Elliott and Jon talk all afternoon and Jon admits he is suffering from something and needs help. The next day, he goes with Elliott to the emergency department of a hospital, where he is evaluated by a nurse and a psychiatrist. They suspect methamphetamine use and ask him to give a urine sample, but he refuses. He is losing weight rapidly, and shows definite signs of paranoia, but doesn't qualify for California's involuntary "5150 hold" for people in crisis because he hasn't threatened to harm himself or others.

The next night, Jon is in Elliott's bedroom at one a.m., telling him he has called the fire department and the utility because power is emanating from under the house and invading his body. He refuses to leave Elliott's bedroom, so Elliott calls the sheriff who comes and talks with Jon and calms him. Elliott decides not to press any charges. The next day, Jon insists Elliott, still home from work, sit with him and watch him orchestrate electrical currents and observe the house and boat change shape. Two nights later, Elliott again must call the sheriff and Jon is placed on a 5150 hold after he tells his father, "You will never see me again." Obliquely, he indicates that he is keeping suicide as an option to escape his earthly torture, but we recognize this signal as only an aspect of his temporary paranoia. Back at Elliott's house a few days later, Jon again enters Elliott's bedroom in the middle of the night. He wants Elliott to watch things move and see the house fall down. He won't leave and, once more, Elliott gets no sleep. Jon stays there all night to make sure his father is "safe." When Elliott suggests to him he may be suffering from a panic disorder, Jon agrees that it is a possibility.

In late July, Elliott discovers Jon has been charging large amounts of money to his credit card at a "smoke shop." Some of these stores are fronts that sell illegal substances packaged as "herbs," "bath salts," or "spice." These substances sometimes contain synthetic cannabinoids (related to chemicals in marijuana plants) that have been sprayed onto dried plant materials. The problem is the cannabinoids are concentrated in vastly higher levels than those found in marijuana, resulting in stupendous and dangerous highs. In other cases, serious trouble stems from the fact that undisclosed stimulants and psychoactive substances are sprayed onto the dried plant material, producing effects similar to those experienced when taking ecstasy, LSD, or other potent drugs. On July 26, at the same time Elliott is uncovering Jon's smoke shop connection, the DEA raids smoke shops in 109 cities, shutting them down and seizing synthetic drugs, bath salts, and spice. In Jon's case, Elliott finds a small, empty package bearing a brand name unknown to us. When I research it, I find it contains khat, a bitter-tasting green twig that grows in the Mideast and East Africa. Its active ingredient is cathinone, an alkaloid chemically similar to amphetamines. It makes a person edgy and strung out. In sufficient concentration, we learn, it can make a person dangerously paranoid, manic, and aggressive. Bingo!

Elliott goes to the smoke shop Jon has been frequenting and asks for the brand name in question. The clerk tells him they don't have that product because it is illegal. Elliott assumes the clerk will not produce the substance because he suspects Elliott is an investigator. The next day, Jon buys more of it, spending fifty dollars for a packet weighing one-half of a gram. The packet is labeled "Not For Human Consumption," a practice later found to be a common one that shippers from China use to circumvent certain inspections. The following day, Elliott takes Jon to a psychiatrist, who prescribes powerful sedative and anti-psychotic medications. Jon sleeps for twenty-four hours and then acknowledges some of the things he has been seeing really cannot be happening. He says it is hard to focus because he keeps seeing strange things, but can't be sure which visions are real and which are not. A few days later, Jon is wound up again and Elliott's credit card shows heavy spending at the smoke shop. The psychiatrist prescribes an anti-seizure medication and tells Elliott if Jon has stopped taking his medications or has returned to using bath salts "all bets are off." We conclude that Eddie's summer visit cannot happen.

On the last day of July, Elliott is clearly frightened of Jon's behavior. He writes to me, "Jon is becoming threatening because I refuse to pay attention to his visions. He is calling me a… drug pusher for trying to get him on medications…If I don't call you by noon, please try my office and ask…if they've heard from me." The Demon is firmly ensconced.

Jon's psychiatrist thinks he needs to go into inpatient treatment where he cannot obtain the bath salts. Although we offer to pay immediately, arrangements are difficult and slow. Four nights later, a frightful confrontation occurs. Jon, angry that Elliott does not believe his reality, throws the vacuum cleaner at a window and a beer bottle against a wall. He gets in Elliott's face and threatens to hit him if he does not treat him with more respect. Elliott calls the sheriff, but Jon hides in the neighborhood until the sheriff leaves. Then he returns, yanks off Elliott's glasses, and stomps on them. He throws a broom through a window and drives off squealing his tires. I advise Elliott to press charges and swear out a warrant for Jon's arrest, something I had thought at the beginning of our long drug odyssey I would never do. "He needs to be stopped – physically," I text to Elliott. "You cannot take this behavior and he needs to be RESTRAINED by the law and forced to dry out." I am not feeling sympathetic to Jon, I tell Elliott, "because of the horrendous fallout on Eddie – no summer trip and no explanation...Bottom line is POOR Eddie – and shame on Jon – to choose drugs over his son!" Elliott agrees: "He is breaking that boy's heart." We are angry, powerless and perplexed. We look for logic in behavior that today we would recognize as drug-induced psychosis. Later, we will learn Eddie had to attend a fairly miserable daycare that summer, with very few activities and long periods of just sitting. What a price this boy is paying – the saddest little victim.

Jon soon returns to Elliott's house after camping in nearby woods overnight. I call him and tell him bluntly his bath salts contain khat and his visions are not real. He admits to me the "stuff" he obtains from the smoke shop is a strong stimulant. Over the next few days, things deteriorate in Elliott's house as Jon steals checks from his father, insults him, and packs to leave but dithers and does not depart. Confrontation comes on the night of August 13, when the smoldering fuse in Jon's brain ignites. He pulls all the wires out of the back of Elliott's refrigerator and microwave because he thinks they are possessed. When Elliott tries to stop him, Jon throws a book and a punch at him. Elliott calls the sheriff, and Jon comes at him with a knife. The sheriff must tase Jon more than once, and, with backup officers, physically drag him into custody. "It was awful," Elliott calls to tell me at five a.m.

At last, Elliott presses charges and Jon is quickly convicted of elder abuse (since Elliott has just passed his sixty-fifth birthday) and spends ten days in jail. The Demon contorts, leaps, bays, and yowls with pleasure. His dangly encrusted limbs flail about as he spins and dances, while father and son fight and swear at each other, their bonds of love stretched to breaking. I support Elliott. "It was awful but necessary," I tell him. "Take care of yourself! You kept sighing on the phone this morning – you sound very worn out."

During this unspeakable summer, as my private tsunami roars through my life, my only refuge is my small support group for parents of addicted persons. This little band of bruised souls is suffering in many of the same ways I endure, but not defeated. With an honest blend of gentleness and bold-faced firmness, surprisingly mixed with humor, they guide me. First and most importantly, they show me I am not alone! Like me, the people in this room are watching as the lives they knew and envisioned disappear in front of their eyes. Some of the outlandish, cruel, unbelievable, twisted, and grotesque scenes that play out in my life have occurred, and still are occurring, in their lives. Some of the conversations we have about the things happening in our homes and families would sound incredible to a "normal" person walking into our meetings. Indeed, these conversations would have been unthinkable to each of us a few years ago, before the Demon tore through our lives. We describe desperate calls to 911, interactions with the police, jails and court system, confrontations with family members high on drugs, arguments with enabling family members, thefts, fear, unimaginable accusations, pleading, tears, exhaustion, and despair. Soon, the people in this group are the only ones to whom I can relate. I feel like an alien with almost everybody else. As Lee Woodruff says, "How do you engage in small talk when you have vanished from your life?"[100]

My group follows a Twelve-Step program somewhat modeled on that of AA and Al-Anon. I get stuck on the first step – powerlessness. I readily admit I am powerless over Jon's drug-using behavior, but I can't progress to any of the next steps. I don't make headway, but I listen, I read, I try, I pray, and sometimes I feel some small shreds of comfort.

After his jail term in California, Jon stealthily returns to Elliott's house and tries to break into his safe. He batters it, but is unsuccessful in opening it. He does manage to steal a few of Elliott's sleeping pills and some cash and food and then sets off driving. We don't know his state of mind, but we warn Jeff to lock his doors and not open them to Jon if he should show up in Seattle. He might be dangerous. On his fourth day out of jail, Jon contacts me and tells me he is driving, but will not say where. I tell Elliott I'm "not sure of his resources, but you know he gets by on barter and fakery." Through me, Elliott offers treatment to Jon at any recovery center he chooses. Jon refuses, but I report to Elliott he seems "REALLY chastised by what has already happened. Seems to believe he can never get a job or have a future with the conviction for elder battery that has just occurred. Very discouraged."

The next time Jon calls, he sounds odd. He believes police are chasing him and tells me that if they get close, he intends to speed up and crash his SUV into a concrete abutment on the highway. He says the confinement of a jail cell almost was more than he could take, and he will never allow it again. Wary of his desperation, I tell him no one is chasing him, his father is not pressing more charges, and he should calm down and be reasonable. I assure him that with a minor conviction, he can still have a positive future. I ask where he most wants to be, and he says he longs to be with Lara. He wants to drive to Billings, Montana, where she lives with her brother's family. I call Lara and we talk. I tell her honestly: "He is my son and I want him to survive so we can have a chance to see whether salvation can occur. My bottom line is different than yours. But I have the same concerns – who is he now?"

When Jon arrives in Billings, Lara agrees to see him and evaluate him. He camps in his SUV in a local park, but spends each day with her. Over Labor Day weekend, they drive into Yellowstone National Park and camp in his SUV. They share a few days of hiking, talking, and renewing. Back in Billings, Jon calls and asks me to pay for an appointment with a doctor. He would like to get some Ritalin[101] for his ADD, to calm down, and focus on a future. He plans to look for a server job there, to stay near Lara and hopefully win her back. I pay for the appointment and the subsequent prescription. I do not know he has promised Lara he will take absolutely no substances. When she learns that he has Ritalin, she becomes very angry and bans him from her presence. He tells me later he, "didn't know she had it in her to be so fierce." Once again, we are all blinded by ignorance about the disease of addiction. When an addicted person is in recovery, his need for "regular" medication to address his underlying problems may be more important than ever. The Ritalin may be exactly the substance Jon needs. But we all still believe the myth that recovery demands complete abstinence from all medications.

Still determined to stay near enough to try to win Lara back after she bans him, Jon goes to Bozeman, Montana, approximately 145 miles to the east. He calls to tell me he plans to get a job at Big Sky Ski Resort, a huge and sumptuous complex located about forty-five miles south of

Bozeman on the way to Yellowstone Park. It will be a good fit for him, he says. He has skills, experience, and energy. Prices are high in the resort village, so he plans to stay in Bozeman and commute.

I am perplexed once again. There are so many logistics. I tell him his old SUV really isn't up to a forty-five-mile commute from Bozeman to Big Sky each day in the harsh Montana winters. I remind him he hasn't located a job or a place to live. I urge him to think of other options, but I send him some money for basic needs while he figures things out. He lingers in Bozeman, camping in nearby woods in his SUV, but spending some of his time in the corner of a Walmart parking lot where local homeless people gather. He sounds clear-headed. He looks for jobs both in Bozeman and Big Sky, but he has no resume or decent clothes with him, so he doesn't look very presentable. After about ten days I tell him I will pay for him to rent an inexpensive room so he can shower and have a place to keep clothes and toiletries. Am I foolish, enabling, or simply helping my son who wants to make a fresh start? Neither California nor Seattle seem like safe places for him, and he doesn't have a healthy track record in Richland either. Maybe, I think, he could fit in a ski town like Bozeman. Once again, I can't possibly know the best course, but I love my son and want him to succeed.

Quickly, he finds an extremely cheap room in a small, rundown house owned by a woman in her fifties. I send payment and he moves in. Within a few days, he asks me to send all his heavy coats, jackets, snow pants, sweaters, gloves, and other winter gear. I pack a huge box and send it by U.S. Mail. The very next day, he calls me, clearly upset. The woman, he says, has appeared naked in his room and thrown herself at him. When he jumped away in horror, she screamed and told him to move out. He is now back in the Walmart parking lot with all his things thrown hastily back in his SUV. Shocked and shaken, I tell him to come home. "Don't even try to get the rent money back," I tell him. "We're done with Bozeman." He readily agrees and begins driving toward Richland. I immediately call the Post Office in Bozeman and ask the manager to watch for Jon's box, coming from Richland to the woman's address. He agrees to stop the box and hold it. However, a routing clerks misses the message to stop the box and delivers it to the woman's house. I call back and explain to the manager that we are quite sure she'll never send it back. In an act of pure kindness and determination, he personally goes to her house, knocks on her door, sees the gigantic box, and walks in and takes it away! I pay him to send it back to us. It is the best thing that happens for us in Bozeman.

As parents, Elliott and I both are exasperated in our own ways. The Demon distorts and deforms our relationship with Jon so much we almost cannot think straight. We are confused, despairing, strained, and taut as we swirl in dysfunction. Yet, we love him so much we continue to provide support in exchange for promises to change. Are we just injudicious or flat-out obtuse? With me, Jon is almost never belligerent. Indeed, he always seems sincere and appreciative of my efforts in his life. Often, I can't distinguish the fine and shifting line between helping and enabling. I – and we – don't know which way to turn. We try to see who Jon truly is, as opposed to our idealized vision of who he was and could become. Elliott texts Jon, "We try to believe you because we want to, because we need to – but…you are just a very clever liar. I am willing to provide you with one more chance." We agree to pay for him to live in a sober house in Richland as soon as he arrives back from Bozeman.

By the first of October, Jon is in Richland and stays at our house for a few days while he secures a room in a men's recovery residence. He does some chores for me to earn money and soon joins some of the other men who have found temporary work picking apples in a nearby orchard. On October 12, he goes to the Emergency Department of a nearby hospital complaining of pain from falling off a ladder while picking apples. He is given hydrocodone and robaxin[102] (a muscle relaxant sometimes used to treat opiate withdrawal). We don't know about this hospital visit. Thinking he is doing better, we purchase tickets for Eddie to visit Richland for Christmas.

By this point, Jon has lived in eight different places in 2012, and, like a surreal character in a movie, appears to land in something resembling a standing position after each crisis. As Congressman Kennedy writes of his alcoholic father, "He managed his life in a way that was full of turmoil, but he always managed to survive, which reinforced his sense that this [disease] was manageable."[103] Such improbable bravado also characterized Jon. Yet the disease of addiction, unless drug and alcohol use are stopped, always progresses.

In late October, I travel to Wisconsin to spend four days with Eddie, hoping to lift his spirits since he did not have a summer visit with Jon. I rent a residence-type motel and we invite his best friend to stay with us. The boys swim in the pool and play video games. We spend one afternoon at a corn maze and pumpkin patch, running through the maze searching for clues, going on a hay wagon ride to pick out pumpkins, and exploring the host farm in the chill sunlight. We live on the fast food that the boys like, and I let them stay up late in the motel. On the last day, Eddie and I are alone, and we go to a movie and then out to dinner. We call Jon, and Eddie is so delighted to talk to him he slips under the table of the restaurant to chatter at length. I tell Eddie he will see Jon in Richland for Christmas.

I return to utter chaos in Richland. At Jon's sober house, seven of the eight residents, including him, have relapsed. The house is being closed by the management. Jon is staying with friends – unhealthy ones. Evan and I go to the recovery house to retrieve Jon's belongings, including the old red canoe. The house caretaker smiles and tries to encourage me as I mournfully remove Jon's meager belongings from the front porch. "There is always hope that he'll get clean and try again," says the man. I am too sad to talk, so I just nod and blink back tears. While we are there, a dilapidated car drives up with Jon in the back seat. The others in the vehicle look surly as they slouch in bagged out sweatshirts. Jon looks the same. He's "going hard," in the lingo of drug use. Evan and I are lifting the canoe into the back of our truck when he walks over. "Taking the canoe, huh?" is all he says. We nod our heads yes and he slinks away. His addiction wants him dead, but will settle for ruining his life and relationships. The next day, I go to the Richland Police station, ask to see an officer, and give a complete description of Jon and his car. I ask the police to be on the lookout for him, as I would rather have him arrested than dead.

In the second week of November, Evan and I travel to Hawaii. Neither of us has been there before and it is a first-in-a-lifetime celebration of paying off the mortgage on our house. We are very anxious to get away. We spend four days on Oahu, visiting Diamond Head, famous beaches, and fulfilling my lifelong dream to tour Pearl Harbor. Then we fly to the Big Island to embark on the highlight of our trip – hiking in Volcanoes National Park. We drive across the island from the airport at Kona to the port of Hilo on the wet side of the island. The vegetation around Hilo is lush and tropical, and we are fascinated as we explore it and the macadamia nut plantations nearby. We find a wonderful little place for dinner and go to sleep with the alarm set for our hike in Volcanoes Park. At five a.m., my phone rings and Dori is screaming into it. Jon has overdosed and is in the Emergency Department of Richland's hospital. She doesn't know his current condition. I tell her I will call some people to go to the hospital to be with her. I call two women from my support group, and both readily agree to go. Evan asks if I need to drive back to Kona and fly home immediately. I tell him I don't know yet.

Over the next few hours, I hover at the phone, learning more details from Dori and asking for updates on Jon's condition. She tells me she received a call from mutual "friends" in the early morning hours, telling her Jon was with them and "acting funny." She went to the address and found a mess of used needles, empty beer cans, and people high on drugs. Jon was sitting on a dirty sofa. As she watched him, he grimaced slightly and pulled his chin and neck sideways and to the left. Then she saw his left fist clench as he grimaced again and his whole upper body pulled sideways. Next, his neck went taut and he jerked hard to the left, his face contorted and stiff. He toppled to the floor. Others in the room barely noticed and told her he was fine. Somehow, with amazing strength, she half-lifted and half-dragged this man who outweighs her by sixty pounds, stumbling to her car. She raced to the hospital, driving up onto the sidewalk at the Emergency Department door. With help, she got him inside.

By mid-morning, I receive word that Jon is awake and being discharged. Meth and heroin are found in his system. Track marks are visible on the underside of his left forearm, and he has marked thrombocytopenia – a low level of platelets in his blood. Acquired thrombocytopenia can be caused by drug use. The doctor notes, "Initially the patient had no verbal response, but would intermittently respond to painful stimuli, then fall asleep. The patient [then] spontaneously began having appropriate speech, is answering questions and appears more awake." As soon as Jon is "alert and responding," he is discharged. Today, we know such crises should be opportunities for the medical profession to guide people toward treatment or at least connect them with trained Substance Use Disorder Peers.[12] However, in 2012, the attitude that drug users choose their own problems and deserve the consequences was still pervasive.

There is no need for me to race home, as I will be back in three days anyway. My friends who have gone to the hospital sternly tell me to finish our vacation and "do nothing...When you get home, tell Jon you thought about him once and that was it...He's an adult and adults pay consequences." Evan and I drive to Volcanoes Park, buy a map, and he plots the route we will walk. I am numb. I walk in nearly total silence all day – grim, stunned, silently praying. Hope bleeds out of my life, as does confidence and any sense that I know how to proceed. I wear the weight of my circumstances like a heavy, dark garment. Satan, the ancient serpent,[104] has come to steal any joy we might have and replace it with despair. At the end of the day, we drive back to Kona. We simply endure the last two days of our trip, resigned and waiting to leave. Nothing in my world is recognizable. Nothing is as it should be. What I had before, I do not have anymore.

I am so defeated. I have utterly failed to help my son via human power. I tell Evan, "I know I have been a good mother and bent myself into a pretzel trying to help. I honestly don't know what else I could have done...it is just so SAD." I have not learned yet that being a good mother doesn't prevent or cure addiction, and there comes a point when help becomes a hindrance. Evan tells me I must detach. Shelley from my support group messages and bluntly advises: "Do nothing more...Let it play out...Stay out of the way...Turn him over to God. That requires

---

[12] Peers are people who have been addicted, but have been in recovery at least one year. They need no college courses or degrees, just a short course to become certified.

doing nothing BECAUSE you trust Him more than even yourself. This Step is just as important for you as it is for Jon."

I am trying. I'm not sure I have a right to boundaries, or that they will keep me safe. However, I tell Evan I have reached my own bottom with Jon: "I need to trust God enough to TRULY let go and let Him work. I'm at the point of not doing anything more for/with Jon...wait and see...no rescues...NOTHING we have done has made him any better." Back home at Thanksgiving, Jon calls to tell me he is hungry, and I meet him to give him a bag of sandwiches, apples, candy, nuts, grape juice, and a small amount of cash. He's crashing hard from his recent binge. He tells Elliott he wants to get off drugs, so Elliott agrees to rent him a very inexpensive motel room for a few days while he tries to get into the local county detox facility. This public facility is very small and spare, but Elliott tells Jon it is the place he will have to go, and he will have to make the arrangements himself. Jon calls and calls, but the center is always filled to capacity. Years later, I will start a movement in our community to build a comprehensive residential detoxification/ treatment facility. As Jon languishes in the motel, we worry that, in withdrawal and with plenty of idle time on his hands, he will give up and go back to using. Finally, on December 1, Elliott and I decide we should get him into a private detox. Hastily I make calls. The next day, I drive him approximately one hundred miles to a nice, well-staffed little detox center. He is pleasant, but subdued on the trip down, obviously in physical withdrawal and mental anguish.

At the end of ten days, I pick him up at the detox center. He seems cheerful on the drive home and looks healthier. Evan again is working out of town, and I agree to let Jon stay in our house while he locates and arranges his next sober house. That very night, gripped by a ferocious compulsion, he goes out and does not come home. In the morning, a call from the local grapevine tells me Jon has relapsed. He has not stayed drug-free even twenty-four hours. Clearly, in the track marks of heroin injections on his arms, legs, groin and between his toes, his cravings are uncontrollable. The Demon cavorts, screeches, slathers, and exults at the utter ruin he visits upon us. We are a family destroyed.

I write to Elliott, "I feel a great foreboding – things are going to take a terrible turn for the worse." I am at FULL STOP as a mother. There is no solid ground, and my beliefs about reasonable cause and effect, effort and outcome, and love and deliverance are completely obliterated. I have been desperate and foolish, trying to control an addicted man whom I am powerless to direct. There is no fairness in this fight. I can't even see my enemy, but this Demon has Jon's attention, displaying his most alluring, festive visage. He has come to seek and destroy, and Jon is in his thrall. I place Jon's belongings on the front porch and lock up the house very tight. In all the circumstances of the long and tangled path of his addiction thus far, I have never been this low.

NINETEEN

BORROWED TIME

Eddie is scheduled to fly to Seattle in just nine days. We consult Diane, who decides Eddie will be too disappointed if another trip is cancelled, since he did not get his promised trip to California the previous summer. She thinks he should make the trip to be in my care, with no contact with Jon. Eddie will be flying alone, using the airline's chaperone service. When we bought his tickets in late October, we listed Jon as the person who would meet Eddie's airplane, but I change the pickup person to me.

It is the evening of December 21, the shortest, darkest day of the year. Evan is supposed to fly home from a business trip, but is snowbound in a Midwest airport. He calls to tell me he will arrive the next morning. I double-check all the locks on the house, even carrying my key with me and locking the door behind me when I put out the trash. I am scrupulous. I am thorough. I have an early dinner. About seven p.m., I am walking through the main entry area of the house when Jon simply opens the door and walks in. "Jon!!" I say, astonished. He has not forced the door, nor has he vaporized through it. He doesn't have a key because we have changed all the locks on our house twice during the past harrowing months. Yet he very plainly has opened the door! He is silent, kind of shrugging, hands palms up, as if to say, "I don't know - will you talk to me?" I am still so astounded at the impossible phenomenon my eyes have just seen, that I simply stare at him for a few seconds, as he looks, downcast, at me. "I wasn't sure you'd answer the door if I rang the bell," he says finally. Later, I will tell this story to a professional counselor. He will ask me quietly: "Did Jon need to be there that night?" When I answer "yes," he will say: "Then it doesn't matter how he got through that door. Maybe angels sent him."

Jon looks cold and haggard. "Why don't you come and eat something?" I finally stammer. He sits at the kitchen table, never taking off his coat, while I fix scrambled eggs. He eats a bit, then pauses for a long time. "Can you eat some more?" I ask gently. He looks so thin and exhausted. He tells me he has been living in his old crate of an SUV, which no longer runs. He has parked it in front of the rented duplex of a "friend of a friend," but the welcome extended to "couch surfers" has its limits. He has no money left and has been sleeping in the dead car in freezing weather. His last meal was pancakes two days ago. Facing another frigid night, he has walked many blocks to my house, not knowing where else to go. Jon looks as forlorn as I have ever seen a human appear. He says little, sighs often, and glances around the warm kitchen, taking in all the familiar Christmas decorations. He sounds resigned, defeated.

He would like to be able to fix his car, but has no money, tools, or place to work on it. I offer to drive him to the place where the car is parked to jump-start it or push it, jump in, and pop the clutch to see if it will go. If we can get it to run, I will follow him back to our house where he can park it safely and use Evan's jack and tools to work on it. Why do I help him when I said I was finished? Any parent knows the answer: he is my son. I love him and he is cold and destitute. Besides, although I don't understand yet the fact that addiction is a brain disease, I know Jon cannot possibly be choosing to live this way. We drive to his car and get it to turn over, but after just a few blocks, its lights go out and it stops. I call my roadside service provider and we wait in the cold. Finally, the tow service comes and loads Jon's SUV onto a flatbed and delivers it to the curb in front of my house. We stand awkwardly in the street. Will it really do any good to walk inside and make him sleep in the frozen car? Finally, I ask if he would like to sleep in a spare bedroom. "Would that be okay?" he asks with quiet amazement. We go inside and I bring out a quilt. Before I can hand it to him, I see his long body sprawled diagonally across the bed. He is already asleep as I drape the blanket over him.

The next morning, Evan arrives home and turns tight-lipped and taciturn when he sees Jon is there. I get ready to drive to Seattle to meet

Eddie's airplane and tell Jon I am leaving and will call him in a few days. His face shows intense, palpable longing, but he says nothing. I hesitate for a long moment in the doorway and then invite him to get in my car. He bounds outside, grabs a backpack from his car, and buckles into my passenger seat. We don't talk much on the drive to Seattle. I don't want to know the horrendous situations he has been living in, and he certainly doesn't want to tell me about them. The Columbia River is a dark, midnight blue when we cross it. The air is foggy and ghostly. As we drive through the Cascade Mountains, Jon sketches scenes of them on a small note pad I carry in my glovebox.

When we arrive at SeaTac Airport, I show the pass allowing me to proceed through a security checkpoint to meet Eddie at his airplane's gate. Jon must wait behind. I am sure he is humiliated that he, the father, is blocked while I go to claim Eddie. However, he says nothing. Finally, Eddie's airplane inches to the gate and, like all chaperoned children, Eddie is among the very last passengers to deplane. He has been told simply Jon is sick and won't be able to see him. However, I tell him his father has gotten well and is actually here. Eddie's little face breaks into a grin so wide he throws back his head and his hat falls off! Tears are streaming down my face when we see Jon's long, gaunt frame down the hallway, waving joyously, with a grin as big as Eddie's.

We get take-out food and go to the hotel where I have secured a wonderful room that opens onto a huge atrium with a giant swimming pool, two jacuzzis, and numerous terraced spaces with tables and luxurious tropical plants. The glass ceiling is several stories above, and the whole atmosphere is warm and steamy. I booked it especially for Eddie. At first, he says he wants to swim, but exhaustion takes over and he lingers on the bed coloring pictures. It's just as well, as Jon and I are depleted, too. The emotions of the past day and night have drained us. We close our big sliding glass door and climb into the two beds – Jon and Eddie together in one and me alone in the other. Jon snores terribly, but we all sleep soundly. In the morning, Eddie wants to wake his father. Jon is sleepy, but plays in the pool with Eddie with boyish enthusiasm, throwing him in the air, swimming after him underwater pretending to be a shark, both of them sometimes sputtering water as they splash each other vigorously. I watch in wonder, just basking. Joy has found me so unexpectedly. I wave and swallow hard so they won't see the huge lump in my throat.

We meet Jeff and his girlfriend for a festive lunch. Jon and Jeff haven't seen each other in more than a year, but if there is resentment, they do not show it. We drive back to Richland through the December chill, the roads crowded with holiday travelers. Jon and Eddie take over the entire downstairs of my house – three bedrooms, a bath, and a large family room with a woodstove. Puzzles, drawing paper, movies, blankets, and pails full of Legos come out, and soon they have a fire going and are fashioning elaborate spaceships, robots, boats, and weapons out of the Legos. Evan is surprised and a bit skeptical, but he sees their delight and warms to the situation. The next day, December 24, I sneak out and buy a pair of warm winter socks for Jon and wrap them up with fifty dollars. That evening, we are opening presents, with Eddie playing Santa. He hands the gift box to Jon, whose head drops sharply down on his chest. "I'm not supposed to get anything," he says softly. "I don't have anything to give you guys." We tell him his presence with us is his gift. The next six days are full of more play, trips to the park and river shore with our dog Mountain, and extended overnight visits from Miles. Jon is like a big kid himself, but also protective of Eddie and Miles, carefully choosing appropriate movies for them and reading endless bedtime stories. The paradox of the addiction plague hits me hard. Jon is being the father all of us want him to be, yet fear is always present. Will he disappear some night? Will he be a different person in the morning, if we see him at all? How much contentment can we allow ourselves to feel?

On December 30, we travel to our cabin with Jon and Eddie. The next day, I drive them to a bus that will take them to Seattle. While we wait, Jon's eyes search the mountain peaks, which are gorgeous, jagged, and snow-covered against an azure sky. He is entranced by such sights, seeming to draw sustenance from them. The massive bus arrives, and they step aboard. Less than two hours later, they arrive in Seattle, where Elliott has flown in and meets them for a brief visit. Despite the awkwardness and hostility from the previous summer, Elliott loves

Jon and wants to reconcile. They go to the wonderful hotel with the tropical atrium and huge swimming pool. It is New Year's Eve and after dinner and a swim, they put Eddie to bed. However, Jon can't sleep. As midnight approaches, he goes into the lobby where people have gathered and strangers are making friends in that special way they do when a festive experience is shared. Jon feels lonely at first, but then thinks to himself that his most favorite person in the world – Eddie – is nearby. He wakes the little boy and takes him into the lobby. There they join others in shouting and cheering as 2013 rings in. They hug each other tight. After about a half hour, they return to their room and go to sleep. It is a memory that both will keep – Jon for the rest of his life, and Eddie longer than that.

After another day in Seattle, Eddie flies back to his mother, and Elliott books a flight for Jon back to Richland. Evan and I are letting Jon stay at our house while he locates another men's sober house. I contact a mental health counselor named Norma and provide the bare bones of Jon's story and struggle. I tell her I can't imagine what his or our next steps will be, as everything we have tried so far has failed. She offers to meet with him, and finds him extremely open, humble, somewhat puzzled by his own condition, and absolutely willing to change. He tells her he has taken essentially any and all drugs she can name "in massive quantities" for many years. He is disheartened by his plight, saying he sincerely has tried and intended to conquer the monster, but can't understand its strange and powerful grip on him. She is discerning, having heard many tales that turned to dust. Instinctively, however, she believes him, recognizes his obvious intelligence, and sees that, even in defeat, he has a spark of wit and humor that bespeaks a love of life. They talk at length about his longing for Eddie and Lara, his loneliness, his current temporary living situation with us, his many relocations, his experiences in sober houses, and his attempts at sobriety. He tells her he thinks he has had ADD most of his life, but now is afraid to take medication for it. He recognizes his own tendency to excess. She suggests he try medication, as part of an overall plan to include counseling with her, socialization in sober circles, a stable living situation, and connection with God.

The connection Norma establishes with Jon is kinetic and almost magical. She believes he needs medication. She knows he might be driven by his addiction to abuse it, but she believes that at this time he does not plan to do so, and she thinks it could help him stabilize. She becomes the first in our experience to cast aside the traditional wisdom that addicted people cannot take any medication at all. She wants my consent, although in a legal sense she does not need it because Jon is way past the age where I can make such decisions for him. I concur with her idea. She quickly renews his Neurontin prescription and places him on Adderall[105] and a mild dose of an anti-psychotic. Adderall, like Ritalin but newer and slightly stronger, treats ADD and increases dopamine and norepinephrine availability in the brain. Jon describes Norma as "awesome...so cool."

I sense in Jon a new and unassuming quietness. He seems lonely, utterly broken, sighs often, and tells me he doesn't know "how many more recoveries I have left in me." I get the radical idea he should live in our house for a few months while he stabilizes, adjusts to his new medications and makes major life changes. When I approach Evan, he looks grim, but he is a good man, and he agrees to a trial period of two months, provided Jon will accept a set of conditions we will impose. Surprised and delighted, I draw up a list of positive requirements and banned behaviors. Together, Evan and I refine it and place it before Jon. Seated at our kitchen table, he signs it immediately, without any objections, and looks at the floor, tugging on the back of his shoes to hide his tears. Just sixteen days after his unexpected arrival at the front door on December 21, he is a resident of our home. It is another time and place where the Lord of the universe intervenes in our lives in a manner so direct and unmistakable that forever after, I will view Jon's story with awe.

Our requirements are carefully designed, born of our long years dealing with addictive behavior. We know many of the signs, trigger points, habits, and omissions that can lead quickly down the slippery slope to relapse. In effect, we get right into the middle of Jon's deep-rooted customs and proclaim a new regimen. On the positive side, he must attend five AA meetings per week until he gets a job; then attend three meetings per week once he is working. He must submit at least three job applications per week, with none being night jobs at restaurants. He must get an AA sponsor within two weeks, keep all medical appointments, and take medications as prescribed. He must rise between eight and nine a.m. each day, do something physical each day, take no naps during the day, and keep his room fairly neat and organized. He must turn over ninety percent of all money he makes to me – not for me to keep but to make a budget for him and teach him how to use it. I pledge to turn over control of money to him gradually, based on performance. He must attend church or do one organized activity per week with new people, such as volleyball, basketball, or a volunteer shift. He will have a curfew of 10:30 p.m. on weeknights except in special cases, such as obtaining permission to attend a late AA meeting or see a friend, in which case his curfew will be midnight. On the negative side, of course he cannot use any alcohol or drugs. We tell him that our alcohol will not be locked up as we don't intend to change our entire lives for him. Also, we will not test him for drugs because we know he is so clever he would be able to fool us. Importantly, he can have no association whatsoever with the circle of friends with whom he used and stayed in autumn 2012, or other drug-using friends from the past. He must delete all these people from his cell phone.

Jon's first order of business is to fix his old SUV, which has sat in front of our house for more than two weeks. He is very thorough, carefully reading the Chilton[106] auto repair manual for his make and model year. He props up on one elbow and stretches out his long legs on his bed while reading, taking notes, and sketching parts of the car's undercarriage and motor. I am so happy to have him home – calm, sober, and occupied – that I can't help sneaking downstairs repeatedly on one pretense after another just to glimpse him. Elliott and I give him money for parts, and we push his car into the garage, closing the door and turning on a space heater. Although it is early January and the garage isn't insulated, it is the most snug and secure working space he has had in a very long time. He plays music on his phone and gets to work. The old SUV crate needs many things, which he discovers one by one as he works underneath it. He wrenches off the ancient, warped bolts and sets out parts on newspapers where he meticulously draws diagrams and labels. One night, he works until three a.m., which upsets me until I hear his triumphant tale in the morning of all the wiring connections he discovered as he worked those many hours.

Through my friend Shelley, Jon joins a social group at a local church and soon becomes an active participant. They hold potluck meals, bowling outings, and do volunteer projects. They also go to Christian concerts in the area, meet for coffee, and take hikes. The church pastor gives Jon three different versions of the Bible and talks to him extensively about the spiritual components of recovery. Some of his counseling mirrors statements by AA founder Bill W. Natural desires exist in all of us, writes Bill W., but addicted people "let these [natural desires] far exceed their intended purpose. When they drive us blindly, or we willfully demand that they supply us with more satisfaction or pleasures than are possible or due us, that is the point at which we depart from the degree of perfection that God wishes for us here on earth."[107] Jon's brilliant mind absorbs the pastor's messages first with curiosity and then with wonder. He reads the entire New Testament rapidly and doodles and draws his questions over every napkin, paper towel, and scrap of paper in his room. The nature of God, His love and sacrifice, His power, redemption, forgiveness, the relationship of soul to body, the character of our fallen world, the nature of Satan and temptation, and many other topics occupy much of the conversations during Jon's sessions with Norma.

I take Jon to yet another church called Home Base that is recommended by a couple in my support group. The atmosphere is casual and the teachings are solidly Bible-based. Jon responds enthusiastically to the Christian rock music, the minister in jeans, coffee and doughnuts during services, and the open expressions of emotions from the congregation. We sign up for a class that meets every Wednesday night and begins with a soup supper. The Jon I see in class is one I have not seen before. He is quiet and reserved, not outgoing and gregarious. He notices it in himself, and calls it "life in the corner." It is, he says, new to him. Usually, around people he does not know, he says his initial discomfort "passes into interest, then into ice-breaking, then into warmth...[but now] I'm content as an observer. I don't exactly know why. Is it a lack of confidence? Maybe...I feel like it's teaching me something. Maybe there are rewards. I'm certainly not reaping them that I know of."

One night in the third week of the class, Jon says silently to himself: "God, if you are real, reveal yourself." Later he will say he immediately felt an incredible peace descend on him. He experienced warmth, a profound sense of acceptance and forgiveness, and a distinct sense that "everything is OK, everything is perfect." Sitting next to him, I look over and see tears in his eyes. I am baffled, not knowing of the deep communion he is having with the Holy Spirit. The rest of the class passes in an ordinary way for me, but the tears remain in Jon's eyes. Walking out to the car and driving home, it is the same. I ask him to tell me what he can about his feelings, but he just shrugs slightly and says nothing. The tears glisten and linger. This boy who has been going rogue all his life is now utterly transformed as he realizes he belongs to Jesus.

Evan notices Jon does not seem to have the enthusiasm he once had for creative cooking or discussing scientific theory, and I observe that he smokes heavily. A ceramic pot outside a back downstairs door fills with cigarette butts at an alarming rate. Jon begins each morning standing outside taking long, deep drags, and, as far as I can see, he is able to go no more than about forty-five minutes between cigarettes all day long. A young girl he meets at AA rejects him when she finds out he is thirty-five years old. Harsh realities of lost years and limitations haunt him. One night, he tells me he is going to use one of his special permission extensions of curfew to see a friend and stay out until midnight. I am not happy that he announces it, rather than asking my indulgence, but I assent to it. I go to bed around my usual time of 10:30 p.m., and find I cannot sleep. I am listening for his car. Very quickly, I become agitated and physically hot. I realize my years of chronic stress have caught up with me, and I cannot stand the uncertainty. By about eleven p.m. he arrives home, and I get up to see him, making small talk just so I can gauge his sobriety. He is fine, but I realize I am not. I am shot through with stress, and my resilience is low. Just as Jon learns some of the constrictions of his age, so do I.

The winter passes, and Jon lives quietly in his tribulation. At the end of two months, Evan and I decide he can stay in our house a bit longer, as things are going so well. He has not found a job, but volunteers with me in a food bank once a week. He is quiet and respectful around our house and constantly does chores for us and other neighbors and friends for cash. He works hard, and no one ever says he is lazy. He volunteers at church, and he and I hike often with Mountain and sometimes with Brett and his dog. Many evenings, to fend off loneliness, Jon takes an old laptop computer we have given him and sits in a Christian coffeehouse practicing his keystrokes and reading. He says he likes it: "The girls are very pretty here. And wholesome. And plentiful...It's enjoyable to chill here. But I bet they wonder why I never buy anything. Cuz I'm broke!"

Jon keeps his hands busy building things at a small workbench he sets up in his room. He fashions minnow traps and fishing lures, and sketches inventions of all types, including a motorized skateboard. In an oblique attempt to get Lara to acknowledge him, he sends a minnow trap to one of her friends he had met the previous summer in Billings. Sardonically, he includes a note in which he refers to himself as Lara's "psychotic, police assaulting, drug addict ex-boyfriend." He provides elaborate comical instructions on how to use the trap. Even after he sends the trap, Lara remains silent and distant.

We don't realize the extent of his suffering. Alone, he writes he is, "wrung out, hanging on a wire...fearful instead of confident...My heart aches and burns. I feel hollow and uninspired. I am in the grip of such turmoil and uneasy, dirty shame. Guilt, regret and indecision wrack my nerves. There can be no deeper state of unhappiness and pain...I'm a shell of what I once was. I'm so lost and so cold and I am broken. I am utterly devastated...So busted up...My best friend is gone. My love is finished...I miss her. I miss what she represents. She was life. She was everything...She is done. Only her ghost remains and the wreckage."

Jon, so forlorn, finds his only hope in Jesus and His word in the New Testament. He writes: "This is where God found me. This is where He came like a flood into my heart washing away the guilt, carrying away the shame...Filling my empty, cut-open heart, sewing up the tear. Pouring new life into the holes, lifting me up. His son bleeding next to me. Bleeding with me. Bleeding for me. The Spirit cleansing my soul...There is no way forward but through God...He has called on me. Despicable me. I am putting my trust in Him...He is beginning to guide me forward. It was too long God. It was too much time in the deep. The wreckage is so stark and icy. Get me out of here please...I have been drowning for so long...Fill me up...I will, in your name, help others."

He is hungry for God's word and studies it with zeal. He writes about grace, sanctification, and the importance of holding on to faith and Jesus' saving power. "Jesus [has] got you. He's got you," Jon writes. Mostly, he believes Jesus means love – a love that is simple, straightforward, and all-encompassing. Jon muses about temptation, scrawling that Jesus, "is able to help those who are being tempted. He is more powerful than the evil, the enemy in ourselves...He has been tempted. He felt it all." Jesus, Jon writes, "will give us rest (peace of mind)," a commodity Jon sorely wants. He still has cravings and clearly is frightened. His cravings, he writes, have "never been completely removed. The only relief has been total abstinence. May be an allergy? Most agree chronic alcoholics are doomed. Even after cleaned up and healthy, most don't make it."

He continues helping Evan and me with chores as spring arrives. Railroad ties that have surrounded our huge garden have aged and rotted. Undesirable Bermuda grass from our neighbor's yard edges through them and produces weedy enclaves. Over several days, Jon digs, lugs, digs deeper, removes the old ties, makes and emplaces wooden forms for a new concrete barrier, mixes and pours the concrete, removes the forms after the concrete dries, and spades the entire garden. It is a tough and muscular job, but Jon volunteers to do it. He contracts a cold during this work, but tells his journal that "I took enough Dayquil[108] to force myself to mix all twenty bags of concrete to do the wall. I...felt like I was coughing broken glass...I hated every second of that concrete but I was glad to be pullin' some weight." He mows the grass, washes windows, and takes our truck to get the snow tires changed. "I feel like I didn't do a whole lot to help," he writes, "but I do anything I'm asked.

I'm so happy to have opportunities to earn my keep...I don't thank her [Mom] enough. If I do I hope she hears me. I hope she knows how much I appreciate her help and all her gifts. All her love...[She] and Evan are so incredibly kind and loving to put up with having me in their home for these last months."

After Jon finishes the concrete work, I buy him two new tires for his SUV, and we go shopping for spring clothes and shoes for him. He seems cheerful, but is profoundly confused and sad. He has feelings he can't understand, as well as feelings he understands all too well. He records that "I'm still paranoid. That won't go away it seems. I still think people are staring at me. It makes me uncomfortable wherever I go... There are times when I hear a burst of laughter from across a room and I'm sure they are laughing at me...I know I have a presence. I always have. But now it's uncomfortable to be looked at."

In late March, he arranges a phone call with Lara, but worries intensely as the call approaches: "I have no idea what to say...There are times when I...truly wish her well and want nothing but the best [for her] and mean it. But most of the time I'm angry...So I can't say anything because I'll feel different twenty minutes later." Is he angry at his disease? Does he feel it sandbagged him as well as her? He writes he has, "almost forgiven myself...[and] have forgiven all others. I have received God's forgiveness...I have." I don't know the outcome of the call or whether it even happens. I do not realize the extent of his loneliness.

Jon asks to resume studies at the local community college and we agree. He signs up for American History and World Civilizations. History, he tells Elliott, "is something I'm naturally passionate about. I mean it's the one subject I've never stopped studying my whole life." Perhaps, he says, he will become a history teacher. Classes begin April 1, and his brilliant mind dives in with enthusiasm. He tackles research and writing assignments in depth, chronicling America's entry into World War I, the submarines and weaponry of World War II, and especially the plutonium production at the Hanford Site near Richland. He searches for illustrative photos and delves into old documents. His writing is personal and vivid. With all his writing assignments, he produces drafts and asks for my editorial help. When I show him grammatical errors, he stares intently at the page and carefully combs back through his sentences to address inconsistencies. He learns PowerPoint[109] for the first time and experiments painstakingly with different fonts, color designs, and layouts. He does well in both classes, especially American History where he earns an A grade.

That same month, Jon signs up with the wildland fire service again and is delighted to pass his pack test. The old red canoe comes out of its winter hibernation under our deck, and Jon uses it to the fullest. He and I also kayak several times, watching the abundant bird life along the Columbia's bountiful shore. Jon has loved the Columbia and Yakima Rivers for a long time, and finds great solace in their waters. At the same time, he is searching determinedly for a regular job in the restaurant business that he knows so well. We have relented in letting him search for serving jobs as his recovery seems so solid. On April 29, he receives the good news that he has been hired at the best, high-end restaurant in our area.

Jon's exploration of Jesus continues unabated. He tells Elliott that "I go to three different churches and am getting myself involved. I'm actually heading up a group of my own this spring...I call it the adventure group...every Sunday for eight weeks I'm going to lead a different hike... [and discuss Jesus]." He has no patience or use for speakers who over-intellectualize the gospel: "I don't want to open Pandora's box...[by discussing] a metaphysical versus a physical universe, its origins, the meaning and purpose of existence, etc...I just want to worship God. It's pretty simple. I just want to take some time and praise God. Give my love and gather together with some other people who also love God...I want to be in His presence more often than I am. I really like church... if for no other reason but I get to be in the presence of the Spirit. I get to feel God in a very real and physical way and I benefit from that immensely...I like church because I can actually feel the warmth, the light and the love of God touch my heart." He muses about repentance. "Radical repentance," he writes, means "turning to God [and having a] changed heart, turned from sin. How can we completely turn from those things? Follow the work of the Spirit...Repentance as a gift... repentance is freeing...God is light and there is no darkness in Him at all. If we confess our sins he is faithful and just and forgiving...There is a promise of forgiveness. Salvation without regret."

Jon counsels with other members of AA, helping members even newer to sobriety than he. Speaking from his own hard-earned experience, he advises that "hitting bottom" is absolutely necessary. He tells one young man that if he is ever to recover, he has "an incredibly difficult battle to sustain for years to come...and that's only if [you]... make the determination that staying an addict is harder and brings more suffering...[You] need to bottom out to the fullest. Need it. It's crucial...because the driving force in someone's heart that propels them through the difficulty of recovery is born only in the crucible [flame] of the bitter end. It can't be talked into someone. It can't be learned through others' mistakes. It can't be scared into someone by threat of penalty of even death...That flame is lit only in the hollow depths of the darkest days of someone's life... Doing anything to 'help' when [you are] close [to surrender] only resets the cycle and pulls [you] way from the only chance." Jon has hit what we thought was "bottom" so many times I wonder where and when he would pinpoint his own bottom.

In late April 2013, through my support group, I am invited to speak to a gathering of parents whose sons and daughters are enrolled in Juvenile Drug Court, a program for teenage offenders who use drugs. Preparing for the talk, I tally up the things that have happened in my life as a result of addiction. I record that Jon, age thirty-five, has been taking psychoactive drugs since at least the age of fifteen, so I've been dealing for addiction for twenty years. He has lived in six different states and in multiple towns and cities as an adult. He moved around so he could have fresh starts and escape drugs, but he always found more drugs. He has been in treatment four times and been arrested four times. He has been in both voluntary and involuntary commitment in hospital psychiatric wards due to bizarre behavior, and has overdosed and nearly died. He carries convictions for elder abuse and destruction of property. This litany shocks even me. I choke while rehearsing my talk at home and cry in front of my mirror.

The small audience is composed of parents, social workers, counselors, and various officials of the court. When I begin my talk, they listen politely. As I continue, their eyes start to rivet on me and their faces gradually change to reflect horror and disbelief. I look so "normal" – like a middle-class mother who probably volunteered to read in her children's classrooms and bake cookies for school. Indeed, I did those things. I am that mother, yet I also am the mother of a deeply addicted man, and I know the mother of an addicted person is never going to be voted "Mother of the Year." We are judged on the results – the reality of our children's lives – not on how much we loved or tried. We are judged for what we did and didn't do, and we are judged because people think our performance as parents must have been faulty. My story frightens those in the audience because the fact that this abomination bloomed and continues in my life means it could happen to anyone. It could happen to *them*.

I send a copy of my talk to my sister Pam and cousin Bart, a clinical psychologist. Both are appalled. Pam knows parts of the story, but never the whole. Bart knows very little, only that I was always too busy to join any get-togethers he tried to arrange. He knows Evan and I passed up invitations to meet and vacation with him and his wife Debra in gorgeous places, including Florida and New Orleans, and he never understood why. Now, as a psychologist who has seen trauma in other families, he realizes I stayed away because of the stress and worry that things would unravel while we were away from home, and the plain exhaustion from dealing with all our crises and episodes. He writes to tell me my testimony is "powerful" and he has "deep sadness that...all of you are suffering so much, and have been for so long." He thinks the aspect of lack of control over addiction and my addicted son is "even more difficult for people like us who are used to taking on the world, working hard and making our own destinies...Then we come up against a situation where no matter how smart or capable we are, we can't fix it for ourselves or those we love the most." Pam calls and says it is important for me to know she loves me and is praying for me. I am beginning to feel shaky. Seeing my situation laid out so starkly in my talk, I don't know how much longer I can ride the rollercoaster.

On Mother's Day in May, I receive a most beautiful card from Jon. He says he can't begin to thank me for all I have done for him. Most of all, however, he is thankful that "you and I have gotten so much closer." He pens incredible words: "When all was lost you lit the way. You helped me through the darkest days. You offered me a guiding hand, even when I could barely stand. And then you say you're proud of me? Well I'm the one who's proud to be your son." This card will stay close to me forever, taking on new and even deeper meaning after Jon leaves us for Heaven.

Later in May, Lara visits Richland. I don't know about her visit until I literally bump into her one morning in the downstairs hallway of my house, coming out of Jon's room with a toothbrush in her hand. She smiles brightly. There is no need to conceal the fact they have spent the night together. Jon works on her car in our driveway whenever he isn't working or studying. He also does some free chores for Kathy and Clark, as part of his Twelve-Step work to make amends for his behavior in their house in 2010. A few days after Lara leaves, I ask Jon about their relationship. "We're in love," he says with sad resignation, "but we just can't be together." There is too much fear of the damage already done – the potential for nagging, worrying, spying, and another relapse, and the possibility of coming to hate each other. Lara even wonders whether she has become a trigger for Jon's destructive cravings.

By this time, plans for Eddie to visit for six weeks during the summer are well underway. All of us had assumed Jon would be living in his own place by now, but he is just starting his new job and has no savings. Evan and I confer and decide Jon can stay with us through Eddie's visit, since his behavior has been perfect and child care will be very difficult for him with his new job. Jon is grateful, even though we all acknowledge it will be prudent for him to find his own place after Eddie's visit. At his age, living in the downstairs of Mom's house is a parody that mocks his pride and just "isn't right."

Jon allows me to guide him in setting up his very first budget. We list income and expenses in two columns, trying to be realistic. It is a very simple accounting, but truly opens his eyes. In the past, he has just spent money impulsively, usually as soon as he received it. In late May, he tells Elliott, "Things are good here." He is working six days a week, "but that's ok...I am making ok money but I'm not able to enjoy it. No time at all between work and school." By mid-June, he has saved 1,000 dollars towards a boat, and Elliott tells him he will match the funds Jon saves if he accumulates a reasonable amount and pays all his other expenses.

On Father's Day, at the end of the third week of June, Elliott does not hear from Jon and becomes concerned. At the same time, Evan and I are disturbed. Jon has stayed away from his work for a week and is very thin. We buy a drug testing kit and surprise him by asking him to submit to it one Saturday morning. He does so, and the test comes back drug-free, but we know he is the world's greatest master at fooling tests, so we aren't completely reassured. I take him down to the dock in our park for a talk. The Columbia is teal blue and running full with spring snow-melt from the mountains. Jon says he accidentally threw away his Adderall about ten days earlier and he wrote Elliott a Father's Day message but the message did not send. Hmmm...I tell Elliott I think Jon is "struggling mightily [and] he is in some kind of...withdrawal." We're worried, but we wait and see.

A few days later, I tell Elliott, "I'm not sure I have the full story. He may have relapsed briefly when he was without his medicine. I may never know. But he has had his med back for three days now and says he is feeling gradually better. Still it seems hard for him to really accomplish much." He goes back to work in last week of June, but in early July, I report that Jon, "is not the person he was a few months ago...It feels like living with a recalcitrant teenager...I do not like what I am seeing." He had promised to wash our windows for pay a few weeks previously, but accomplished only about one/quarter of them. One day, he says he will fix a problem with our boat's engine, but goes to sleep instead. When I wake him up, he is rude and argues with me. Emotional dysregulation shouldn't be a surprise in a person with Jon's chemical history. Still, we wait and wonder.

Eddie arrives in Seattle on July 14, and Jon joyfully picks him up. Fun begins immediately. They again take over the entire downstairs of our big house. Jon has a fish tank and terrarium, and he and Eddie head to the Columbia River right away to hang their traps beneath the dock. Over the winter and spring, Jon has filled many of his idle hours by fashioning several varieties of traps. Eddie is impressed! Mountain often accompanies them on their jaunts to the river, plunging in to cool himself and fetch sticks for Eddie. In the old red canoe, Jon takes Eddie fishing for brown catfish in the muddy delta of the Yakima River, just as it empties into the Columbia. Known as channel cats, these hefty, speckled fish love smelly bait such as hotdogs or common worms and require no expensive lures to catch. The catfish outings occur most evenings when Jon is not at work, and come to represent some of his and Eddie's fondest memories. Miles stays overnight at our house many times, and I often take the boys to a swimming pool in the late afternoon as Jon heads for work. We come home for late dinners on the deck, yard play, video games, and silliness that is enchanting to watch. I am busy with two difficult, demanding consulting jobs, but feel so blessed to have these hours with the boys.

The first weekend Eddie is with us, Jon takes him on a camping trip to a state park with his church group. They splash in a waterfall with other families and stay up late with campfires and camaraderie. They come back with dirty clothes, sandy towels, and a smelly tent that must air over the deck railing for many days. Both seem extremely happy. However, Jon is making some poor decisions about his work. The second week of Eddie's visit, he works only two nights and then takes Eddie on a four-day trip to the Oregon coast. I warn Jon not to go, because he may lose his job due to excessive absences. When he comes back, he learns one of the shifts he thought he had covered with a substitute actually was left with no one showing up. Restaurant management had to scramble and was not happy.

In early August, Evan and I fly east to meet Pam and Fitz, and travel with them to a beautiful vacation home that Bart and Debra have built on an island off the coast of Maine. We have a magical visit, catching up with each other, watching whales in Bart's boat, eating fresh lobster dinners, hiking, and sitting lazily in a gazebo overlooking the spectacular Bay of Fundy. All of us speak of our children and their lives. With tears in my eyes, I tell them of my distinct joy at being able to state that Jon is doing well.

The week I return home, Jon is fired from his job. Although both

Elliott and I have advised him he has one of the best restaurant jobs in our area and should give it primacy in his life, he had continued to trade away shifts. He also argued with the management when they gave him shifts other than the most desirable ones. Later, he writes, "I got fired because I was too aggressive." Learning he has been let go, I tell Jon in no uncertain terms, "We cannot have an extended period of unemployment." I insist he pursue "LOTS of jobs – not just the best, high-end ones." I say I will watch Eddie every afternoon so he can look for jobs. Initially he is defensive, but then says he will do so. No doubt his pride is hurt.

Jon, age 33, birthday, with Lara

Jon age 33, with Eddie and Miles

Jon, age 33, catching crabs with Eddie

Jon, age 33, teaching Eddie about tide pools.jpg

Jon, age 33, with Eddie at Pacific Ocean

Jon, age 33, with Eddie

Chalk drawing of Golden Gate bridge made by Jon for Eddie

Jon, age 34, catching river creatures with Eddie.jpg

Jon, age 35, birthday

Jon, age 35, Christmas

Jon, age 35, with his dog in California

Jon, age 35, with his dog

Jon, second from right, age 35, with Jeff, Elliott and Eddie

TWENTY

FIGHTING FOR THE POSITIVE CHOICE

I t is a time of ultimate irony. Eddie's summer visit with us ends and Jon takes him to Seattle to catch his airplane back to Diane. We don't know Eddie and Jon will never see each other again in this world. Jon returns from the trip a changed man. He sleeps all morning, ignoring our agreement to get up and be productive. He does not eat, do promised chores for us, or search for work. He is surly or sarcastic when I prompt him to do things, and when I insist, he simply drives off in his car and sits for hours in various parks. Within a week, his cheeks are sunken and gaunt. His actions and demeanor certainly look like drug-using behavior to me, but I still don't understand all of the twisted contours of mental distress that accompany years of drug abuse. He may be suffering from hyperkatifeia, an extreme sensitivity to emotional distress that can follow opioid misuse. He says he is just very depressed about Eddie leaving and surely that statement is true.

Jon is obviously struggling to maintain control of his stress and simply may be unable to handle the grief of separation after having seen and experienced the joy of his beautiful, burgeoning son. His years of addiction mean he has bypassed many of the normal milestones of emotional maturity, so he does not know how to regulate his feelings. He also may have paranoia from his long years of drug use. Or, he may be using drugs to cope. I can't tell. However, for us it is a distinction without a difference. We have clear conditions for him to live in our house and none of them are being met. I sense the trickster Demon is close, shape-shifting in some new form designed to confuse us and defeat Jon. I'm weary and scared we are starting the terrible cycle of addiction once again, and I fear I don't have the strength.

We will learn later Jon did misuse his medication when Eddie left. He doubled his Adderall for a few days and then ran out. No doubt, his huge mood swings were due, in part, to the effects of these rapidly changing amounts of medication. However, perhaps the fact that Jon had lived for eight months in an organized, productive manner in our house by the time Eddie left allowed him to truly feel his love for his son and realize his deep sense of loss, maybe for the first time.

Jon's behavior manifests as paranoid. He believes his phone has been hacked by someone who means to harm or embarrass him, and he harangues me, trying to convince me. He follows me into the yard, into the driveway as I am backing out my car, and to the park when I try to walk Mountain. When I am not home, he calls me and talks repetitively and obsessively about his phone. Jon is not the same person who has been living peacefully and productively in our house for the past eight months. The situation deteriorates rapidly. I'm taut, alert for a danger I cannot see, but that I sense is near. Perhaps, to my shame, I react too quickly. I tell him he has two weeks to move out. He insists he is not using drugs and hasn't for nine months. Perhaps this is correct. We do not know for sure. Four days later, using the money he has saved over the summer, Jon rents a place in a large rooming house in Richland and moves out of our home. Outwardly, he is polite and quiet as he leaves. No doubt there are other strong emotions boiling inside.

Perhaps Jon just could not find his bearings when Eddie left, and lashed out. His emotional age no doubt is much lower than his chronological age, and it may be as low as that of a teenager. In the past, as do many people addicted to alcohol or drugs, he simply buried his feelings with substances and stunted his emotional growth. Perhaps he couldn't handle the sophisticated job at the restaurant over the summer, and the strong emotions of being a father trying to make up for lost time and have tons of fun – all the while being an emotional teenager. I feel sad and defeated that, after eight great months, we have parted with Jon on a sour note. He is distant and we don't see much of him in the early autumn. I hope he may be fine if he sticks close to his church groups and school and finds work. As for our "trashed relationship," I resolve to just wait and give things time.

We continue our pledge to support Jon in school, and in September, he begins taking Introduction to Philosophy and General Psychology at the community college. He now wants a degree in social work, particularly in drug and alcohol counseling. "I know that sounds cliché," he writes, "but I believe it is my calling. I trust God. I believe God has called me to...articulate this subject. To help people understand what they are battling...This is no easy fight. There is no comfort in any of this [drugs]...the Trail Head out of addiction begins in the worst possible despair. You have to be [completely broken] before you find it."

In mid-autumn, he begins coming over to ask for my help with assignments. Working together, searching the Internet, finding interesting items, re-working sentences for better writing, we begin to relate more positively to each other. For the Psychology class, he researches brain science, neurons, synapses, chemical messaging, and brain adaptations, learning some of the new findings about addiction. He especially likes the Philosophy class, which explores big questions, such as the nature of morality, the purpose of life, the existence of God, whether human beings are free, and how to determine the ultimate standards of conduct. When the question of God is discussed, Jon always writes "yes" in the margin and sometimes draws a little smiley face saying, "Hi God!" He writes at length about grace and love. To Jon, the message of Jesus is quite simple: "love...love and...love." He still misses Lara and doodles messages to her in his school notebooks, telling her how much she means to him. He appears to be sober and working hard in school.

In November, Jon takes a job delivering pizzas in the evenings. Elliott has moved overseas to take a job that will last for five years, leaving his dog Buster in a boarding kennel in California. Just before Thanksgiving, he reaches an arrangement wherein Jon will travel to California to get Buster, and Elliott then will begin to pay Jon's rent in exchange for dog care.

During the first week of December, Jon drives to California, taking with him a friend named Alice who is on her way to spend the winter in Mexico. They stop at Shasta Lake, the beautiful wilderness gem north of Redding to look at a marina. Ever curious, Jon asks detailed questions about the boats' engines and gets down on hands and knees to inspect motors and designs. This intense inquisitiveness is one of the traits she finds most endearing, Alice will tell us later. They arrive in San Francisco and retrieve Buster on a remarkably blue and sunny day, taking several pictures of Jon overlooking a city scape with Buster and his old SUV. He looks healthy and strong. The following December, he will be deceased. He parts from Alice and drives north with Buster. An unseasonably cold, early storm moves into the Siskiyou Mountains as he enters southern Oregon. Out of money, Jon and the dog spend a frigid night sleeping in their vehicle. The following evening, he arrives back in Richland hungry and broke. He calls me and I go to his rental, bringing dinner for both of them and gas money to get him started the next day. He finishes his classes very well, getting an A in Philosophy.

Jeff comes to Richland for Christmas, and we have a nice time with all our five children. Evan's daughter June has recently married Ron Morris, who was a school friend of Jon and Matt. The reunion of Jon and Ron is fun for them and delightful for all of us to watch, as they laugh and remember old times at school. This Christmas is the first time all members of our family have been together in a very long time and every bit of each activity, meal, joke, and conversation seems sweet. We don't know it will be the last Christmas we can all share together. Buster plays with Mountain and Brett's dog. We take frigid hikes with them and come back for steaming hot tea and Christmas cookies. At night, we watch movies, draped all over sofas, blankets, pillows, and dogs. I tell Elliott things appear to be good with Jon, but, "the only thing suspicious...is that he is ALWAYS flat broke and always on his phone."

As 2013 comes to a close, the Alcohol and Drug Abuse Institute at the University of Washington in Seattle compiles some frightening statistics. Between 2002-2004 and 2011-2013, opiate-related deaths in Washington State increased by thirty-one percent. Our county has seen a seventy-five percent increase. From 1999-2010, treatment admissions for prescription opiate addiction increased by seventy-three percent and treatment admissions for heroin addiction increased by nearly 104 percent.[110]

In January, Jon begins his next quarter in school taking Business and a sociology class called Social Problems. In the rooming house, he moves from his single room on the second floor to a two-room suite on the ground floor with enough room for Buster. The new location allows Jon to put the dog in the yard right outside his window for some romp time. The two of them take walks together most days, gaining exercise and endorphins. Dori and I pitch in and work on Jon's new place intensely. We paint; scrub floors, and shop for lamps, curtain rods, a clothes hamper, trash can, sheets, and rugs. We find a huge, used blue sofa and go get it in my truck. By the time the three of us force it in the door, Jon's place is looking quite good. I tell Elliott it is, "funky in the Jon style." Jon and Dori begin seeing more of each other, and their relationship seems positive. They often hang out together, get take-out food, or walk Buster. Even more often, they simply text silly quotes, videos, or cartoons to each other from their separate locations.

In the winter, June and Ron move into a new house and invite friends to help with painting and set-up. Jon joins the crowd of young people and soon becomes a star because he is the only one tall enough, with arms long enough, to paint an area high above the entry staircase. He rigs up an uncertain scaffold out of boards and ladders and climbs up, dangling precariously. "Take a video of me while I'm doing this," he jokes, "so I can watch it when I'm in traction in the hospital." When I hear this story, I ask myself why it doesn't occur to Jon that his school friend Ron and all the other young people there are moving ahead with their lives – getting married, buying homes, holding steady jobs. How can he be his cheerful and good-natured self when he sees this discrepancy with his own life? Later, I would learn he certainly did see the disconnect, and it bothered him immensely.

Later in February, Dori and I drive to Seattle to visit Jeff. He has just bought a new desk and donates his previous desk to Jon, loading it into my car for transport back to Richland. At the same time, Jon lets me know he has decided on the birthday gift he wants from his father. He describes to me a high-resolution projector that can attach to his television and project shows onto the wall. Elliott is amenable and asks me to purchase it because he is overseas. He will reimburse me. After arriving back in Richland and dropping off Dori, I go and purchase the unit and take it to Jon. He is as excited as a small child and tells me more than once he intends to host movie nights for friends from school and church. By this time, it is late in the evening and I'm tired and hungry. Yet I linger, delighted with his boyish enthusiasm. When I finally arrive home, I am exhausted, but content. I seem to have three happy children – a situation more positive and hopeful than I have had in a very long time. It will be the last time I feel this way.

Late that winter, Jon writes for his Sociology class a well-researched, strongly worded paper entitled, "Drug and Alcohol Addiction: Everyone's Problem." In many ways, his treatise is remarkably prescient. Ahead of the time much of the nation realizes the problem, he presents statistics showing that addiction is a widespread issue in the United States. He then makes the point that pain-killing prescription drugs are as potent and addictive as many street drugs and contain the same basic opioid ingredients. He speaks of the "physical and psychological agony" of withdrawal and states that addicted people battle through it with "indomitable will" and "the stark realization that it is likely to be for nothing anyway." Here, he hints at the dark secret he carries -- that he feels he may be doomed by his addiction because he can never be free of it. He points out the futility of law enforcement efforts to reduce the supply side of drugs, calling it an, "outright failure...illegal drugs are widely available. The market is fully intact...The only rational approach...to the drug problem is to divert...resources to efforts aimed at decreasing demand." He proposes making treatment always and easily available to anyone wanting it.

However, some of his behavior is odd. In March, walking with Buster late one moonless night in a dense forest preserve along the Yakima River in Richland, Jon sees some very large footprints. He texts me and Dori excitedly: "Whatever made this [the footprints] was VERY heavy...700-800 pounds...It clearly moved through there on two legs, not four...Dori what is this?...Nothing that size could live in [the preserve]... The evidence suggests it is migrating. On the last pitch-black night before spring. In a calculated and deliberate attempt to go undetected... Headed west toward the Cascades." Dori asks him whether he is hinting the prints belong to Big Foot, but he doesn't answer directly. However, he scours the internet for pictures of mysterious footprints and insists the prints he saw were "four times bigger." The next day, he returns to the spot and photographs the footprints, taking measurements and comparing his own prints to the large ones. Soon he is texting the photos to me, Dori, and many other friends. Most of us, including me, are turned off. Some friends distance themselves. This strange and extreme interest makes him seem foolish.

Throughout the late winter and early spring, Jon and Dori maintain a silly dialog of friendly texts. He repeatedly tries to get her to canoe in the river, hike with him, and visit a small island in the Columbia that he calls his "own." In March, he tells Elliott he is working on "the book I was meant to write." It is called the *Bright Grey*,[111] a reference to an album of the same name by acoustic fingerstyle guitarist Derek Patton. The album is lyrical, emotional, quiet, but sometimes emphatic and dramatic. It contains no electronic assistance from music synthesizers, other instruments, or vocals. Although not known as an exclusively Christian musician, Derek Patton clearly shows his faith on this album. Some of the songs take their inspiration from Jesus being betrayed and arrested in the Garden of Gethsemane, faith and acceptance in the face of loss, and the famous quotation from Saint Paul that "These three remain: Faith, hope and Love. But the greatest of these is love."[112]

Jon's *Bright Grey* narrative begins with a sub-section that he titles "Eden," dealing with creation and the emergence of life from the sea. Life forms, he defiantly asserts, are not the result of, "random mutation and natural selection...There is a single and infinite power driving everything." He affirms that evolution is evidence of God's perfect design. "The DNA [deoxyribonucleic acid] inside all living cells contains God's physical writing...How can we say that DNA is a self-writing, self-editing code that is the blueprint of all living things and then say there is anything random about it... We are not simply the sum of all our parts. We are so much more...The fact is, there is one ultimate truth...There is a positive power that is the source and the creator of all things, [and] we are part of it." He emphasizes that God is love and "there IS a shining light. It is all around us...It knows you well. It loves you unconditionally. It can make people whole again...Love is light in action...The light can do the impossible, it can cleanse us, heal us and even bring the worst of sinners back from the brink of oblivion."

In making his case, Jon exercises his brilliant mind to describe the structure of cells, DNA, and the role of carbon and water in life. He compares the salt balance in human blood and salt with that of sea mammals; explains gravity, plate tectonics, and the role of the moon in tide swings; illustrates the mathematical challenges of putting men on the moon; and elucidates other aspects of scientific knowledge that few people understand. Considering his relative lack of education, these understandings are all the more impressive because he figured them out on his own, simply by reading and thinking. Science, he says, is "truly awesome." Still, he insists, "Science has always had it out for God... [science] is constrained by the long-standing paradigm of materialistic, reductionist, deterministic theory."

He then turns to the nature of evil in a sub-section titled, "The Lie and The Light." Evil, he says, is all around us. "Evil is insatiable and unquenchable...in its true naked form it is a void, a singularity, it grows hungrier the more it pulls in. It is rot, decay, as much pain as possible to destroy each of us. The darkness does not want to kill us. It feeds on our pain, it can use us to propagate. It wants to keep us alive, alone and out of the light. This hungry darkness is parasitic in nature. It is cunning and patient, it can adapt and learn, it aims to find and exploit our individual weaknesses to the fullest." There is, he writes, a "spiritual war raging all around us...what we do here and now, in this life, is way more important than we may think...how we behave, how we treat one another really matters. It means everything." To gain favor with God, he asserts, humans need to be kind to each other and, "We also need to ask. We need to properly receive."

At this point, Jon's narrative trails off. No doubt he means to add to it later. As it stands, it is an open allegory of his life. It clearly illuminates his views and perspective, based on the suffering he has endured in his addiction. This once carefree, footloose teenager and young man has lived in abject misery; been possessed, driven, and mastered by his Demon; and has fought through both physical and metaphysical agonies to find Jesus. Clearly, he knows the nature of evil. Having found the Lord, he wants to celebrate his joy and freedom from the clutches of evil, and he wants to teach others his view. Quite simply, he believes, evil exists, God exists, and to have life one must follow the light of Jesus.

TWENTY-ONE
RELAPSE

Addicted people and addiction counselors will tell you that a relapse happens in the mind of the addicted person long before a drug is ingested physically. During the spring of 2014, I begin to see troubling signs in Jon. The Demon is slithering closer, and I feel his cold tentacles reaching for my son. As usual, the transition is marked with confusion. In early March, I tell Elliott I "have been concerned that Jon may be using. I bluntly told him my suspicions and he said he is just busy and distracted. I just don't know – time will tell I guess." I arrange to take a walk alone with Jon to observe, talk, and form my own ideas about how he is doing. Afterward, I report that "I could be wrong, but there were no big red flags I saw." However, between our walk and Jon starting some chores at our house, I relate, "he was 'absent' for about forty-five minutes, which did make me wonder. But overall he made sense and had energy."

In March, Jon's report card shows he has earned good grades in both his classes. I take him for a celebration lunch, and soon afterward, I suggest to Elliott that we buy Jon a newer car because his is "a total tank – loud, heavy and the gas mileage is awful." However, Elliott tells me that, based on phone conversations with Jon, he thinks his behavior is "suspiciously lazy." A nicer car would be an asset Jon could sell, and he fears the enabling possibilities. As happens to many families of addicted people, we are on and off the fence, not knowing whether we are being fooled or whether Jon is just being quirky and private. Elliott suggests we wait and see about a car, because, "I really don't know but I am tending to think that the signs are bad."

Inklings deepen in April. Dori and I ask Jon about the fact that he hasn't been attending AA or NA meetings and does not have a sponsor.

He is defensive, saying there are no men in the local groups whom he respects enough to be his sponsor and that the nearest AA group is not meaningful. Dori hears through the local grapevine that he is smoking marijuana and has been seen with a girl with whom he had many misadventures back in high school. Like Jon, she became addicted to hard drugs in the ensuing years and still lives in Richland. Jon's new association with her cannot mean anything good. He spends a lot of time alone with just Buster, often camping out on his small island in the Columbia River. He calls it Jon Island, as it has no name. He gets few hours at work, often finishing shifts by 7:30 p.m. He often appears spacey, disorganized, and late. But – is he using drugs occasionally? I just don't know.

For the community college spring quarter, he is taking an anthropology class called Religion and Culture, in addition to an Art and Design class. He is once again doodling eyeballs on trees in his school notebooks. He likes both classes and is writing a story called *Pika-Don*. The word Pika-Don was devised in the Japanese vocabulary after the atomic bombings of Hiroshima and Nagasaki in 1945. Translated, "pika" means brilliant light and "don" means boom, the phenomenon seen and heard when the bombs exploded. Jon's story is dark and disturbing, and is never finished. Reading it later, I see that he is trying his hand at creative writing, developing his characters slowly, giving them multi-faceted personalities that are not easily labeled as entirely good or bad. He includes small, interesting details that humanize them, and inserts some of their silent thoughts as a technique to engage the reader and create some level of suspense. However, I am most struck by obvious ironies in the story. An American sailor thinks he is safe in waking from a nightmare, only to be killed in the next instant. The citizens of Hiroshima are smug and complacent, sure of their nation's victory, when obviously they are wrong and in grave danger. Does Jon feel that nothing in life is as it seems? Does he see misplaced hope and destruction as inevitable? Why does he set his story in a city that will become the epicenter of catastrophe?

One morning in the third week of April, I stop by Jon's rooming house to drop off some clothes I have mended. I find him asleep when he is supposed to be in class, and tell him clearly that I am not happy. School is a privilege and skipping school is not an option. I tell him he knows what he needs to do and "not do." Up until this day, I have been supportive. However, something has shifted in me. I want a bottom line. I don't want to live with a question mark and a lump in my throat all the time. I don't want to feel out of control and always at the mercy of events caused by others. I truly need something to really change. The next day, Jon tells Dori that I undoubtedly came to his rooms to toss them to look for contraband. I'm hurt he would say it, because as many times as I have been the steward of his belongings, I have never violated his privacy. Dori finds him to be "confrontational, snippy, angry – uneasy like his old self." Anger and exasperation mix in my feelings.

We inform Elliott, who says he will talk with Jon "as a father – not a prosecutor – and tell him it's time to recognize that no matter how smart he is he can't do sobriety alone." He will insist that Jon move into a sober house, "where he can give daily focus to his addiction and recovery... In one month he must have to have a real job...No soft landings! But no disregard of his disease either." I respond that I agree with the plan. I write back that "if we, who have decades 'down the road' with this disease, fall for his [Jon's] weak excuses, then shame on us. We would be helping him to die of his disease." I worry that "we are giving him a safe, comfortable place to use and that is unconscionable."

I'm changing from completely broken and dependent on circumstances I cannot control to being more resolved. I'm tired of being disheartened and helpless. My anger is taking the place of distraught sadness. Perhaps being tough and insistent is a way for me to foster some sense of control. I want to love my husband, love my other children, not be broke, stop having chest pains and sickening thumps in my heart, stop feeling wrecked and blown apart, take walks, go skiing and boating, and see God's handiwork in our beautiful world. Slowly, I'm moving toward detachment. I'm choosing not to board the Titanic with my son. Perhaps I'm just at the end of my rope, my compassion fatigue gone to bone-tired exhaustion.

A man in my support group says, "Tough love sometimes works, but enabling never works." Another man, addicted but with long years in recovery, advises me: "When a person is using or refusing to follow a program or deceiving/exploiting you, walk away until the person figures out not to do that." I listen. I nod quietly. I'm at a turning point, and I don't think I can stand another hurricane. It's a common phenomenon in families of addicted people, as the family members come to resent their powerlessness.

My group discusses the futility of trying to make reasonable agreements with people in active addiction or relapse. Logical discussions don't work when the manipulation and hidden agendas of these people are directed at the singular goal of obtaining and using drugs. They're smarter than we are in all the ways that matter, and we flail around trying to out-guess them and driving our stress levels into the red zone. Floods of cortisol, the hormone released during stress, exhaust key receptors in our brains, causing depression, fatigue, heart arrhythmia, and other diseases. Suppressing emotions makes our bodies vulnerable, and, all the while, we're not helping our addicted loved ones. Staying "in the game" with them – tolerating, enabling, excusing addictive behavior – leads to continued drug use, with all its perils and perhaps deadly consequences. These discussions affect me powerfully. Perhaps they occur at just the right (or wrong) time. Power, choice, and self haven't been part of my lexicon for a long time, and their appeal is strong.

A few days later, Dori hears that Jon and an acquaintance with a history of drug use have had a terrible fight, which involved screaming and throwing furniture in a yard. My heart wrenches down and sideways in the familiar, crooked pita-style fold. In a year, this acquaintance will be dead of an overdose, leaving behind a daughter. Dori confronts Jon with the news about the fight. He tells her he won't be seeing his old friend anymore and firmly denies he is using drugs. However, the episode causes Elliott to text Jon that "I am cancelling the payment of your rent in your current apartment and applying it to rent at a... [sober] house. You may think this grossly unfair but I am doing it for you because I believe that your behavior is strongly suggestive of what you and I experienced in California. That is just too scary to imagine... If I'm wrong there is no harm done – you simply live in a community of recovery...I know you're going to be demanding to push back. However... you're too important for me to change my mind."

Of course, Jon reacts immediately, pleading with Elliott to be able to keep his rented rooms. The accommodations are humble, he says, but they represent independence, dignity, and privacy to him, and the location is ideal because it's on a direct bus line to the community college. He doesn't even seem to take Elliott's dictum seriously. "Dad C'mon. You know I'm not going to move into a sober house," he texts to Elliott, following this sentence with a symbol for a small smiley face. He adds that he may have a good server job "on the hook" and "may have found a nice girl." He asks for alternative ways to prove himself.

Elliott and I confer, and, confused as always, we decide that a set of strict conditions will suffice on a trial basis, instead of immediately making him move out of his rooms. He is so clever that we can't possibly know for sure whether he is using, so we will give him a chance to meet some new standards I can verify. We devise the same old set of conditions – attendance at AA or NA meetings, getting a sponsor and a better job with more hours, submitting to random drug tests, getting A grades in both his classes in school (an easy task for him if he tries), and not associating with anyone using drugs. We are still unbelievably naïve. We think our prescription for sobriety will work, but we are dealing with an incredibly intelligent, practiced, and wily manipulator. We don't know at this time that we should stay out of the business of micro-managing a recovery. Every addicted person must find his/her own way, and the path of discovery is an important part of successful recovery.

On the last Sunday of April, Evan and I host a belated Easter dinner with all our children, as well as June's husband. Jeff comes over from Seattle, and Jon, having achieved compromise with us, is pleasant and cheerful throughout the evening. He wears clean clothes, but his hair is longer and his skin has a tinge of that waxy, greasy sheen we have seen earlier when he was using heroin. We take pictures of our whole family – six young adults in all. Jon, who is tallest, stands in the middle, stretching his long arms behind and around the others. These photos become the last ones showing all our children together.

On April 30, I hand Jon his rent check in exchange for his initials on his new compliance plan. I tell him bluntly of five red flags I have seen in him that indicate "using behavior" – seeing his old acquaintance, settling for his crummy job, not going to AA and NA meetings, not having a sponsor, and displaying angry outbursts. He has answers for each of these items. Most are vague. Dori hears through the grapevine that he is seeing a young woman with a very unsavory reputation, which upsets me greatly because I believe her reputation is deserved. All my reserves – mental, emotional, and physical – have been stretched thin for a long time. I'm trying to make critical decisions in a world I do not understand, with parameters and challenges constantly shifting. I feel depleted, old, under siege. Evan and I talk about it and realize that our years of dealing with addiction have worn us very thin.

As Jon's deadline of June 1 to meet our conditions approaches, Elliott and I confer. We clearly are more worried than Jon, who still doesn't seem to believe we will follow through. We ask Jon about his new girlfriend but he insists he has stopped seeing her. He does not answer the question of why he hasn't gotten a sponsor. I suppose we shouldn't be surprised that Jon is stubbornly insisting on managing his life his own way. He has been obstinate since infancy. In the meanwhile, he has been spending more time on his small island. He says he is building a natural bridge there as a graphic project for his Art and Design class. He says his instructor has approved the plan, provided he takes adequate photos of it to turn in for his class project. He also is negotiating arrangements with Diane for Eddie's summer trip. I tell him his father's and my position: "We cannot help you bring Eddie here as long as...you have not done the things we asked of you five weeks ago...And the woman you have been seeing...is an absolute show-stopper for us in terms of Eddie...We wish with all our hearts that you had made different decisions, as we would love to see Eddie, and would love to see more of you, but cannot under these conditions." He looks dumbfounded. He cannot believe our ultimatum was serious, and walks away from me.

A week passes and we hear nothing from Jon. In my calculus, the next move must come from him. Elliott asks me to check on Jon's art project on the island, but I tell him I cannot since none of us knows

Jon's hidden spot. However, I say the idea that "a campsite could be an art project is ingenious, and, knowing Jon's creative spirit, could be true." Within the next few days, I learn through the Richland grapevine that Jon indeed is using drugs again and is back to seeing the unsavory woman. Dori persuades a formerly heavily addicted man named Asher, now in recovery, to visit Jon for a "Twelve-Step call." It's a cold call wherein people in recovery invite a person of the same sex in active addiction to talk and consider attending AA or NA. Asher arrives at Jon's door unannounced, and Jon invites him inside. They have a good talk, ranging over their years and experiences of drug use as they verify each other's "street credibility." Jon tells Asher of some horrific experiences, cementing in the older man's eyes that Jon is a genuine veteran of the ages, stages, cunning, ferocity, and desperation of the drug world. He admits to using occasional violence against small time dealers when they "stepped on" (diluted or contaminated) his drugs. Jon says that "my family hates me," but Asher reassures him that statement is untrue – we just hate what he is doing right now. They agree to talk again and perhaps attend an AA meeting together. Afterwards, I cling to the small hope the connection with Asher provides. He tells me Jon "is in pretty bad shape." Final exam week comes and goes at Jon's community college, but we hear nothing from him.

It is the fourth Monday in June, and I am at my volunteer shift at the local hospital. I keep sensing an array of colorful lights when I glance to the right. I'm wearing a necklace of multi-colored stones and I think the hospital must have brightened the ceiling lights over the weekend in the room where I work. My necklace must be playing off the new, high-powered lights. The problem is I keep seeing the strange lights as I walk to my car after my shift and also while I drive home, have lunch, and do errands. At the end of our dinner that night, I mention the odd lights to Evan, and he jumps to my side in alarm. At least one of my eyes is detaching, he tells me, and the condition is serious. It could be the retina. He has known people who have experienced this phenomenon and then lost their eyesight. He calls our eye doctor and has me lie down, propping pillows right there on the kitchen floor. The doctor is equally alarmed. He asks Evan to pull me up and stand behind me and then puts us through a series of sweeping arm movements, asking me what I can see each step of the way, where the arc of my vision cuts off, whether I see anything double or anything that looks like it is missing a piece or is cut off in the middle. After several minutes, he says I do have a problem, potentially serious, but can wait until morning to see him. He instructs me to go to bed, lie in the dark, and not read or watch television.

We arrive at my eye doctor's office the next morning stunned and scared. After a thorough exam, he tells me I have posterior vitreous detachment (PVD) in my right eye, a precarious condition for which there is no treatment or cure. While detached retinas can be repaired surgically, PVD cannot, although PVD can lead to retinal detachment or retinal tears. It happens when the vitreous fluid in the eye loosens from a jelly-like consistency to a thinner, more watery density. It is related to age, but also to strenuous activity and stress. The doctor, who knows me well, pins the underlying cause squarely on my stress levels, which have been extreme and prolonged. Now that my PVD has announced itself, he says, I will have to make some lifestyle changes. No more running, he says, and no aerobic exercises that involve jumping, dancing strenuously, kicking, or twirling. There is no time limit. These restrictions are permanent. It sounds so final. Now there are things I can never do again, and I am shocked. Perhaps the worst part is that I suddenly feel fallible and vulnerable. Ever since my tribulations began, Evan, Pam, and others have told me prolonged stress breaks people. However, I didn't really believe it could happen to me. I was so energetic, resourceful, determined, and positive that I could fix things. I exercised, ate healthy food, used sunscreen, never smoked, and drank coffee and wine in moderation. My worst vice was using real butter. But stress had found a back-door way to confound me.

My eye doctor doesn't know whether the tearing and detaching in my right eye will stabilize or continue. To give myself the best chance, he says I should stay as still as possible for at least three weeks, including some bed rest each day. He gives me several cards with emergency numbers printed in bold, telling Evan and I to carry them in our wallets and cars at all times, and post them on our refrigerators at home and at the cabin. A cold dread of the future steals through me. I have been a reader, researcher, and writer since I was four years old. I can't even approach the idea of being without my right eye, and I surely can't consider the possibility that my other eye will detach in the same way. I leave his office determined to stay as quiet as I can, cancel commitments for a few weeks, and literally tiptoe through my life.

I am lying in bed about two hours later when my phone rings with an unfamiliar number. It is Jon, asking to meet. Despite my recent anger and exasperation at his crises, I am flooded with relief. I quickly decide a quiet lunch can't hurt. However, I tell him that "I am not into rescuing and short-term fixes. Are you ready to make major changes?" He says yes and tells me he agrees to move into a sober house. I need to pick him up as he has almost no gasoline. I arrive and he opens his door looking awful. He is pale with sallow skin, his hair is long and stuffed messily into his hat, he is wearing a coat even though it is summer, and he is unsteady on his feet, trembling slightly. He will never look like a healthy young man again. "I've missed you," he says tentatively. I hug him, feeling through the coat that he is very thin. I suggest we go get some food. Sitting across the table from him at a casual restaurant, I watch his hands shake as he pushes his food around the plate. He ought to be ravenous. He tells me he quit his job a few weeks ago and is out of money, food, gasoline, Neurontin, and his phone doesn't work. He also has no food for Buster. I know these conditions indicate a brutal relapse, but still I ask questions. Although I know the Demon well, I never stop being amazed at the traps, humiliations, and sufferings he imposes on his addicted victims.

Jon says he has been sick with a terrible flu, but has not been using drugs. He tells me he left his job over a dispute about whether he was late one evening. It was just a misunderstanding about the time his shift was to start, he says, but the manager was rude to him, and he walked out. Later, I will learn he was fired for habitual lateness and/ or not showing up at all. The manager will tell me gently that the staff liked Jon so much they gave him more chances than policy allowed, but after a while, they just could not depend on him. Jon is not sure of the grades he got at the end of the school quarter, but says they "maybe aren't great." I will learn later from his professors that his attendance in class declined in May and stopped altogether in June. Throughout the quarter, the projects he turned in "didn't fit the bill" because he wasn't in class enough to listen to what was assigned. He never showed up for his final exams and did not turn in his final class projects. They had no choice but to fail him. I ask about his phone and discover it is broken and he thinks someone sent a virus to it. He had called me on his landlord's phone. I know the foul Demon I am dealing with. Jon's body and mind have been battered by this horrific relapse, and there is no use continuing to question him.

I tell him I have been diagnosed with an eye problem and must take it easy, but that we can still go get a few things he will need. I slip seamlessly into helping mode, but I don't consider it enabling. He has agreed to go into a sober house, and I know he won't get any better if I leave him sick and penniless. We get his prescription filled and try to buy a new, inexpensive phone. He wants to keep his phone number, but learns it will take at least twenty-four hours for it to transfer. However, if he accepts a new number, we can get the phone working right away. He ponders. Finally, he shrugs. "Okay," he says. "At least with a new number maybe certain people will stop calling me."

Next, we get his SUV and drive to a gas station where I tell him to fill up. I see a tear escape his eye as he bends to insert the gas hose. I decide to program his new number into my phone as we stand there. However, I can't seem to get it right. I am confused. I try at least three times, juxtaposing numbers, but I still can't program the correct number. Finally, I just hand him my phone and his big fingers quickly punch in the number. He looks at me quizzically. "Mom, are you okay?" he asks. He has never seen me less than competent. I tell him I'm fine, just a little worried about my eye. I want to go home and rest. I give him cash for food, and he agrees to come over the next day and paint a ceiling for me. I watch him drive away toward the discount grocery store, head characteristically titled slightly to one side. For the first time, I wonder about my own breaking point. Up until now, it has never occurred to me that I have one.

TWENTY-TWO
END OF DAYS

During the next few days, I see Jon several times. We go to the bank and withdraw the very last of a stack of savings bonds I had bought him several years earlier. I let him have it on the condition that he pays two months' worth of child support, which he does. He comes to our house and does the painting, I fix him eggs and tacos, and send him for a haircut. He comes back looking much better. Dori stops over and they joke around. Both express shock at finding me resting on my bed in the middle of the day, because it is something I never do. Evan takes them aside and tells them my eye problem is more serious than it seems, and they must not upset me. Jon attends an AA meeting with Asher and visits him at the sober house where he lives, meeting and talking with the guys there.

One day, Jon sits on my bed while I am resting and guides my hand to feel three pea-sized lumps on the side of his neck. He tells me they have come and gone a few times in recent months, and they worry him. I tell him to make an appointment to have them checked. Another day, he tells me with wide-eyed joy that Lara is going to move back to Richland in mid-summer. Her mother needs cancer care here, and Lara and she will get an apartment together. He also tells me he has a new job prospect that looks likely.

Soon, Jon learns Dori has gotten an apartment and we won't tell him the location until he has been sober for ninety days. The news upsets him tremendously. He is the big brother and yet he is failing, going back to a sober home, while his little sister is moving on with her life. It wounds his pride deeply. He becomes surly and stubborn with me and, a few days later, has a terrible outburst aimed at Dori. He tells her he will sell all his possessions to pay for staying in his rental and will never agree to "take a step back" by moving into a sober house. Later, Evan and I consult Asher. He tells us he thinks Jon is "not done using drugs." He advises us to "let him go" for now, and let the summer pass.

My heart, as it has done so many times, thuds sideways and down. I slide low in my chair, the wind sucked out of me. Jon has been back in our lives only five days, yet already we are enmeshed in outbursts, situations we cannot sort out or fix, and our stress levels have climbed to the red zone. His diatribe against Dori makes me think he has taken a substance – an upper – but I may be wrong. His excessive anger may be the result of the extreme emotional volatility that follows a heavy relapse, and/or brain damage from protracted drug use, and/or complete frustration and anger at himself. I am terribly sad.

The next day, Jon says he needs to talk to me, but it has been only a few days since my eye diagnosis and I feel overwhelmed with the new avalanche of conflicts and problems. I need to rest. I tell him I can't take stress, not even a stressful conversation, and ask him to wait a few days. He tells me he won't be moving into a sober house, and I feel betrayed because I thought that agreement had been sealed. He texts: "I would much rather put a bullet in my head. I'm not going to lose everything. I'd rather die...I don't want to live like this." Ominously, he concludes: "But here's the thing. I don't have another one of these in me. I'd be better off dead."

In truth, I don't take his death threats seriously. Death simply is not something that enters even the most remote corner of my mind (unless it might come accidentally, from an overdose). Still, I write back to him: "You have mentioned death several times - I sincerely hope and pray you don't do anything foolish!"[13] Heartsick, worn out, feeling futile and confounded, I go to bed. I just want to hide.

Jon still cannot pay for Eddie's summer trip by himself and appeals to Elliott who adamantly says no. Jon calls him several times in Seattle, but Elliott will not answer. He also calls me many times, but I feel defeated, depleted, scared, and cornered. I'm beyond the outer reaches

---

[13] I now know that is the worst way to frame a question to people mentioning suicide. It makes them defensive and embarrassed to answer truthfully.

of my capabilities and I have nothing left. I do not take his calls. He texts to let me know that he has secured the new job and once again asks to talk. I write back that I'm not ready to talk yet. "I do not want to see you until after you change your life," I write. "Go figure out how to be a responsible adult who pays your own bills and doesn't blame others. Until then, do not contact me." He asks me to, "please drop the tough love stuff. C'mon. It's never been necessary with me you know that. Good Lord...I'm Jon, remember. I'm not working some angle." A terrible storm is brewing.

On July 4, I am resting at home, feeling sad, impotent, and perplexed. I cannot make sense of my son and the apparent fact that he doesn't understand his own actions have caused his parents and sister to distance themselves. In my head, I turn around the events of the past twelve days, from re-engaging with a grateful and broken Jon to our current whirlwind of conflicts. I have no answers, but my head spins. Evan does quiet chores in the house. We see Jon walking up the driveway and I go into my bedroom and shut the door. I tell Evan I am just not up to a discussion – I'm played out, I've got nothing. Evan tells Jon that I'm resting, but Jon insists and a dreadful quarrel ensues. He shouts to me through the bedroom door, demanding that we talk. "You won't even come out and look at me," he says. Later, I will realize that what my son actually meant was: "This thing [the addiction] is eating me alive and I'm terrified, and you're not fixing it!"

Evan tells Jon to leave me alone, and, appallingly, they nearly come to physical blows. Evan calls 911, and Jon leaves. The police ask us to describe his car, and they soon stop him a few blocks away. The officer writes Jon a very expensive ticket for having no vehicle insurance and several other violations on the decrepit crate that serves as his SUV. He then calls us to ask whether we want Jon to be arrested for domestic violence. We say: "No, do not arrest him. Just tell him not to come back to our house." I don't know rage and aggression can be signs that a person is contemplating suicide. Shaken, despairing, mournful to the core, Evan and I lock all our doors and hold each other. I cannot comprehend my life and I can't process anything. The jolts and lurches of this journey make me feel that I have no substance – I could disintegrate and not even feel it.

That night, Jon texts me, again asking to talk. He speaks of "cataclysmic disaster" if we do not, but I don't respond. I have no answers. I punish him for displaying the symptoms of his disease. I disconnect from Jon not because I don't love him. I disconnect because I think I must in order to survive, but it is the worst thing I will ever do. I will never talk to him again.

In the autumn, after Jon's death, I will learn he was very close to suicide right after his last conversation with me. However, he held off because he knew Lara would be moving back to Richland. He spends the summer working at his new job running a tasting bar in a liquor store. I learn later he is very popular with the customers, and the owner and staff like him very much. When Lara arrives, he begins spending time with her, her mother Alyssa, and sometimes Kathy and Clark. One of the first things he tells Lara is that he wants a bench placed on "his island" and named for him when he dies. No one tells me. He and Lara walk and swim with their dogs in the river shore parks, paddle around in the old red canoe, watch movies on television, begin to ferment grapes to make wine together, and share an occasional glass of wine. However, they are just friends, not boyfriend and girlfriend. Lara has a long-distance boyfriend who sometimes visits her in Richland, which Jon does not like, but must tolerate.

One day, sitting in a park with Alyssa, Jon confesses he "really blew it with Lara" and asks what he can do to win her back. Alyssa wisely tells him just to "stay the course, keep being friendly, and don't pressure her." She reminds him that Lara spends almost all her free time with him, certainly much more time than she spends with her boyfriend. Kathy reassures Jon privately they have forgiven him for his relapse in Seattle that broke up his life there with Lara. She says the relapse was a mistake and all people make mistakes. "Yes," he says tellingly, "but those mistakes are going to keep happening, and they're going to be the end of me." After his death, she will tell me he "tried to act like his old self [that summer] but couldn't quite pull it off...the spark and quick grin were gone."

I don't know Jon is making and drinking wine, but I do know he works at a liquor store, and I think that is a very bad idea. To me, it seems foolish and arrogant for him to work managing a tasting bar, conversing with people about various wines and other alcohol, their tastes, and their "bouquets" all day long. It seems the opposite of the humble surrender to powerlessness that saves many alcoholic and addicted people.

In the first few weeks after the July 4 confrontation with Jon, I stay shut down. I'm very depressed and see only Evan and Dori. Soon, Evan and I go on our annual vacation to the island off the Washington coast. This island knows us well. At various times, it has brought us solace, family fun, tension, terror (the year Jon was homeless in California), relief, and renewal. This year, it brings just quietude. The weather in my life has changed so many times, so precipitously, that I am numb. I watch the deep green, swirling water of the ocean as we drive our boat, the dark forests of cedar trees and Douglas fir with their crooked tops, madrona trees with their smooth orange limbs, and the huge black rocks along the coasts. I survey the deer as they munch grasses and leaves near our cabin, and the sun as it traverses the yard and sets red and gold in the late western evening. I don't discuss Jon with Evan, because every time I try to sort out the most recent events, my mind literally hurts. I cannot make sense of Jon's extreme anger.

I don't yet understand addiction as a disease that affects maturity and impulse control among other things. I look for logic. Why does a thirty-six-year-old man blame me and Elliott because he can't afford a trip for Eddie this summer? If he would just grow up and support himself like a "normal adult," I ruminate, none of these questions would matter. I am annoyed, irritated, deeply exhausted by our long history, stymied, unable to figure a way forward and, for the time being, unwilling to try. A self-perpetuating downward spiral in our relationship is in play. His anger exerts a reciprocal influence on me, and I withdraw.

I don't intend to stay apart from Jon indefinitely, but when we return from our week on the island, I still don't feel ready to engage. Almost as soon as we unpack, Evan and I are thrust into an urgent, high-profile consulting job. Evan is highly stressed. I tell him to calm down – we will do this task together. We get busy. We work feverishly for most of August and are finally done in the second week of September.

Once again, events overtake us. We have made reservations for a trip to Canada for ocean fishing at a spot Evan has wanted to visit for many years. I know that when we return, Dori will be starting back into community college, so I order a computer for her at a local store. The computer will be held in secret until we return from our trip. I also need to purchase and send birthday presents to Eddie, as all these dates are converging. We go to Canada. I'm no longer avoiding Jon, just postponing a talk and perhaps a reconciliation with him until events calm down. Jon, for his part, stays away from us and does not communicate. He tells Lara that it will be up to us to approach him. My refusal to talk to him in early July hurt him deeply. In addition, part of his stoicism may be a desire to hide any signs of his despair because he wanted me to believe he was strong and doing fine.

Elliott's feelings vacillate. In July, he was adamant we stay away from Jon. However, in mid-August, he writes to me that "I can't help worrying about him." Yet in mid-September, Elliott's anger rekindles as he thinks about the collateral damage to Eddie. Like the rest of us, he is trapped in this vortex. With naivete that today seems preposterous, we are still texting each other with lists of conditions we might use to motivate Jon. As if more insistence on AA meetings, a different job, inventories of dos and don'ts, and good grades in school might finally vanquish the monster devouring him. We are so ignorant about this cruel and wily disease.

Back from Canada, I take Dori to the computer store to pick up her gift. The store is located almost next door to Jon's liquor store. Dori and I are just emerging from the computer store when we see Jon walking from his store to his car. It appears to be a day off for him, as he is dressed casually. His hair is short, and his clothes are neat. We don't want to run into him then and there, as we worry that he will see the computer and reignite his resentment toward Dori. It would be better to see him another time, we say to each other, so we duck away. We see him open the passenger door of his car, bend over, and lean in – his long frame stooping down, his right leg bent upward at the knee. He retrieves something from the car and walks back into the store, head bent characteristically slightly to the side. He has ten days to live. We have no idea.

Three days later, Elliott emails me to say Jon has called him twice, wanting him to call back. I counsel Elliott to "take the call, LISTEN first because maybe he wants to apologize and get back on track...Please leave yourself open to that...Remember – our emotions don't matter as much as getting this young person on the right track. Maybe this is that chance." He does take a call from Jon on September 28, and they have a long talk. Jon says he would like to go back to the community college, and Elliott agrees to help him, provided, "he makes a commitment to school...He would have to work but I would pay tuition...I need a roadmap of his future and I won't invest in anything less." Elliott also states that "I continued to press for a sober house [but] he [Jon] was not hearing any of it...He is Absolutely unwilling to consider [it] because it would set him back." At the end of their conversation, Jon says "thanks Dad." Elliott will never hear from him again.

I'm glad they are talking. It seems like such a waste of a summer for all of us to be so estranged, although I know I'm the one who cut off conversation with Jon. Elliott and I text about our mutual confusion. "The question we have is what do we do now?" he writes. "Jon has become such a con artist that we can no longer simply have a discussion and determine among ourselves how to go forward." It is October 2. We are standing on the fault line of an earthquake, but do not know it.

What does Jon hear in the conversation he has with his father? Does he detect the skepticism in Elliott's voice? The edge? The fatherly duty to instruct and guide, as well as love? Does Jon know or feel he is slipping again? Or does he just know that someday, at some point, he might? Does his Demon's constant shadow over his life fill him with such shame and fear he can't think straight or thinks of simplistic solutions? What about me? What about the fact that my own exhaustion and stress, as well as the press of events throughout the summer, have kept me from reaching out? I had no solutions, but I could have offered love. I could have gone to him and said, "I don't know what we are going to do, but you're not alone. We'll face this thing together." But – I did not. I did not follow Jesus's dictum to point out a fault, discuss it, and forgive.[113] How many opportunities did we miss that summer? I don't know. I just know we failed.

Jon has got to have love in his life. He is withering without it. His employer will tell me later that in late September, he had some phone calls at work that upset him deeply. He would go outside the store and pace up and down, talking animatedly. His manager liked him very much, so she offered to counsel him, give him extra time off, or loan him money if he needed it. Intensely proud, he always told her simply that his problems were "personal." A torrent is building inside him. He decides to propose to Lara, go for broke, be open and vulnerable, tell her he has always loved her. On October 5, he buys a bottle of very nice wine and sets out two wine glasses on his coffee table. Nervous, he rehearses, scribbling the words and sentiments he wants to convey. She can't or doesn't want to see him that night.

The next morning, he asks her to meet him on the Columbia River shore, at a place near his island where they have often launched the canoe. In words too private to repeat, he confesses his deep, abiding love for her. He says he has stayed away from her for the past two years because he wanted to spare her from his curse. "It's all out of love," he has written in a note he never gives her. However, he has discovered he is nothing without her. He asks her to accept him exclusively, but she says she just cannot trust him. She has an edge to her that day. She has responsibilities and must get to work by noon. She is supporting herself and her sick mother, and she has no safety net. She knows if she doesn't work, no one will rescue and pay their rent. Memories of the disastrous experience with his relapse at their apartment in Seattle rise in her mind, making her angry. It will take longer for him to prove himself, she says. Later, she tells me part of her wanted to accept his offer of a future together, for she surely loved him. She just wasn't ready. There were too many ghosts. Lara goes to work, but soon receives a text from Jon saying, "Take care of Buster, he's your dog now." Seriously worried, she tells her manager that she must leave work and goes back to the river shore.

Lara and Jon talk more. She can smell liquor on his breath, but he is not drunk. He tells her he has been thinking of suicide all summer, ever since his blow-up with me, but that he held off because she was moving back to Richland. Now, he says, there is no reason not to do it: "Why shouldn't I? My family won't speak to me, I can't see Eddie, and you don't love me." She tells him to be positive and responsible. "Don't be foolish," she says. "Think of Eddie." She persuades him to walk up to his car and suggests they go for a quick lunch. She thinks he has agreed, but suddenly, he turns swiftly on his heel and strides down to the canoe at the river shore. A bulky sleeping bag lies in the bottom of the vessel, hiding in its folds a large rifle. He has been caretaking his rental house while the owners were away on vacation. They have given him a set of keys to every room. Inside the closet of an Iraq war veteran stood a 357 rifle. Jon has bought a box of cartridges.

As Lara watches, he leaps into the canoe and paddles rapidly away from shore. He throws his laptop and phone over the side. "Tell my Mom I love her," he calls over his shoulder. Lara screams his name over and over, but he does not stop. She runs out on a narrow strip of land that leads to an island near his, yelling his name. She considers jumping into the water and swimming between the two islands. Instead, she calls her mother and begs her to come to the river shore. About twenty minutes later, Alyssa arrives, and Lara drives off to find me. At first, Alyssa stands, straining forward and scanning the tree line on Jon's island. She sees the red canoe beached under some bushes. Then she sits down on a bench, shoulders slumped, elbows on her knees. Jon claims his fierce grace. A single shot punctuates the still air.

TWENTY-THREE

UNDERSTANDING ADDICTION

After Jon's death, I writhed around in pain, reading, walking, talking, praying, never sleeping. I could not stand to be in my own skin. Looking for some understanding, I called a psychologist whom I trusted, and he made room in his calendar to see me almost immediately. He spoke some of the first words that brought me anything that might be called comfort. "It sounds like your son had brain damage," he said when I told him the basics of Jon's story. His words had an electric effect on me. "Tell me more," I said simply. He recounted Jon's increasingly mercurial behavior during the last year of his life, emphasizing the outbursts towards Dori, friends, me, and Evan. Diminishing impulse control, he said, could indicate impairment in the frontal lobe of Jon's brain – impairment consistent with findings in the new science of research on addicted brains. I was fascinated by this small flicker of understanding. Something was starting to make sense logically and it met my need for rational process.

I soon developed an unquenchable appetite for more knowledge. I read voraciously, learning new terms and taking notes with a diagram of the human brain by my side. I wrote to researchers and government officials involved in this work. The information I learned was, and is amazing, and it literally grows by the day. Dr. Nora Volkow, Director of NIDA, states plainly that alcohol or drug abuse disrupts the brain: "Science has shed much light on addiction. We now understand that changes in brain networks needed for self-regulation cause substance use to become compulsive in some individuals — despite their best efforts to decrease or stop use."[114] In other words, she says, the behaviors that break moral codes are symptoms of disease, and the person is sick with the psychiatric disease of addiction. Addiction is not a moral failing as has been said throughout history. Dr. Volkow became my heroine, and I wrote to tell her so. Her staff called me to suggest additional leads.

I learned that, like cancer or heart disease, addiction is a physical illness that needs treatment and help, and people usually do not recover without these interventions. Although the Diagnostic and Statistical Manual of Mental Disorders, the standard classification guide for psychiatric conditions and diseases, has named addiction as a disease since 1968, this determination was based simply on observation of aberrant behavior. In the late twentieth century, science began discovering that addiction is a disease that literally and measurably changes the brain. It damages the organ by disabling some abilities and reinforcing other urges and desires to supersonic levels. Neuroplasticity is the term applied to brain changes in response to stimuli. It means that the brain is malleable – it can heal or partially heal after injury or stroke by developing new neural pathways. It also can change in maladaptive ways, developing neural pathways that reinforce drug use and make it first habitual and then essentially automatic. The adaptable ("plastic") brain can be shaped by experience and changed by developing new neural pathways, for good or ill.

Behavioral neuroscientist Judith Grisel carries the concept one step further. Thoughts, memories, and feelings are not just intangible and theoretical, she says. They have real, measurable, physical effects on the brain and its plasticity. "The brain is no more static than a river," she writes, "as currents constantly form from the flow of our experiences."[115] In other words, once addiction takes hold in a person's brain, the brain has been changed, and a disease is present and has a life of its own. In the 1990s and early 2000s, almost no one outside of a small slice of the scientific community knew of brain neuroplasticity in addiction. Certainly, we did not.

Today, MRI technology, PET scans, single photon emission-computed tomography (SPECT) scans, and quantitative electro-encephalograms (QEEGs) map the deterioration of the brain in addiction. However, as Jon's addiction moved from seed to weed, we did not know. Human beings are programmed to repeat behaviors that bring pleasure, and most of those activities promote the continuation of the human species. Activities such as eating, having sex, holding babies, and relating to other people are pleasurable and contribute to the propagation of the species. Performing these functions releases the chemical dopamine, which makes people feel good, in the brain's limbic system, particularly the nucleus accumbens (NA) and ventral tegmental area (VTA). These functions also release serotonin, endorphins, and enkephalins – all natural brain chemicals associated with pleasure. Drug use mimics these chemicals and floods the brain with excessive amounts of them, thus producing the "high" (intense euphoria). Maia Szalavitz says excess dopamine stimulation of the NA provides "the chemical signature of bliss...the currency of pleasure"[116] The limbic system, sometimes called the reward center or pleasure center, processes emotions, stress, desires, motivation, conditioning, and reinforcement. It also includes the hippocampus, hypothalamus, and thalamus.

Dr. Robert Lustig says simply dopamine is a "Jekyll -Hyde neurotransmitter...There really can be too much of a good thing. It can even kill you."[117] When the brain is blasted with dopamine, it seeks stasis or normal balance and begins producing less dopamine on its own. Dopamine D_2 receptors in the brain actually shrink or deactivate. As Dr. Lustig states, "There is a price to pay for reward... [and] it's measured in neurons...If you open the dopamine floodgates repeatedly...with multiple rapid firings...the dopamine-receptor neurons go into overdrive, leading to cell damage or death."[118] Soon, only high amounts of dopamine generated by drugs can bring feelings of pleasure. As addiction grows, people develop tolerance, which means they need more and more drugs to experience the euphoria of their first use. They no longer are moved by ordinary, healthful processes that bring pleasure, and they lose interest in activities that normally would inspire them, such as fun, productive work, and even eating. Thus, perhaps, Kurt Cobain's anhedonia. In advanced addiction, the brain has been "hijacked" to the extent that it actually "thinks" that taking drugs equals survival, because drug use is the only action that brings pleasure. Sam Quinones says that drugs "perform literal brainwashing" on people, causing them to act contrary to their own self-interest.[119] Thus, end-stage addiction patients do not care if they eat, have warm clothes or shelter, or companionship. The drive to seek and ingest drugs replaces all the logical and necessary activities needed to sustain life.

Additionally, repeated exposure to dopamine-enhancing drugs causes the brain's amygdala to adapt. *Mu* receptors in the amygdala and thalamus, act as "keyholes" into which opiates fit like perfect keys. Once a drug enters and binds to these receptors, it overwhelms normal feelings, overriding and blocking the actions of natural brain chemicals. With natural dopamine and serotonin production decreased, depression and anxiety increase. In addition, over-stimulation of the limbic system by drugs increases production of the brain chemical corticotropin-releasing factor (CRF, or corticotropin-releasing hormone – CRH), thus elevating stress. Patients are driven to use more drugs not just to "get high," but to obtain relief from stress and withdrawal symptoms. "Thus," says Dr. Grisel, "the most profound law of drug use is this: there is no free lunch…the benefits that drugs confer will have to be paid back."[120] To make things worse, stress activates receptors that remember and crave opioids in the brain's VTA, a key part of the "reward center." Stress can damage or weaken neurons in the brain to the extent that actions become almost involuntary. This cascade of stress chemicals in the brain explains why addicted people seem to relapse at the worst times – just before a big interview, test, or family reunion.

Another drastic consequence of drug use is its effect on memory. Twin processes take place, each in the wrong direction for health. Memory is diminished by drug use, but also enhanced. During drug use, the hippocampus, as a site of memory and learning, suffers damage, often because it is stressed. Some drugs, notably marijuana, block the glutamate receptors that build synapses during the memory process. Synaptic connections are eliminated, and the hippocampus actually shrinks. However, conversely, the brain chemical adrenaline (epinephrine) enhances memory, and the brain's amygdala (site of processing of emotional memories) literally grows in physical size. A memory made in the presence of adrenaline and/or dopamine is strongly remembered and becomes "over-learned" and almost permanently etched into the amygdala. Dr. David Kessler, former dean of the medical schools at Yale and the University of California at San Francisco, says these memories tie the drug together with a host of good and desirable feelings in the brain of those who are addicted.[121] Overlearning of a memory explains why addiction patients experience cravings when they encounter sights, smells, colors, persons, or places that remind them of drug use. Overlearned behaviors and associations are extremely resistant to change.

The final area of the brain damaged by drug use is the frontal lobe or prefrontal cortex (or more precisely, according to some researchers, a sub-area known as the orbitofrontal cortex) located just behind the forehead. It is often called the site of "executive functioning" – decision-making, self-regulation, inhibition, assignment of relative value, modulation of reward, and ability to anticipate consequences. When drugs or alcohol are used repeatedly, the neural pathways leading to the frontal lobe are damaged and some of the cells are impaired or go dormant. In terms of the effects of drugs/alcohol on the frontal cortex, neuroplasticity is negative. Impaired signaling of dopamine and glutamate, caused by drug use, weaken the ability of addicted patients to make logical decisions, weigh consequences, defer gratification, and inhibit impulses. In end-stage addiction, MRIs and PET scans show marked dark areas, indicating lack of blood flow and functioning in the prefrontal cortex. Three-dimensional SPECT scans actually show lesions and holes in this area. These physical changes explain why addicted patients can be sincere in their desire and intention to cease drug use, yet at the same time, so impulsive that they cannot act on their resolve. They literally are out of control. From these observations came the popular term of a "hijacked" brain. As reporter Sam Quinones says, "An addicted brain is one where a raging primitive reward system has silenced the prefrontal cortex's wise counsel."[122]

When a weakened or partially disabled prefrontal cortex is combined with a limbic system whose cells have changed so they can be stimulated only by floods of dopamine from drugs, and a memory both unable to recall negative consequences yet finely tuned to pleasure-seeking cues, the "perfect storm" of addiction is complete. Addicted people have acquired what the American Society of Addiction Medicine defines as a *primary*, "chronic medical disease involving complex interactions among brain circuits, genetics, the environment, and an individual's life experiences."[123]

At this point, addicted patients are their own worst enemies. As the limbic system gets stronger and the prefrontal cortex gets weaker, people lose themselves. They will break all social barriers to obtain drugs; leave behind other responsibilities and loyalties; spend money recklessly on substances; violate moral codes by stealing, lying, and manipulating to get drugs; and repeatedly ignore pleas to stop these behaviors. These people look like they have no morals, standards, or consideration for others, when in fact, the behaviors are caused by brain-based compulsions, drive and disrupted self-control. Sometimes people very simplistically refer to the "go" part of the brain (the reward or pleasure-seeking center) and the "stop" part (the frontal cortex with its role in inhibitions). In addiction, again simplistically, the "go" portion easily overwhelms the "stop" portion, and the affected people are virtually defenseless against themselves.[14]

The emerging science of epigenetics ("on top of" or "in addition to" genetics) is starting to yield more molecular clues to the brain changes that occur in addiction. According to Dr. Grisel, even though the field is just "beginning to scratch the surface, epigenetic research shows that cellular and physiological changes can be caused by external factors that switch genes on and off," and affect how cells "read genes." DNA is the long, double-stranded nucleic acid molecule that is the main constituent of our chromosomes. It carries our genes as segments along its strands. Epigenetic studies demonstrate that external modifications to DNA can affect how cells interpret or "listen to" genes, without actually changing the DNA sequence. In other words, epigenetic research seeks to understand dynamic alterations in cells. Addiction has been shown to alter brain cells, perhaps when enzymes add or remove chemical tags in DNA, blocking production of certain proteins. Withdrawal from drugs

---

[14] Material in the preceding seven paragraphs is drawn largely from the work of Dr. Nora Volkow, Director of NIDA, and her colleagues.

possibly can trigger an epigenetic mechanism that keeps genes turned off. Histone acetylation makes genes more accessible to being turned on or off and is present in higher levels in the brains of addicted people. The neurotransmitter glutamate plays a key role in these changes and is present in overdrive in addicted animals. Understanding these changes is a key building block from which, hopefully, research can proceed to modify, reduce, or expand the actions of proteins and other brain chemicals that affect drug-seeking compulsions.[124] The hope is that research can find ways to block or promote the changes necessary to bring an addicted brain back into healthy stasis.

Worse yet for Jon, I learned that the speed and strength with which addiction takes hold and advances are accelerated when drug use begins in the teenage years. The brains of teenagers are still developing, have more plasticity, and are particularly susceptible to damage from drugs in several ways. The teenage brain produces even larger amounts of dopamine than the adult brain when stimulated by drugs, precipitating stronger and faster addiction. Dr. Grisel states: "The "neurobiological consequences of drug use are much more profound and longer lasting when exposure occurs during adolescence than when it occurs after about the age of twenty-five."[125] Even the U.S. Supreme Court agrees teen brains are especially malleable. In 2005, it outlawed capital punishment for crimes committed before the age of eighteen, finding that incomplete frontal lobe development in the brain can make teens more impulsive and less responsible for good decisions than adults.

Very importantly, research has found that teen brains have an undersupply of white matter, or myelin, a sort of connective insulation that helps information flow efficiently from one part of the brain to the other. Myelin is made of tightly packed cells that surround the ends of neurons and allow faster speeds of signal transmission. Essentially, myelin "greases the wires" to hasten communication by neurons in the brain. Neurons are brain cells that communicate thoughts, feelings, movements, and moods by sending electrical messages to one another. Without insulated connections provided by myelin, signals coming from one area of the brain have trouble linking up with other parts of the brain. For example, signals of fear and stress coming from the amygdala have difficulty reaching the prefrontal cortex's sense of judgment. Complete myelination of the brain does not occur until people reach their early thirties, and the prefrontal cortex is the last area of the brain to be fully myelinated. Research shows that drug use actually inhibits the formation of myelin and the normal maturation processes in the prefrontal cortex.

Likewise, alcohol use in adolescence can affect the size and functioning of the prefrontal cortex (executive center) and the hippocampus (memory). The U.S. Substance Abuse and Mental Health Services Administration (SAMHSA) states: "The use of substances may also compromise an adolescent's mental and emotional development from youth to adulthood."[126] Research shows that teens who begin drinking alcohol before the age of fifteen are more likely to develop alcohol use dependence later in life than those who start drinking at or after age twenty-one.[127] Teens, inexperienced, perhaps dared by friends or maybe believing that "everyone does it," often drink to excess. When the less-than-fully-developed pre-frontal cortex of a teenager is combined with the impulsiveness, inability to focus and follow through, and temptation to engage in risky behavior that is characteristic of the age group, peril already exists. The danger of addiction becomes exponential.

The disease of addiction, science now knows, leaves its victims or patients looking like themselves, but vastly changed inside. Their behavior is destructive and seems to defy logic, yet they pursue it relentlessly, acting against their own survival. They become unable to respond to normal consequences, to the pleas of their loved ones, to threats and punishments from the law, to physical distress and illness, and to any barrier that stands between them and their drug use. Normally, the ability to persevere despite negative consequences promotes survival, but in the twisted circuits of an addicted brain, persistent drug seeking promotes the opposite and can lead to death. Was Jon's brain addicted after he used marijuana, speed, LSD, and methamphetamines as a teenager in high school? Probably not, but some seeds of addiction at least had become buds. With abstinence from drugs and limited drinking, could he have led a normal life? Almost certainly yes. What about after his time in Sun Valley? What about after his stressful time alone in Richland grieving the absence of Eddie? Dr. Lustig says simply that "stress promotes faster addiction to drugs of abuse."[128] Probably Jon could have recovered with intensive treatment and the support of a community of other addicted people. However, none of us knew the science, the field, or the odds. We tried methadone and had hope and love. None of us knew what the future would bring.

Some researchers see addiction as a coping mechanism to calm and sooth a person whose environment seems overwhelming, too busy, and full of stimuli. They say taking drugs can represent a safe haven, a way of managing one's environment. Jon had ADD, but we did not recognize it. He focused intensely on tasks he liked, but could not focus on those he disliked. He was extremely creative (an attribute sometimes associated with people who suicide) and abundantly stubborn, again traits he could have addressed by self-medicating. In addition, Jon was prone to depression, especially when he was isolated. The fact that he craved and sought company and sociability may have been a coping mechanism that came automatically to him. Finally, he was extremely gifted. Research has found that more intelligent adolescents can be more susceptible to drug experimentation, partly because they require more stimulation to keep from becoming bored.[129]

Yet another factor probably was genetic. Dr. Volkow states that researchers are "gaining an understanding of the genetic, developmental, and environmental factors that cause susceptibility to drug experimentation and to the brain changes underlying addiction."[130] It's not simple and straightforward. There is no one gene, or two, that contribute or predispose to addiction, but there is a correlation. NIDA explains that it has been "extremely difficult to identify the possible genetic contributions to addiction because it likely involves a combination of inherited variants in multiple genes."[131] Dr. Grisel adds that "hundreds of genes…are involved…a particular strand of DNA may enhance a liability for addiction but only in the presence (or absence) of other specific genes."[132] Jon's father smoked for fifty years. He tried many times and many methods to give up cigarettes, but found quitting a monumental task. Likewise, Jon took to cigarettes very young and never stopped smoking. Some research has found that smoking cigarettes activates the dopamine system, and statistics show smokers are more likely to use and abuse other substances. NIDA affirms that genomic variants "influence smoking or alcohol use...many locations [on the genome] influence synaptic transmission which could hold a key to understanding inherited traits in addiction...locations associated with smoking and alcohol use affect several other chemical functions."[133] Some research demonstrates that nicotine can increase tolerance for alcohol, so it takes more alcohol to produce the same effect in smokers than in non-smokers.

In addition, research has identified certain personality dimensions associated with thrill seeking, sensation seeking, and impulsivity as being found more commonly in addicted people than in control groups from the general population. A high desire for intense and novel experiences, being extroverted, being uninhibited, having low ability to control behavior in the face of cues for rewards, and being prone to anxiety and depression complete the personality profiles of people who may be likely to gravitate to drug abuse. Some research has found that young teens with "exaggerated sensitivity to reward," and a love of risky behavior, are more likely than others to develop substance use disorders.[134] Essentially all of these characteristics fit Jon and had been displayed since a very young age. Should we not have seen Jon's emotional dysregulation as early as elementary school? Probably yes. Other research has found physical characteristics of alcohol metabolism in the liver that distinguish alcoholics.

Given all these factors, might we, or a perceptive counselor or doctor, have identified Jon as a person prone to addiction early in life? Maybe. However, we might have been wrong. And if we had been right, what could we have done? This trail of thoughts led me into the "shoulds" and "what ifs" – impassable terrain for a grieving parent. The fact is that I was never in control.

As much as I learned about the science of substance abuse, I innately realized it is not just a physical and psychological ailment. It also has a spiritual dimension. It seems perfectly designed by Satan to destroy not just health but relationships as well, thwarting sympathy and justifying rejection and ugly judgment. Jon thought so also. He wrote in the last year of his life: "Addiction is a psycho-socio-spiritual malady that brings wreckage and decay to the afflicted as well as everyone and everything around them. Its pathology is clear and stark." To me, the spiritual aspect of addiction is evident partly in the behaviors of addicted people, which often are immoral, even if the people themselves are not. Addicted people do terrible things to their families – ruining trust, finances, marriages, health, reputations, property, confidence, and many other foundations of life. They exhaust, defy, and spew hateful distortions, crumpling their families' view of themselves as loving, functioning units. The affliction of addiction captures their characters, turning them into liars, thieves, manipulators, cruel verbal jousters, and dividers, and makes hash of their family relationships. In a sense, they become very like Satan himself, the disrupter and "father of lies."[135]

Another spiritual dimension of the disease concerns the way others perceive and treat addicted people as bad, failed, embarrassing, or derelict. Harsh judgments follow an addicted person, with the worst verdicts delivered by him or her self. Even in modern times, many people believe in the "just world" theory that bad things only happen to bad people, and misfortune is the result of misbehavior. We expect fairness in reaping the rewards or the torments of our choices. An addicted person must have done something to deserve his affliction. As long ago as Biblical times, Job's friends advised him to confess his secret sins to be cleansed of his troubles. "Consider now," said Job's friend Eliphaz, "Who, being innocent, has ever perished? Where were the upright ever destroyed? As I have observed, those who plow evil and those who sow trouble reap it."[136]

In our world, the stigma attached to an addicted person for being "out of control" and disgusting shows itself in so many ways. When a family member has cancer or an auto accident, helpful and sympathetic friends bring food and cards, and they stop to talk. However, when addiction is the illness in a family, there is no such warmth and sympathy. Silence descends, and the family is left alone because addiction is not seen as a disease, but a moral failing. Dr. Volkow states bluntly that "stigma pervades medicine, policy, and communities."[137] She continues: "Little progress has been made in removing the stigma around substance use disorders. People with addiction continue to be blamed for their disease. Even though medicine long ago reached a consensus that addiction is a complex brain disorder with behavioral components, the public and even many in healthcare and the justice system continue to view it as a result of moral weakness and flawed character."[138] Jon wrote about this very condition during the last year of his life: "We tend to view addicts as lacking morals or being weak-willed. It certainly does appear that way on the surface. Often people compromise their morals to feed their addictions. This tends to further distance them from the love and care of family, friends and the rest of us. Guilt, shame and remorse pile up and help fuel the destructive cycle that fuels addiction...The fact that millions don't do what we think we would do and just quit leads us to believe they have little or no willpower instead of leading us to the more rational conclusion: quitting must be exceedingly difficult if even possible."

As I read and learned, late autumn came on. It was getter darker, and I was missing my son. Guilt tore at me. When Jon was alive, I didn't understand, and our tragedy compounded. Knowledge about the true nature of addiction might have saved us. Yet I had resented my son because he couldn't fix it. What if we had known earlier, when it might have done him and me some good? My university's motto was "knowledge is power," and I have always believed it. My thoughts contort, tangle, and devolve. There is nothing as expensive as ignorance.

TWENTY-FOUR

UNDERSTANDING SUICIDE

In addition to studying addiction after Jon died, I read a great deal about suicide, which, like addiction, has a biological basis in damaged, dark, or non-functioning portions of the brain. Hopelessness, despair, anomie, and "last straw" triggers accompany suicide, but defunct synapses play an important role. According to the statistics and research, Jon's self-murder was somewhat "typical." It occurred on a Monday between nine a.m. and four p.m., it was done by a youngish male with a gun, he was not married, he left no note, and his act followed a prolonged period of depression and dysfunction but was immediately preceded by a precipitating event (Lara's refusal to accept his proposal for an exclusive relationship with him). Two-thirds of gun deaths in the United States are suicides. In addition, according to Dr. Volkow, "People with a prescription opioid use disorder were twice as likely to attempt suicide as individuals who did not misuse prescription opioids...[and] people with substance use disorders...are twice as likely to have mood and anxiety disorders, which are independently associated with increased suicide risk."[139] I also learned that people who suicide often have a profound depletion of serotonin and dopamine – brain chemicals that produce feelings of pleasure and well-being.[140]

Princeton Professors Anne Case and Angus Deaton explain that "when the euphoria fails to materialize or wears off, or when a person relapses in the struggle to remain sober and so experiences shame, worthlessness and depression, death can seem better than another round of addiction."[141] Another psychologist who has studied suicide extensively,

Dr. Thomas Joiner of Florida State University, says prolonged drug use reduces the brain's natural production of pleasurable chemicals, thus inducing depression and disturbing sleep, appetite, digestion, moods, sexual function, and even cognitive thinking. Extended drug use also literally hobbles faculties in the pre-frontal cortex, the part of the brain that allows humans to think, plan, organize, inhibit destructive impulses, foresee consequences, and defer gratification. When the pre-frontal cortex is damaged or loses essential pathways of communication, then impulsive, thoughtless, random, and erratic behavior results.[142] Many other researchers agree with Joiner's studies. Autopsies of the brains of people addicted to opiates have found damage similar to that seen in elderly Alzheimer's patients.

Dr. Victoria Arango, a psychiatrist who has pioneered autopsies of the brains of people who have taken their own lives, states that "there is a specific biological vulnerability to self-destructive behavior." She points out "localized changes" and measurable deficits in the cells of the orbital cortex, a part of the pre-frontal cortex located just above the eye, in people who die by suicide. Cells have been lost in this area, and the signaling systems that allow neurons to communicate with each other have been disrupted. She can document these changes under the microscope. I am virtually certain Jon developed some level of these and other brain impairments as a result of his prolonged drug use. Dr. Arango continues by stating that suicide is the result of brain disease, and therefore, "finding something biological in this [new understanding] should help remove the stigma associated with suicide."[143] Many other researchers have identified abnormalities or alterations in brain chemistry as causing suicide ideation, and have associated such aberrations, after the fact, with suicide itself.[144] Dr. Kay Redfield Jamison, a Professor of Psychiatry at the Johns Hopkins University School of Medicine who tried suicide herself, points to "genetic vulnerabilities," upsets in the serotonin balance in the brain, as well as "acute psychological stress" to understand suicide.[145] She adds that suicide is "always an irrational choice."[146] Sue Klebold believes her son's primary motivation in his Colorado rampage was suicide. "Most people believe suicide is a choice," she says. "Yet we know from talking to survivors of suicide attempts that their decision-making ability shifts in some way we don't well understand."[147]

Most suicide researchers identify hopelessness as a necessary component to completing the act. Dr. Paul Quinnett, a clinical psychologist who specializes in studying suicide, says that "Hopelessness is the ONE common thread among the majority of those who commit suicide- they despair of any future solution – 'What's the use? I might as well be dead'...the state of hopelessness is the most dangerous one."[148] Many people are depressed and do not suicide. However, they are able to tolerate depression if they feel things will or may improve. Dr. Jamison finds that the ones who kill themselves seem to be convinced their situations will not change and there are no solutions to their problems.[149] Dr. Quinnett writes that "It takes time and losses and failures and repeated defeats to fall into the hole of hopelessness...[these people] believe that no matter how hard...[they] try, trying doesn't matter." Their deaths of despair occur because they feel they are a burden to others in their lives. They give up on themselves.[150]

Such people simply cannot see anything beyond wanting the pain to stop, and suicide is the ultimate escape from mental torture. Dr. Jamison says that when people are suicidal, "their thinking is paralyzed, their options appear spare or nonexistent, and hopelessness permeates their entire mental domain." Such people may see suicide as "the only solution possible to an unendurable level of mental pain."[151] Sue Klebold writes that "Suicide is the result of a person losing a long and painful battle against their own impaired thinking. A suicidal person is someone who is unable to tolerate their suffering any longer."[152]

Hopelessness can stem from depression, substance-induced depression, and, according to SAMHSA, "in particular there is a heightened risk of suicide when relapse occurs after a substantial period of abstinence – especially if there is concurrent financial or psychosocial loss."[153]

Jon had had many relapses, with the concomitant stigma and losses, and many times when drugs had so worn down his body that getting high or euphoric wasn't possible. Certainly, he was intelligent enough to see the long pattern of breaks and failures in jobs, school, relationships, finances and other areas that his drug addiction had brought into his life. He saw his brothers, sisters, and some of his friends achieve goals and pass the mileposts of adult life. He saw the contrasts with his life, and it hurt. It cut, confounded, and shamed him.

Additionally, researchers say that most of those who suicide are somewhat brave and perhaps combative people. They are decisive and impulsive. They simply will not accept and allow themselves to live in situations they see as insupportable, miserable, or failed. They refuse to exist at a gravely sub-par level and cannot accept lives that don't meet their own standards or self-concepts. Again, these profiles applied to Jon. He was depressed for a long time at his inability to resist drugs, he was aware of the drain that drugs placed on every aspect of his life (school, work, finances, relationships, reputation, general health and strength), and he was proud and defiant when challenged. He also was resolute, often not in a good way. He would quit jobs or situations he considered untenable, rather than stay and compromise or submit. He was an "all in" kind of guy, and he led with his heart and his fists.

At its most basic level, suicide is a way to take control. Suicide can be seen by some desperate people as a way of re-constituting selves that have been shredded by the experiences of their lives on this earth. Dr. Quinnett affirms that people who suicide "have decided that, if they can control nothing else in their lives, at least they can take control of the how and when of their dying."[154] Tellingly, Jon had written earlier in his struggle with addiction that "I had...decided that if I was goin' out at least I'd have a say in when and how." Kathy, Lara's aunt, believes Jon saw his suicide as the only way to be honorable and not fail and disappoint people anymore: "He wanted to go out proud."

As for thoughts of family and other loved ones, people who are suicidal often or usually believe they are burdens to their families and convince themselves their loved ones would be better off without them. Dr. Jamison says that, for people actively considering suicide, even the warmth and understanding of family cannot "compete with a relentless and ruinous disease."[155] Dr. Arango states that "If you are the person left behind, it's normal to wonder why a loved one would hurt you in this way. Well, the person really didn't. He or she just didn't know what else to do."[156]

These conditions also applied to Jon. I have absolutely no doubt that he loved me fiercely, and loved Eddie, Dori, Lara, and others. Yet, he saw himself as so bankrupt, so empty, so unworthy that he couldn't even imagine positive, healthy relationships with us. Probably, inside the dark, constricted cocoon of his mind, he couldn't imagine anything good. Before he left us, he was already gone. In a confessional moment with me four years before his death, he told me that sometimes he had "taken ridiculous amounts of drugs...when I was so crushed and desperate from the weight of this [addiction] that I didn't care to face another day...There was no malice involved toward you or anyone." Indeed, in one of his journals, he had described exactly how previous thoughts of suicide and self-obliteration had blotted out considerations of family: "When it came down to my family I was so [far gone] already that I didn't care enough to pause...too lost, too hollow, too despairing to think about...[their] loss." Perhaps he thought we would suffer more if he stayed with us.

In addition, a good share of researchers believe that people who suicide have practiced self-injury before the final act, and have become inured to fear. The "forbidden" factor slowly disappears when people get used to dangerous behavior. NIDA studies "non-suicidal self-injury" and finds it is associated with addiction, although not causative.[157] Jon had harmed himself every time he tied off a vein with a big inner tube from a bicycle tire and forced in a needle of heroin, methamphetamine, or other poison. Additionally, in the drug world, he had seen and participated in some level of occasional violence and, like most other young Americans, had become comfortable with at least the images of violence shown every hour on television. Unfortunately, with an impulsive person used to injury or violence, ready access to a gun or rifle can propel unguarded thought to action. Professors Case and Deaton state that "Suicide is more likely when the means of death are easily available."[158] For Jon, the rifle in the closet of a housemate became that answer.

Research also shows that most people who suicide have talked of, fantasized about, or tried suicide before. Jon had not tried it, but I learned after his death that he had talked and thought about it sporadically for nearly nine years, written about it at least four years beforehand, and described his probable method at least three years earlier, during a time of extreme despair over another relapse.

Most experts agree that the process of suicide starts long before the act. A precipitating disappointment, rejection, or failure can tip the scales. As Dr. Jamison states: "Much as a compromised immune system is vulnerable to opportunistic infection, so too a diseased brain is made assailable by the eventualities of life."[159] Even when suicide is planned, she says, the ultimate timing and final decision is often impulsive. Suicide results from "a brash moment of action taken during a span of… suicidal hopelessness. Sudden death often waits in the wings for those whose…brain chemistries predispose them to impulsive suicide; they are like dry and brittle pyres, unshielded against the inevitable sparks thrown off by living."[160] In part, then, and after the fact, I "understood" Jon's suicide as being logical in his own diseased mind. The "why" of it did not puzzle me endlessly, as it does some family members of those who have suicided.

However, despite some modicum of understanding, Jon's choice gutted me. Suicide is "a death like no other," says Dr. Jamison. "It rips apart lives and beliefs, and it sets survivors on a prolonged and devastating journey…always asking why…the agonizing question… Suicide carries in its aftermath a level of confusion and devastation that is…beyond description…For surviving family members there is a hole in the heart that can never be filled."[161] The emotions of grief and bereavement are widely acknowledged to be confusing, non-sequential, and mercurial. Yet when suicide is the cause, these feelings are not just stronger, but tossed in a blender of tornadic speed with guilt, shame, and questions that no one can answer. The family members left behind "enter a time of great and unremitting sadness," says Dr. Quinnett. "Unprepared as they are, the pain can be almost physical, and despite an occasional good day or light moment, the sadness sweeps over them, again and again."[162] For parents of those who suicide, there is despair so dark that it has no bottom. Gloria Vanderbilt, whose son jumped to his death from a fourteen-story ledge right in front of her, described herself as being "below sea level, centered there, balanced in a pain that will never leave me...I don't understand anything anymore. All I understand is pain."[163]

Did Jon hate himself during the summer of 2014, as he fought his darkness? Did he think about all he had wasted and squandered (time, money, relationships, jobs, education, self-esteem, and health)? How heavy was his guilt for the lies he had told, items he had stolen, family and friends he had manipulated and used, excuses he had made to Eddie? Did he feel like an emptied-out shell (which is how he looked)? Did he see absolutely no hope of peace and wholeness here with us? Did he believe he was forgiven in a metaphysical sense (but not forgiven by us) and simply longed for the peace of the great God of the universe? We know he feared the future and the Demon who pursued him. He wrote at the very end of his life that he never wanted another relapse, because he saw the destruction it rained on the people he loved. However, he wrote, he couldn't keep us "safe from ever going through that again...I would never be sure. Absolutely sure...that there was[n't] any risk of that happening again." We know he wanted to spare us. Did he see killing himself as the only way to kill the Demon?

Ultimately, I realize, I will never *really* know why Jon took his own life. I know a lot, but until I see him again in Heaven, I won't truly get the answers. "Each way to suicide is its own: intensely private, unknowable and terrible," says Dr. Jamison. "Suicide will have seemed to the perpetrator [as] that last and best of bad possibilities, and any attempt by the living to chart this final terrain of a life can be only a sketch...incomplete...No matter how much we may wish to reassemble the suicide's psychological world, any light we gain is indirect and insufficient: the privacy of the mind is an impermeable barrier."[164] Gloria Vanderbilt, writing of her son's suicide, says that "I still don't know, none of us do, the *reason* why it happened or what demons took possession of his fantasies."[165]

"Suicide is ugly," writes Sue Klebold. "It's wreathed in disgrace. It screams to the world that a person's life ended in failure...As a culture, we believe that people who die by suicide are weak, that they lack willpower, that they've taken 'the coward's way out'. We believe that they are selfish...if they cared about their families...they would have found a [different] way."[166] My son Jon was not weak nor a coward nor selfish nor uncaring. He was terminally ill, and he knew it even when I did not. As he lived in the crucible of addiction and grew to despise himself, he was most of all tired – weary of fighting himself, covering up, being broke and needy, starting over, believing his best times already were behind him, wanting the peace he could not have, fearing and facing his Demon, and always wondering why. The dichotomy between the man he wanted to be and the things he knew he had done and wasted, the lies he had told, the dishonor, and the shame, became too much for him.

Most psychologists and psychotherapists who have studied and written about suicide say that the hardest task of a surviving family member is to forgive one's self. Forgiveness is a two-sided labor for me. The question of forgiving Jon for ending his life is almost easy. In his mind, I believe, he could endure his torture no more, and he depended on the rest of us to take care of his son and to cope. Judith Fox and Mia Roldan each lost a parent to suicide and then interviewed other survivors of family suicides. They offer the perspective that when people are suffering great physical pain at the end of their lives, most of their loved ones can be grateful that the suffering is finally at an end when they die. So, perhaps, we could or might be grateful that people suffering great mental torment are finally at peace when they die, even if by suicide. In those cases, forgiving and understanding that they needed to end their pain might be the highest form of love. Forgiving does not make anything alright. It means simply that the survivor comes to see suicide as the sad, but inevitable, outcome of an illness that no one could fix.[167]

Yes, I can do that. I do believe Jon's illness was incurable by the time we got to 2014, and he knew it and he chose not to live in the morass. However, with the merciless power of hindsight, I will never forget that I, his mother, abandoned him at the end when he was too sick to fight anymore. He gave warning signs, and I missed them. I failed at my most essential duty, and forgiveness of myself is a brutal task. So far, it is insurmountable. I should have been close to him, I should have walked through the fire with him, and I wasn't and I didn't.

TWENTY-FIVE

COPING

Who am I now that the boy who filled and expanded my heart has broken it? "Grief is an alchemist," writes Lee Woodruff. "It will change you - morph you into someone more empathetic, more aware of what is precious, and more clearly able to see your priorities."[168] God, the open-heart surgeon, has transformed me from the confident, optimistic young mother I once was. The refiner's fire burned so fiercely in my life that the heat will never leave me. Deep grief can and does break people. George Lardner, Jr., a Pulitzer-prize winning journalist for the *Washington Post* whose daughter was murdered by a stalker, says simply: "Nothing can prepare you for the death of your child."[169] Famed agent and psychological profiler John Douglas, who dealt with all manner of death and trauma during his years with the Federal Bureau of Investigation, calls the death of a child "utterly transformative" for the parents. "It is an experience that turns the natural order upside down, that demands more in the way of strength and emotional resources than any rational person has to give...It leaves none as they were."[170] Gloria Vanderbilt writes that the suicide of her son "exploded the core of what I had known myself to be...[It] stripped me bare, the loss that had no echo...a loss I thought I could not survive."[171]

How did I cope with Jon's death? How did I go on? Well, the truth is that even though I did "go on," I often did not cope very well or at all. Peace was elusive and still is much of the time. Just as Jon the addicted man had struggled in treatment with the "war between the conscious mind – knowing better – and...need at any cost," I struggled – and still struggle – between knowing my son is better off because he is whole and disease-free in Heaven, and my overwhelming need to have him here with me. My beautiful, doomed son, desperate and sick unto death, had truly walked in misery here on earth. Why would a loving mother want to drag him back into that pain? At one point in the winter after Jon's death, a wise and loving counselor looked straight at me and said: "I challenge you as a Christian. If you truly love your son and truly believe he is safe and whole in Heaven, why don't you rejoice for him?" And yet I wanted him back. My heart literally had beat for his, my lungs had breathed for his. He had lived inside my body. We were joined for all time, and his loss to me was an amputation. I simply could not fathom going on without him. I certainly could not rejoice.

It is not lost on me that Jon died by a shot to the heart. Why did he choose his heart? Heart is one of the most freighted concepts in all human understanding. Ancient civilizations in Babylonia, Egypt, and India believed that pain was experienced in the heart, and its presence evidenced an emotional imbalance or an invasion of evil spirits. Ancient Greek medicine saw the heart as the center of the soul and the source of heat within the body. Some ancient cultures who believed the same thought it was necessary to eat the heart of a defeated enemy to totally vanquish him. Medieval societies saw the heart as the seat of courage. A warlike virtue was to have "the heart of a lion" and to be cowardly was to "lose heart."

The Latin root word for heart is "cor" or "cord," which became "coeur" in the French language, "cuore" in Italian, and "corazon" in Spanish. All hint at the heart as being the core or center of emotions. The Bible contains the word heart 725 times, often using it to indicate the inward nucleus of a person. "People look at the outward appearance, but the Lord looks at the heart," said the prophet Samuel.[172] King Solomon advised people to, "Above all else, guard your heart, for everything you do flows from it."[173] Indeed, the heart as the container of feelings is almost a universal concept throughout humanity.

Most of all, the heart is seen as reactive. It slows, quickens, or tightens in response to emotions. It can thud and seem to jump out of the chest when a person is startled or upset. It is said to "stop" or "pound" with fear or "rage" with anger. It can "break" when a person is hurt badly. It can "flutter" or "swoon" when a beloved person or object is sighted. It can "sink" with sadness or "swell," "soar," or "be full" when a person is happy. A generous person is said to have a big heart, but a miserly person's heart is small. The heart of the Grinch, created as the embodiment of stinginess and lack of love by author Dr. Suess, was said to have grown three sizes when he found the spirit of Christmas.[174] The heart can be warm or cold and it can "melt" with tenderness or "turn to stone" when a person is unfeeling. Jon was a very emotional man, and I came to see his death as a "heart condition" prompted by his feelings of failure, rejection, and loneliness. The thought of my child in so much pain doubles me over.

Grief is a psychic blow. It bruises and requires long, slow healing, just as a physical blow to the body brings bruising and needs long, gentle restoration. Yet, I was positive I would never be restored, nor even come close. I did not want to heal or go on. The Serenity Prayer famously says that "hardship [is] a pathway to peace,"[175] but I just wanted to dissolve. Too much had been lost. I hurt to my very core and back out to the fibers of my skin and hair. There was nowhere to turn to escape the hot flames of pain. The rest of my life, I was sure, would be simply a slow march through misery and darkness, punctuated by sharp spikes of torment at every reminder of the void. Joy was out of the question. The beautiful boy and man I had brought forth and proudly called my own, even when he was terribly sick, had taken away with him all my stamina, hope, delight, sustenance, and marrow. I would no longer have him as my companion, friend – or as anything – at all – ever. We had lost our future – the plans and hopes for everything that would not happen.

Thanks to generous caring at the Home Base church, Jon's memorial service was beautiful. The minister, Mason Inman, assured us the sin of suicide is forgiven by Jesus' sacrifice on the cross, just as any other of our sins. In the case of a person so sick, hopeless, and desperate as to self-murder, Pastor Mason promised us, God is more in the business of forgiving than judging. In other words, this profound man banished the panicky thought that suicide is an "unforgivable sin" that condemns the one who commits it. This reassurance was the first good thing that happened. Along with the solid knowledge that Jon had experienced the Holy Spirit and the peace of God in the church in 2013, Pastor Mason's firm confidence made me sure that Jon is with God. I knew it in the core of my being, and I clung to it. I cling to it still.

Jeff, Dori, and Elliott helped me prepare a photo montage of Jon's life, and, with their suggestions, I wrote the story of Jon's life for Pastor Mason to read. I chose quiet, lilting songs that spoke of coming home and the knowledge that the "language of the heart" can be spoken across great distances. We "got ready," and I think we honored Jon and captured some of his unique spirit in his memorial service. However, there is a huge difference between getting ready and being ready. I would never be ready to bury my son. We kept Jon's death out of the newspapers, fortunately sparing us the scrutiny of curious and ill-founded gossip. We recognized that when there is suicide, many people assume the parents did something terribly wrong. A loving family could never have produced such an outcome. There must have been some secret dysfunction, abuse, or neglect. We knew those things weren't true, so we told only those people whom we wanted to know, and nearly every one of them came to the memorial. Some, including old school friend Matt, flew in from great distances. We brought in Eddie and his mother and paid special tribute in the service to Jon's titanic, out-sized love for Eddie.

Most of all, we were honest about Jon's addiction and his suicide. In the service, we spoke of the Satanic curse of his addiction and the fact that he could no longer endure its pain. Pastor Mason, we, and others spoke of Jon's great faith and the blessed assurance we now had that he had escaped his anguish on earth and ascended to victory with Jesus. Sometimes, God sends death as a mercy to those who are suffering intolerably, and death is the only door that leads to Heaven. As we commended our son's soul to his Lord Jesus, we also released his pain, fear, shame, and sickness, which we knew had already vanished. As the Book of Wisdom tells us: "The souls of the righteous are in the hand of God, and there shall no torment touch them. In the sight of the unwise they seemed to die: and their departure is taken for misery, And their going from us to be utter destruction: but they are in peace."[176]

Jon's landlord designed and brought a large, creative floral arrangement that included river shore plants and some of Jon's boat floats, crab traps, and minnow traps. It served as the centerpiece of the altar during his service, along with photos of Jon and an urn containing half of his cremated ashes. We spread the remainder of his cremains in the royal blue Columbia River – his refuge, his joy, and his choice for his final earthly encounter. Two months later, in a private family service, we buried his urn in the cemetery plot where my earthly remains will rest one day.

Fall came on quickly after Jon left us. The days darkened and nights came earlier and lasted longer. Fall is the worst time to lose someone, as it presages the beginning of a long, hard winter. For me, autumn and grief are forever entwined. Never again will autumn be a time when the bracing chill, comical pumpkin faces, and brilliant oranges, yellows, and reds signal a welcome change from summer's heat. There is no anticipation of frosty walks and comforting nights by a cheery fire. No, autumn is somber, gloomy, and unbearable. Death has no respect for love.

After losing Jon, it seemed that winter would never end, and sometimes just surviving through another day and night was a huge accomplishment. So began life in my brutal new world. There was no solid ground in my landscape of grief and often, I felt as if I had vertigo. I had lived a long time with dread as my companion, but now I was flat, almost dead myself. Jon's death stole so many things from me – not just himself, but peace. Life seemed capricious, unreliable, ready to trip me up with no warning. How do you process your child's dead body?

I lived in Jon's aftermath. I had an insatiable desire to speak to everyone who knew him. I spent much of the autumn and winter meeting with people who had interacted with him in the last two years of his life – his employer, Lance, Shelley, other members of the church group, Jon's landlord and another resident of his last house, Kathy and Clark, a few other friends, our neighbors for whom he had done odd jobs, Norma, and of course, Lara and her mother. I visited the professors from his final quarter in school to ask about his performance and attendance, and spent a long lunch with Matt's mother, who had known Jon as a teenager. I asked everyone I sat with about his behavior and demeanor – events in the last months clues, hints, and things he had done and said. I implored them to tell me about the last time they saw him and any anecdotes they remembered. I had a great need to talk about him, and many people gave generously of their time. Still, at the end of our conversations, I had to go home and live with my grief, while they did not.

I also scrambled, literally, to collect and back up all emails and text messages from, to, or about him in the past several years. I archived his school papers, journals, letters, postcards, treatment reports, medical records, photos, old bus and airplane tickets, tax returns and legal papers, and any scribbles and doodles I could find. Without knowing it exactly, I was preserving him as best I could so we who love him could know him better. He was a real person, much beloved, and I needed to make sure he did not simply disappear. A big part of honoring him, I sensed, would be remembering him and speaking his name. I spent much of the late fall and all the winter typing out text messages to, from, and about Jon on the phones of all our family members and Lara. I filed them chronologically and then cross-filed by the people involved. I organized everything methodically so I could read and re-read, wringing out every bit of information, inference, and item. Allowing him to recede into the distance was not an option until I learned everything possible about him.

Evan and I visited Sun Valley that winter of 2015. I wanted to experience a day of skiing on Baldy and a night in the town where Jon had reigned supreme among the young revelers. As it turned out, being on the mountain was fine, but being in the town haunted me. It had changed so much since Jon's era. Quiet, expensive bistros dominated, instead of the raucous beer pubs with swinging doors. No longer did we see and hear the spirited, often drunken, uproar spilling out of open portals. The town had grown weary of the young partiers and opted instead to cater to a wealthier, more stable group who wanted to spend its money in quiet comfort. Some of these retirees on the younger side took jobs at the ski resort as lift operators and ticket scanners to stave off boredom, giving the entire place a different feel. In the late afternoon, I wandered some of the side streets, but their ghosts proved too much. Tears stung my face, and I was glad to leave in the morning.

Shock is the reaction that occurs when things we take for granted are taken from us suddenly and completely. I experienced shock when I first heard myself refer to Jon in the past tense – not saying "he is..." but "he was." It sounded so discordant. My universe simply did not work without Jon. I could no longer hope he would get well, parent his son, enliven my mind with brilliant philosophical discussions, crack me up with laughter at his ironic wit, or enfold me in his huge bear hugs. His death was definitive, absolute. I hurt in every part of myself and needed to be around others who were hurting. I attended support groups for people in grief and specifically, for survivors of family suicide. I clung closely to my support group for families of addicted people, and many of the members cut short their own stories to let me talk. As I listened in the group to others going through the fear, the sleepless nights, the worry and aches of the addiction roller coaster, I thought about the nearly unbearable stress Jon's illness had brought to all of us close to him. Even still, I wanted him back. I knew that in a heartbeat, I would trade all the quiet and calm in my life now, and willingly take on the stress and anxiety all over again, if I could have my Jonny back.

For me, life was bifurcated by the loss of Jon. There was a then and a now – a time before his death and a separate time after it. Before was difficult, but after was unbearable. During that first horrendous year after he died, I read many books by parents who have lost children, looking for clues and wisdom about how they coped. I found howls of pain, quiet resignation, lives that were openly broken, and those with a hidden hole in them that was known only to close friends, pastors, and other family members. Some parents of lost children have anger, I learned, but all I have is a deep-seated, never-ending sorrow. The grief is relentless, malignant, predatory, knee-buckling, and fierce beyond words. I almost never had anger at Jon after his death, except that I felt like shouting at him: "You think we didn't love you???!!" However, most of me knows he HAD to realize we loved him, and that knowledge probably made even more unbearable his sense of having failed to get well and re-join our family in a meaningful way.

Some parents of children whose deaths were mysterious spoke about the need for closure, as if knowing the details of the child's condition, intentions, or whereabouts would help them cope. I can't speak to their yearnings since all of us grieve and process loss in different ways. However, our family had closure, and it didn't help. We knew with absolute certainty that Jon had suicided. We knew the exact place, time and method, and the position of his body. The police released his remains immediately, as there was no suspicion of foul play or evidence of a crime. I had all the closure anyone could ever want, and for me, closure was over-rated.

Jon's death remained outrageous and unbelievable – a cruel, tortured hallucination from which we would surely awake. I felt the immutability of it, the fact that it cannot be re-wound, deleted, edited in any way, or undone. I could not un-see, un-know, or un-feel the darkness. Jon was irreplaceable. Nicholas Wolterstorff, a Yale Theology professor whose son died in a mountain climbing accident, writes that "It's the *neverness* that is so painful. *Never again* to be here with us...All the rest of our lives we must live without him...A month, a year, five years – with that I could live. But not this forever."[177]

As I continued sorting and cataloging Jon's journals and other communications, I read God's word, often from the very Bibles and handbooks he used and underlined. Not surprisingly, these readings brought me the closest I had come to some semblance of peace since his convulsive departure from us. Through many years of struggle, I had kept an index card taped to my bathroom mirror, reminding me of Jesus' words: "In this world you will have trouble, but take heart; I have overcome the world."[178] He spoke these words at the Last Supper, trying to prepare his disciples for the terrible loss they would suffer in His crucifixion. They had to remain behind, living in the fallen world that contained so much human sin, despair, and grief. He wasn't telling them they would not suffer in this world, only that their troubles would come to an end someday in His triumph over death.

Living in my broken world after losing Jon, I held to His sustaining promise. Saint Paul tells us that we can approach God freely and ask Him for anything. He may not give us specifically the things we request, but He will give us His peace: "The peace of God, which transcends all understanding, will guard your hearts and your minds in Christ

Jesus."[179] And sometimes – occasionally and fleetingly – I did feel some peace, and I didn't understand it. I was scarred for life and irretrievably broken. How could I ever have peace? But sometimes I did, and it was a restful, bountiful gift. However, the greatest gift of all came from the mouth of Jesus himself, who said, "I am the resurrection and the life. The one who believes in me will live, even though they die; and whoever lives by believing in me will never die."[180]

As much as I read about suicide, depression, brain chemistry, brain science, neural pathways, addiction, and behavioral patterns, and recognized Jon in the descriptions, I could not see anything "typical" about his death and simply could not believe it had happened. Why was Jon afflicted with the disease of addiction? Despite the knowledge I had gained, the inklings from his boyhood, the clues from his big and audacious personality, his copious journals, and the quiet confidences he shared with me, I have no answers. However, Saint Paul reassured me that I did not understand the full scope of God's plan, but He did and there was purpose in Jon being taken from us. "For now we see only a reflection as in a mirror; then we shall see face to face. Now I know in part; then I shall know fully," promises Saint Paul.[181] As an earthly mother, I could not see the whole picture from my limited perspective, but someday, I would know not just the plan, but my son and my God. For now, my questions were irrelevant. Gloria Vanderbilt felt the same, writing: "Someday...we will understand the tragedies that come to us – understand *why*...[and] when it will be made clear...I believe the answer will be so simple, so right, so true that...we shall no longer cry out *Why, God, why* – for with understanding we shall be out of pain, out of darkness into light."[182]

Psalm 46, most likely written by King David, says simply: "Be still and know that I am God."[183] Sometimes when I was the most tormented in my yearning for Jon, almost crawling out of my skin with the raw, wracking ache, every nerve fiber broiling inside me, I would simply try to be still and wait. This experience was very like the drug cravings that Jon wrote about in his treatment center in 2010. A wave of grief would hit me, then build unbearably, then reach a crescendo when I almost couldn't breathe, and then ease down to ordinary misery. Like my son, I would wait it out.

Sometimes I could not calm down, but sometimes I could, at least partially, and that was progress. Sometimes I almost could sense God telling me: "It's not your call – it's mine." He didn't make this bad thing happen, but He allowed it, according to the laws He established for our world. Physical organisms get sick, solid objects collide, decay takes place, we are not fitted here on earth with the bodies that will take us into the next world, time is not on our side, and we are all terminal. "Play it as it lays," said the great 1920s golfer Bobby Jones when he contracted syringomyelia, a debilitating spinal disease. "Give me a choice and I won't" allow it, my sister Pam said when the third member of her family developed cancer. "Trust in the LORD with all your heart and lean not on your own understanding; in all your ways submit to him, and he will make your paths straight," my friend Sarah said in 1987 as I set out for Richland, cringing at my fate. "If God is for us, who can be against us?" asks Saint Paul.[184]

As Jon studied the teachings of Jesus in the last years of his life, he was struck by the famous words usually (but erroneously) attributed to Christian philosopher C.S. Lewis, that "we are not a body with a soul; we are a soul with a body."[15] At his violent transition on the small Columbia River island, the bond between his soul and his earthly body dissolved. He no longer inhabited the body that I had borne, but Jon himself – his essence – simply went to a place I could not see or follow. When the police found his body on that island, they did not find him, for Jon – my son – was already gone. This realization comforted me, especially when I found the eloquent poem by nineteenth century minister Henry Van Dyke, titled "Gone From My Sight:"

> I am standing upon the seashore.
> A ship at my side spreads her white sails to the
> morning breeze, and starts for the blue ocean.

---

[15] Actually, these words were written originally in 1867 by George MacDonald in *Annals of a Quiet Neighborhood* (copyright expired).

She is an object of beauty and strength, and
I stand and watch her until she hangs like a
speck of white cloud just where the sea and
sky come down to mingle with each other.
Then someone at my side says: "There! She's gone!"
Gone where? Gone from my sight — that is all.
She is just as large in mast and hull and spar as she
was when she left my side, and just as able to bear her
load of living freight to the place of her destination.
Her diminished size is in me, and not in her.
And just at the moment when someone
at my side says: "There! She's gone!"
There are other eyes that are watching for
her coming; and other voices ready to take
up the glad shout: "There she comes!
And that is — "dying." [185]

Ash Wednesday 2015, found me sitting in the sanctuary of the church that had held Jon's memorial. I was quite miserable. The lights were dimmed and all I could see as I looked at the sermon platform were the photos of Jon and the huge natural plant arrangement that had served as the backdrop for his memorial service. Of course, these items were long gone. I hunched lower and lower, not sure I could move from that spot, feeling trapped and drawn in at the same time. The next time I looked up, I saw Jon, seated cross-legged on a floor at the foot of a being who was dressed in white in a chair. Jon clearly was in a seminar or small group teaching situation of some kind. He wore the medium blue sweater he had worn every year for several winters, his hair was clean cut, his high forehead handsome as ever, and in his right hand he held up an open book. His long fingers were splayed across the back of the book, with his thumb to the forefront, holding open a page. He obviously was referring to the book as he dialogued and learned from the being. His face registered enthusiasm and enjoyment of spirited discourse. I had the distinct knowledge that he was being fitted for service in God's kingdom, undergoing a tutorial to prepare him. The vision didn't last, but it was so distinct and real that I never doubted I had seen it. I already believed that our time in Heaven will not consist of lying around in filmy robes singing hymns, but instead we will be busy performing tasks in the kingdom. Now I actually had seen my son, but I was hesitant to talk about it. When I finally confessed the glimmer to a friend two years later, she told me simply to regard it as a gift and give thanks for it.

The first spring after Jon's death came, it seemed to me, with more audacity than usual. How dare the sun shine with warmth and brightness, when my world was dark? How dare flowers bloom and buds become tiny shoots and then supple, full-bodied leaves? What nerve possessed the duck, geese, quail, and other wildlife to bring forth their fuzzy young and then scramble around feeding and protecting them? As I looked out at my leafy yard, I saw Jon everywhere – spading the garden, trimming bushes, washing windows, lying on the grass ruffling Mountain's ears. I told Evan I could not stay in this house. Twenty-five years after Evan and I had built an addition to the house to accommodate our burgeoning family as I moved in with Jon and Dori, we decided to buy a lot in another part of town and build a new house. That same spring, we brought home a new Labrador puppy named Lankston, soon known as Lanky. We had contracted for him while Jon was still alive, and we knew Jon would have reveled in his soft fur, his wide eyes, his curious nose, his warm tongue. Lanky blessed us with new life at the same time he tugged us backward to our never-ending thoughts of Jon.

At last, in the second year after Jon's death, I began to write about him, his life, and our lives together. I loved the process of writing, forming sentences, thinking about their structure, and trying different ways of expressing feelings, events, and conversations, turning all of it over in my head. I have always loved writing, but this task was more than special. I knew my effort would not be perfect. However, it would be "all me and all Jon," describing and remembering and portraying him for all time in ways that felt true to the lives we had lived together.

In this process I tentatively – with trepidation and the utmost caution and dread – approached the no-fly zone of the "what ifs." What if I had leaned in instead of letting go in the summer of 2014? What if I had brought Eddie to Richland for a visit? Would Jon still be alive? I know now that one of the worst failures an addicted person can feel is being denied the chance to parent their child. What if I hadn't gotten so tired of the outward antics of addiction? What if I had known it was a brain disease and compulsion? What if I had realized it is chronic, and that relapses are part of it? What if I hadn't seen his erratic behavior as something he was doing *to me*, instead of as the tortured flailing his ravaged mind was inflicting *on him*? What if I simply had gone to him that summer and said, "I don't care what you said or did, I don't even understand it, but I just love you?" What if he hadn't felt so alone? What if the last, weak vestige of his identity as a valued member of our family hadn't been taken away? There are so many woulds, shoulds, coulds, whys, and maybes…and they dare me not to disengage from them.

Psychologists tell us that dwelling on "what ifs" and "if onlies" is a way of trying to exert control over events and circumstances we cannot and could not control. My insights are flawed and incomplete, but I know I am guilty. It is a mother's job to protect her child. A mother is supposed to know her child well and perceive things. A mother is supposed to look beyond bad behavior and forgive. My wise father told me that often when a child is acting the worst is when he needs love the most. He also told me that every parent makes many mistakes, "but if your child knows in his core that you love him, he will forgive all your mistakes." I always thought parents were in the business of making dreams come true. During Jon's last summer on this earth, I know that love and acceptance might have helped him as he got sicker and his self-image plunged. I am his mother, and I failed him. I stood on some lofty, logical ground of consequences, and I lost my sick, suffering son. Nine years later, we know so much more about his fatal illness. If only I had known then what I know now – I still wouldn't have had a solution or a cure – but at least I could have faced his terrors with him. If only stigma and shame hadn't reflected back at him every time he ran out of gas, relapsed, couldn't pay a bill, or failed to keep a commitment. Once again, I knew I couldn't go there in my head. My heart is too fragile and always will be. I wrack my brain until my head aches.

My grief has shaped me as a different person. After the trauma of losing Jon, I live more in the moment than I ever did before. I have to, because I know that no one has a contract on the sunrise, and no one knows what each day will bring. I approach the world tentatively, taking only bits of pleasure in small things. The color deep forest green is one of those small things. It can be a shiny forest green car, an evergreen tree, a sweater, hat or mitten, or an extra dark emerald in a piece of jewelry. I follow the color with my eyes, relishing it. I also love to look at Lanky's furry, chocolate brown profile as he leans out the car window to sniff the air, ears flying backward, blocky nose stretched forward. Sometimes, I glance at him so often I almost swerve off the road. I like the crystalline aqua color of the swimming pool viewed from underwater when I get to do laps on a sunny summer day. I like to watch airplanes glide in a long, even descent as they prepare to land. I love just looking at photos of Jon's son or texting with him. As a sturdy twenty-one-year-old with a deep voice, Eddie has the looks, mannerisms, quick intelligence, soft smile, and boundless curiosity of his father. He has endured so much, yet he is kind, hard-working and respectful – an enormous blessing.

I read and follow the many positive developments that have occurred in the nation's fight against opiates in the nine years since Jon's death. The attorneys general of more than forty states, along with hundreds of counties and cities, have sued the makers and distributors of opiate pain pills. By 2018, 2,600 jurisdictions had sued Purdue Pharma and its owners, the Sackler family.[186] In 2021, Purdue was dissolved in court, and the Sackler family was ordered to pay more than four billion dollars from its personal fortunes to forty-eight plaintiff states. (However, many of the Sacklers' assets had been moved offshore and the family remained fabulously wealthy.) In addition, the family had to relinquish control of the business, which would be transformed to a "public benefit company" with profits going mainly to addiction treatment and prevention programs across the country. After appeal, that figure required from the Sackler family was raised to six billion dollars in 2022. Many other significant judgments have been won against drug distributors Cardinal Health, Amerisource Bergen and McKesson, as well as pharmaceutical giants Johnson and Johnson, Teva,

Mallinkrodt, Insys, and others. Drug distributor Morris and Dickson, Co.™ was stripped of its license to sell addictive painkillers in 2023.[187] Pharmacy chains such as Walgreens, Rite Aid, CVS, Giant Eagle, and Walmart also have been sued successfully for failing to flag and report extraordinarily large orders. Even the Joint Commission on Hospital Accreditation was sued for the pain management standards it imposed in hospitals. In 2016, the CDC issued prescribing guidelines for chronic pain. "Nonpharmacologic therapy and nonopioid pharmacologic therapy are preferred for chronic pain," said the CDC. "If opioids are used, they should be combined with nonpharmacologic therapy and nonopioid pharmacologic therapy."[188]

Many other beneficial changes have taken place in public policy just the nine years since Jon died. These corrections gladden my heart, but are both ironic and bittersweet. Yes, I want to see people recognize the addictive properties of opiate pills, close that barn door (albeit too late for the more than one million people who have died since 1995), and attack addiction for the scourge that it is, instead of attacking addicted people. But yes, I have to wonder whether my son, a casualty not only of disease but stigma, shame and ignorance, might have had a different outcome if enlightenment had come sooner.

I take some encouragement in the reminder from Dr. Vincent DaVita that things can change in the world of medicine. Dr. DaVita spent his fifty-year medical career as a cancer researcher and recalls that "in the 1940s, cancer was such a dreadful diagnosis...that many people...couldn't bring themselves to utter the word...as if there were something shameful about it...As late as the 1960s, the chief of medicine at Columbia University refused to let his medical trainees make rounds on the cancer wards, lest their careers be tainted by the futility they would encounter there...When I entered the field, cancer cells were essentially black boxes – mysteries...Now...we have a much greater understanding of why cancer happens and how it behaves, on a genetic and molecular level – an understanding that has led to a breathtaking array of new treatments."[189] Well said, Dr. DaVita. I pray the same trajectory of learning and hope can be true for addiction.

But in the end, my grief is still private, not amenable to the balm of lawsuits, government edicts, and science. Perhaps the nature of my grief has changed in nine years. Maybe it has become intrinsic to me, permeating every part of me in a quiet stoicism. It ebbs and flows, develops a shape, and then loses it, only to surface again in some new permutation. Sometimes, my grief maintains almost a respectful distance from my surface, but then a memory or a color or a car or a word revives it, and it rushes in for the kill.

Yes, I am still haunted and yes, I definitely have PTSD, as I think do all close family members of addicted people. We have lived on the front lines of a covert war, all the more insidious and brutal because it was undeclared. Research shows that PTSD is most likely to affect those who feel, rightly or wrongly, that they bear some responsibility for the disaster. It is also more prevalent in people whose trauma is individual and isolating, rather than produced by a shared community catastrophe such as a hurricane.

I look alive, but am I? There is no way to measure that. I know I will never be the same. I laugh sometimes, but I always carry the weight of my circumstances. I have very low tolerance for stress, as if my lifetime of ability to bear it has been used up. Little stresses, like aftershocks of an earthquake, upset me more than they should or would have earlier in my life. I also have intense distress at surprises that suddenly bring me up close with the past. When Chris Cornell, addicted lead singer of the original Seattle grunge band *Soundgarden*, died by suicide in May 2017, I was pulled back to Jon's first stint in treatment in 1994, when Kurt Cobain killed himself. The memories were haunting, because at that time and place I knew so little and hoped and believed so much.

However, nothing compares to the anniversary of October 6, in reviving my nightmares. In terms of jittery despair, Jon's birthday is second only to the anniversary of his death. During the run-up to these dates each year, a grim fatalism takes up residence inside me, and becomes more constricting each day. Finally the day arrives, and often the only thing I can tolerate is a long, solitary walk with my dog. Sometimes the pain is sharp and hot, but other times it manifests as a hollow, vacant, empty despair. My grief is cavernous, filled with a dreadful nothing. It is a blunt force with no schedule, but it is always there. It is a glutton – it takes and takes. I live with my grief, still never understanding it. My feelings are different each "normal" day. There is no straight line out of this morass.

Saint James tells me to, "Consider it pure joy...whenever you face trials of many kinds, because you know that the testing of your faith produces perseverance."[190] Likewise, Saint Paul advises us mortals to "glory in our sufferings, because we know that suffering produces perseverance; perseverance, character; and character, hope."[191] In the same vein, Bill W. writes that "The grace of God...can sustain and strengthen us in any catastrophe....By God's grace, we can take troubles in stride and turn them into demonstrations of faith."[192] Yes, my faith is strong – even absolute, and yes, I know God is good all the time, even when it doesn't seem so. But I cannot get to joy or feeling glory in what happened to us. I can't even get to acceptance.

Many people, both famous and ordinary, have said that grief teaches people valuable lessons, especially about compassion for others. Yes, I hope and think I am more compassionate. However, part of my mind rebels against this line of reasoning. It is too cerebral. It does not acknowledge the raw, open wound that is grief. Jon's death was not symbolic or emblematic of a lesson. He wasn't figurative, allegorical, or metaphorical. He was a real boy. His cheeks flushed when he was embarrassed, his shoulders shook when he laughed, his eyes grew wide when he was surprised, his voice choked and croaked when he was sad. He was mine, and I would rather have him back than ever learn another deep truth in my life. Clearly, I'm not as strong as a co-worker whose son was killed in war in Iraq. After a few years of grieving, this man told me he, "finally moved from sorrow that I lost him, to gratitude that I knew him."[193] Yes, of course I am grateful for my years with Jon, but I have not moved past sorrow. I'm sure I never will.

I ruminate about the times of my life with Jon over and over – our conversations, our fun, our arguments, trips, rescues, and our hugs. I think of what I had, and do not have now. I know that less-than-perfect people have faults and foibles. They make mistakes and often badly hurt the ones they love. Both Jon and I were such people, and we loved each other fiercely. We tried to hang on together in the face of an incredible storm, until I let go, and he fell. Dealing up close with his addiction exacted a huge cost on all of us, but it was nothing compared to the cost of disconnecting. There are times, even with all my understanding of disease, of the will of a sovereign God, and of the joyous reunion with Jon to come in Heaven, that I just "lose it." *I want my son.*

My marriage has now endured more than thirty-four years, and has included some of the most horrific experiences two people could live through. Grief sometimes fractures a family, but it did not break ours. The longevity of our vows is all thanks to Evan's immense patience – with me, with Jon, with things we didn't understand, with disruption and absences and expenses and stress and worry and, at times, with absolute terror. We slogged and struggled so long through the mess and turmoil that comprise life in the families of addicted people that we learned not to even fight our conflicted emotions. We adapted because we had to make room for the mercurial moods as the traumas came and went. Sometimes a glance was enough, or a slight tap on the shoulder, or a sigh. By these signals, we let each other know we were entering or enduring the tunnel of another bad experience. After Jon's death, each of us could read the other's subtle signals to realize that a sick feeling had sucked the life out of an otherwise ordinary day. We didn't need to dissect or explain these emotions to each other. We just knew and we let them go, allowing silence to be our private language. The spoken word is inadequate for some sorrows.

During Jon's life, we hoped for and even expected a cure – an issue solved, wiped away, put behind us. Steeped in the twentieth century American idea of progress, we believed problems had to be uprooted and eradicated and that anything less was unacceptable. But life doesn't always – or often – work that way. Perhaps instead, we could have supported Jon emotionally and remained a close, friendly presence in his life, giving him hope while maintaining some reasonable boundaries, until he found a way to manage his addiction. Letting a thoroughly addicted person "hit bottom" is very likely a death sentence.

"Death be not proud," said seventeenth century English poet and cleric John Donne, because, "those whom thou think'st thou dost overthrow, die not."[194] "The tomb is not a blind alley, it is a thoroughfare," wrote nineteenth century French author Victor Hugo after his daughter drowned. "It closes upon the twilight, but opens upon the dawn."[195] Even more eloquently, Saint Paul tells us that when the trumpet sounds to herald the return of Jesus, "the dead will be raised imperishable, and we will be changed...When the perishable has been clothed with the imperishable, and the mortal with immortality, then the saying that is written will come true: 'Death has been swallowed up in victory. Where, O death, is your victory? Where, O death, is your sting?'"[196]

I believe them all, and I wait for the time of victory when I can see my son again and ask his forgiveness. I believe with absolute certainty that God, the Great Grave Robber, has my Jon right where he should be. In the meantime, in Jon's name and in his honor, I will do what I can to fight the disease of addiction. A bereaved mother can bring a terrible rage. So, to the best of my ability, I will rip away the stigma and advocate for addicted people to be treated with the dignity and sympathy of patients. I will speak, write, advocate, organize, and testify about this cruel condition, and do anything else that seems likely to help. I will join with others who love or have loved an addicted person – warriors without training, troops, battle plans, armor, or maps. I must try, because if I do not, then death might as well be proud.

I cling to the promises that Jesus made to me and my son (and to all who believe in Him). Almighty God, pledged the prophet Isaiah 700 years before the birth of Jesus, will never leave his people. "When you pass through the waters I will be with you: and through the rivers, they shall not overwhelm you; when you walk through fire you shall not be burned, and the flame shall not consume you; for I am the Lord your God."[197] Jesus, who fulfilled the Old Testament prophecies, said that He is, "the light of the world. Whoever follows me will never walk in darkness, but will have the light of love."[198] "Those who mourn will be comforted,"[199] He promised, and, "Those who weep on earth will laugh in Heaven."[200] I believe. I will wait.

TWENTY-SIX

SOLUTIONS: WHAT WE CAN ALL DO TO FIGHT ADDICTION

My fellow Americans, this battle is up to us. The experts haven't solved the addiction crisis in our nation or our families. Science may yet help the next generation of potentially addicted people, but we can't wait. Law enforcement personnel can't arrest their way out of the addiction flood, because jails aren't equipped to offer workable, long-term treatment. And we surely can't stop the deluge from the supply side, as long as desperate, poor, and/or predatory countries and individuals see profit and political motives in hurting us. Throughout human history, drugs came from plants – poppies, coca leaves, cannabis, mushrooms, and others. But today, eradicating poppy fields that grow the plants used to make heroin and other opiates is ineffective because the value of the crop is low until it has been highly processed, and other fields are always available.

Besides, it is now so easy to manufacture the powerful synthetic opiate fentanyl that poppy fields and huge labor forces are not necessary. Ephedrine is no longer required to make methamphetamine, and, thanks to chemistry, many other synthetics need no more than the space of a trailer to prepare. Additionally, new synthetic drugs, known as "designer drugs," are being invented every day, usually by changing just one molecule or one part of one ingredient, to make the drugs harder to profile and trace.

We have to focus on three things: Education, Prevention, and Treatment. There is so much we can and must do to save our children and our communities. It has now been nearly thirty years since Jon started taking drugs. First, I suffered in distracted confusion, but once I learned about the brain science of addiction, I started to volunteer in addiction advocacy. For the sake of all of us parents, grandparents, teachers and other school personnel, law enforcement and emergency responders, doctors, dentists, nurses, cities, counties, state legislators, employers and business people, faith communities, and everyone who has ever loved another human, I offer the solutions my long trail of tears have taught me.

SOLUTIONS FOR EVERYONE

1. Start with your own medicine chest.

    Keep all narcotics or other controlled substances in a lockbox. Include even soft medications like prescribed and over-the-counter sleeping aids and cough medicines advertised for night use. Lockboxes can be purchased at any hardware store or online. Deposit any and all types of medications you haven't used in more than sixty days in designated drop boxes in your community. Usually, such boxes are located in police stations and pharmacies, but if your community doesn't have any, then attend city council meetings or make an appointment with the police chief to ask for them. Then, once you get them, contact local media and ask them to publicize the boxes. Post about the boxes on your own social media and ask your friends, workmates and church, synagogue, or mosque to do the same. Maybe even get together with friends to make colorful posters to display next to the boxes.

2. Talk with your own doctor, dentist and advanced registered nurse practitioner (or anyone else authorized to prescribe).

    Tell them you prefer non-opioid pain relief should you have an injury or surgery. If you absolutely need opiate pain medication, say you want it in the lowest dose for the shortest possible time. And tell them why you feel this way – you are concerned about the drug epidemic in America, you oppose overprescribing, and you hope they are adopting this philosophy throughout their practices. Ask if they are registered and actively participating in your state's Prescription Monitoring Plan (PMP – all fifty states now have them). Be especially careful when you or a family member has so-called routine surgery such as hernia repair, stitches for a minor wound, laparoscopic procedures, or wisdom tooth removal. These procedures don't necessarily require opiate pain relief, and if they do, it's only needed for a few days. One of the most prevalent pathways to teens beginning drug use is opiate pain pills prescribed after wisdom tooth removal.

3. Educate yourself about the disease of addiction.

    The brain science of addiction is interesting, readily available, and you <u>can</u> understand it. It's available now on websites, articles, blogs, TED Talks, and YouTube videos. This information is just as important as information about heart disease, cancer risks, and diabetes – all of which were subjects that weren't discussed or known about when I was a child.

4. Recognize addiction as a disease: Don't judge people who have it or their family members and don't gossip.

    Don't bury addiction in whispers as if it is shameful. It's a disease, not a disgrace; a sickness, not a sin; and a medical issue, not a moral issue. The causes of addiction are multi-faceted and not fully understood, but we know that some are genetic and biochemical, some are caused by life events, and many other factors. If you know of an addicted person, reach out to the family to ask if they want to talk or if they want help looking for treatment resources or support groups. If there is an overdose, arrest, or other crisis, bring dinner just as you would for an auto accident. Above all, don't make pronouncements about what people "should" do, as they probably are barely coping and just need friendship.

5. Fight stigma in multiple ways.

Say the words "addiction" or "addicted person" out loud. If someone is addicted and in treatment or struggling, you can say they have the disease of addiction, as long as it's not in a gossiping way. Say it matter-of-factly just as you would when mentioning a person with a broken leg. If you hear disparaging words such as "druggie," "junkie," "stoner," "tweaker," "pothead," "acid head," or other slang about an addicted person, mention to the speaker that such words are offensive. And never let people who know nothing about addiction offer cheap advice about causes or cures. We wouldn't listen to an uninformed person give advice about the causes or treatments of heart disease. In the same way, we can't let people who are spouting cliches about addiction go unchallenged, because their words reinforce stereotypes. Speak up (albeit quietly – not in an argumentative way) and offer to help them become more educated.

6. Form an advocacy group.

Just get a group of friends together and agree that each of you will invite two local people who aren't your friends to a meeting. Invite teachers, nurses, police officers, auto mechanics, administrators, postal carriers, carpenters, or other people in trades, grocers, or basically anyone. Each of the friends in your original group should keep asking until at least two people commit to attending your meeting. Develop a message – such as "our town doesn't have a detox center" or "there are needles in our school yards." Then at your meeting, ask those present for their ideas on what to do about the problem you've identified. Don't let the meeting degenerate into complaints. Tell the people you're looking for suggestions and solutions. Most local libraries and community centers will let you hold meetings for free if you reserve a room ahead of time. Who knows where your efforts will lead – maybe to substantial local action.

7. Run your group meetings well.

    Be <u>organized</u>! Prepare an agenda and notes to yourself as to what you're going to say and a rough timeline of how many minutes you're going to spend on each segment of the meeting. Keep the meeting to one hour (or just a bit more if necessary.) Always start with introductions, letting each attendee say his or her name and why they are interested in this cause. Make sure to keep each person brief. If someone starts telling their entire story, gently but firmly tell them the group needs to move on. Then announce some ground rules. Be sure to say this meeting isn't a support group, but an action and advocacy group. (Tell people that if they need a support group, you will help them find one.) Other helpful ground rules include not letting people use your meeting as a marketing opportunity for their business or practice and being respectful to all members present (i.e., no interrupting or arguing). Also, while you are speaking, don't make side remarks such as referencing inside jokes with your close friends at the meeting, as this will make the new people feel like outsiders. Be sure to give all attendees something to do, such as inviting others to the meeting, researching the cost of certain services in other communities, or making a list of needs, goals, and pertinent questions. Collect names and contact information of attendees and definitely set a time for the next meeting. Then stay in touch to confirm seven to ten days before the next meeting.

8. Speak up to politicians and law enforcement.

    These contacts are most effective at the local level, but can be extended to your state legislators too. Attend meetings of city councils, county commissions, local health boards, school boards, and other governing groups. Police chiefs and sheriffs usually attend some of these meetings. Don't speak up at the first few meetings you attend. Listen first and get to know the local officials. Pretty soon, you'll figure out which ones might be open to your cause. When you do speak up, make eye contact with those people and speak directly to them. Be polite, logical, and offer suggestions and solutions instead of just complaints. Then stick around at the end of the meeting to engage in friendly chit-chat. Ask if some of them might attend a meeting of your group or have coffee with a few of your members. Making contacts can be a step-wise process, eventually getting you connected with state representatives. Remember, elected officials want to please the voters, so if you present yourself, your group, and your mission in a helpful, public-spirited way, there's a good chance you'll be heard.

9. Get formally organized (if you're going to raise money).

If you decide to pursue a major goal such as raising money for a program, get formally organized by becoming a non-profit corporation. Forming a corporation is easier than it sounds, and many times local attorneys will donate their time to help you set it up. The point is you're not going to get any substantial donations unless you are a tax-free, non-profit organization. If you do become a non-profit organization, then don't be afraid to ask everyone you deal with for a discount or a contribution – a local store where you buy office supplies or an insurance agent if you need insurance to hold events.

10. Use the media.

The media – both social media and the "old-fashioned media" such as newspapers, television, and radio – can make or break your efforts. Once you know what you want to accomplish, such as establishing a detox center or establishing a speakers' bureau to give educational talks about addiction, then call the local media and ask them to let you write a guest editorial or speak about the problem and solutions. Most local media will do public service announcements (PSAs) if you explain that you're just educating and advocating, not asking for money. A good time to ask is when you see a local news article about addiction or drugs. Post it on your social media with a comment offering a solution or suggestion and use that opportunity to announce your next meeting. Just raising the visibility will help! It will bring new people to your group and cause others in the community to think twice or wonder what more can be done locally. Lastly, it's especially effective if your PSAs feature real local addicted people and their families. Some such people will want to keep their privacy, but many will be glad to speak out.

11. Network with hospitals, local doctors, and treatment providers.

SAMHSA has a list of addiction treatment providers organized by zip code on its website (https://www.samhsa.gov/). Find the providers in your area and contact them to ask what kind of treatment services or referrals they have or are using. What do they do when they encounter a person who has overdosed? Do the same with hospitals, any doctors you know personally, the local medical society, and the local health department. It's best to ask for short, in-person meetings, because telephone inquiries can arouse suspicion in the medical field. There are strict privacy restrictions in this field, but if you meet face-to-face and assure them that you're seeking only general information, and you're not a competitor or an inspector, they may help you to the extent they can. Like most professions, medical and treatment providers have a network and your contacts may expand slowly, but they will grow if you're polite and careful to explain that you just want local community information.

12. Talk to landlords, press for more lighting, and start neighborhood watch programs.

   Landlords at apartment buildings are often corporations located nowhere near their properties. If you suspect drug use in a property, contact the landlord and remind them of their potential liability. Ask them to be proactive, such as installing more lighting, hiring security guards, or asking for regular, visible police patrols. If you know of drug activity at a specific apartment or house, call the police and press the landlord for eviction. Neighborhood Watch programs involve more than just a sign on a corner. People have to walk around, observe, get to know their neighbors, their vehicles and their frequent visitors, and – without being a snoop – interact!

13. Don't give cash to panhandlers.

   People with signs asking for money or help now wait at exits to store parking lots in numbers not seen until a few years ago. However, it's not a good idea to give them money because those funds could very easily go for drugs or alcohol – you'll never know. Instead, you can give money to a local homeless shelter or church that serves food to the homeless. If you really want to give something to a person who looks needy on a one-on-one personal basis, then carry small bags in your car containing granola bars, toothbrushes, soap, or gloves and socks if the weather is cold. You can hand those bags out through your car window and know you're not contributing to deepening someone's addiction.

SOLUTIONS FOR PARENTS, GRANDPARENTS AND FAMILIES

1. Don't be naïve!

    Your job is the hardest of all! You are faced with the biggest drug epidemic in United States history, combined with pernicious and ever-present social media. The plain fact is that deadly drugs are available to your children over the internet, at school, in playgrounds, at workplaces where they may have afterschool jobs, at church, from friends and neighbors, and essentially everywhere they go or look. The most important thing you can do is be aware of these facts and never think it can't happen to your family. The most loving, careful, involved, supportive families are still vulnerable, and you'd be surprised who else is using or offering drugs.

2. Educate yourselves about drug signs and lingo.

    The drug world has its own signs, symbols, and slang, and it's always changing, so you may not be able to keep up with all the specifics. That's the point – a subculture wants to identify itself as distinct and doesn't want everyone else to know the keys to its identity. Still, do your best. A federal program called Community Anti-Drug Coalitions of America (CADCA, at https://cadca. org/) has an interactive exhibit called "Hidden in Plain Sight" that shows a mock teenage bedroom containing all kinds of indicators of drug use that parents probably don't recognize. There are also videos of the same topic on YouTube (Example: https://www.bing.com/videos/search?q=hidden+in+Plain+Sight+exhibit&docid=608015568095415547&mid=B8D510277E89B2C22296B8D510277E89B2C22296&view=detail&FORM=VIRE). There also are many exhibits of still photos on the internet (Example: http://powertotheparent.org/be-aware/hidden-in-plain-sight/), and other ways to access this information. Items as innocent-looking as apples, aluminum foil, clothes dryer sheets, plastic tampon holders, bent soda cans, and many others can be signs of drug use, especially if several of the items are present.

3. Talk to your children – about everything!

The surest way to be successful as a parent is just to stay close to your kids and talk to them – period. Eat dinner together, take walks, cook, or do woodworking or work on motors together, and just make sure there are plenty of opportunities for free and easy exchange. Don't be afraid to talk about drugs. In fact, you must! Don't think talking about drugs will put ideas in their heads – they already know and have many other sources already talking to them about drugs. Let your children know you will pick them up anywhere, anytime they find themselves in an uncomfortable situation with friends – and you are fine with them making you the bad guy. They can say, "My ridiculous parents told me to I have to babysit," "My mother got sick and Dad says I have to go stay with her," or whatever gets them off the hook with anyone who is tempting them. Also, let them know they can come to you if they have made a bad decision, and you will help – not punish.

4. Stay rooted.

Children don't do well when they are frequently uprooted from school to school, house to house, church to church, or anywhere else. Even short distances such as across town can effectively cut off a child or teen from seeing friends, being on the same teams, or attending after-school events. Then they are thrown back on the internet for companionship, and we all know the hazards that creates. Constantly having to make new friends causes anxiety, even if it doesn't show.

5. Get involved at school, church, sports or in the neighborhood.

    You've got to have a network to share and confirm information. Some children welcome their parents' participation in their activities. However, some – especially teens – may find your presence intrusive and may not even want you at their school. Find a way to make an inroad anyway. If your child is into sports and doesn't welcome you being their coach, then volunteer to shelve books in the school library. This contact with the school gives you a network and you'll hear things. You'll get to know who and where the problems are at that school, and get familiar with the staff so you can ask questions in a friendly, easy manner. The staff isn't going to give you any important information if they've never seen you before and you just walk in and ask questions. The same is true with any network – they have to know you before they'll share information.

6. Set an example.

    Don't get drunk at home, neighborhood barbecues, work parties, or anywhere. There are lots of good reasons not to do this, but the most important one is that your kids will think it's okay, normal, and maybe even funny if you do. And if you smoke, give it up! Smoking and drinking often go together and just set up your children to think the activities are acceptable, and thus gravitate toward the wrong crowd.

7. Let your teens know that not everyone is doing it.

    Studies have shown that teens and college students wrongly believe nearly everyone in the high school or on campus is drinking to excess on weekends or at parties and many/most are doing drugs. Yet, according to the CDC, only small minorities of teens and college students binge drink, get drunk frequently, or use drugs (especially hard drugs), although nearly half in these age groups have at least tried marijuana. The myth that "everyone is doing it" needs to be corrected because it can lead to a self-fulfilling prophecy. Young people want to be accepted by other young people, or be cool, or wired in. Letting them know it's really only a vocal minority of their peers getting drunk or using drugs can be very reassuring.

8. Don't dismiss behavior changes as "normal teenage rebellion."

Everyone knows that teenagers want privacy, prefer their own styles, spend more time with friends than with family, and often argue back at parents just to assert themselves. Yes, every parent is probably going to see these behaviors, but don't be complacent – be *careful*. If your teen's hair is longer and unkempt, it might just be an okay thing not to argue over. If his or her room is more messy, if he prefers cash to other gifts, if she sleeps in a lot, if his taste in music grates on your ears, these things also could be normal. However, they might not be. Dig deeper and ask questions of your teen. Check with the parent-school-church or neighborhood network you have established. And I'm not against snooping now and then in your teen's room or computer. (Yes – you should have their computer passwords – all of them – as long as they are minors.) If you find information that contradicts what your teen has told you, go back with the evidence and ask him/her again. Don't just assume the new behaviors are simply ordinary aspects of being a teen.

9. Act fast if you find your child or teen is using drugs.

You'll never have more power than you do when your child or teen is under eighteen. Use it! You can compel treatment, even confined inpatient treatment, when a minor is under eighteen. Do this if it's needed! They may not like it and might beg you to let them leave, but keep them in treatment anyway. You can take their anger, but not their death. Even though the success rate for teen abstinence after one month in treatment is very low, they'll learn something, hear something, or see someone that might stick with them at an important moment in their future. Even after your teen turns eighteen, you still have more power than you think. They need shelter, food, and financial support at the very least, and you'll still have more resources than they have for a number of years. You can withhold vital resources they need to coax them back into treatment, to AA/NA groups, or into sober group homes. Don't dangle your resources in a punitive way, but let them know you're not going to make them comfortable if they're risking their lives (and your happiness) by using drugs.

10. Don't fear crises, and be ready.

Crises can be great opportunities. In the addiction world, these are times called "moments of clarity" or "windows of willingness," when an addicted person gets so tired, sick, broke, cold, hungry, or discouraged that he or she decides it's time to try treatment. These times usually occur after crises, such as getting evicted, getting arrested, overdosing, having a spouse walk out, or any number of other devastating events. Such wake-up calls sometimes bestow "the gift of desperation," and the addicted person is ready. But you have to be ready too, because these windows can be very, very short. If there are dozens of logistics and obstacles to wade through, the chemical cravings will take over and the addicted person often will just go back to using. So develop a plan beforehand including who you're going to call, what treatment centers are available that you can access, rules and requirements of those centers, transportation and logistics, and any other practical matters that could slow down or even destroy your opportunity. There might be animals to care for, employers or landlords to notify, vehicles to store, short-term medications to pick up, etc. Be sure to work through all these issues and talk to whomever you need to, so that when your addicted loved one says "Yes," you can make it happen.

11. Try to analyze your own personality style.

Many tests exist on the internet to help you do this. It's important to know yourself well because your personality style determines your "default mode" on how you will respond when something happens. Be especially careful if you find you need and seek closure – if you like things to be over and done with, neatly tied up and put away. Addiction and recovery are long games and often need years to resolve. Or, they may never be resolved. If you find it hard to tolerate lingering situations with not much, if any, closure, it is good to recognize this trait in yourself and build in breaks (time-outs) and deliberate coping mechanisms (such as meditation or other relaxation strategies). Otherwise, your need for finality may cause great harm to you and/or your addicted family member.

12. Drug use explodes families, so do three things to survive.

Family turmoil will ensue one hundred percent of the time when someone in the family is using drugs. Marriages break up or other children in the family (known as "shadow children") are ignored and may develop problems of their own. Stress causes physical ailments, finances are strained, other relationships outside the home can wither, and it's absolutely a sure thing that family members will disagree on how to handle the addicted person. There is a continuum from the enabler (the "Dove") to the tough love advocate (the "Hawk"), and every family is going to have some members all over that spectrum. How is a family going to survive? There are three necessary things:

A. Make decisions as family and stick to them: Family members must sit down and decide how they are going to handle situations that come up. What are you going to do if the addicted person asks you for money, steals from you, you find him or her sleeping in your garage after you've said they can't be at your house while using? You <u>must</u> have your answers agreed upon before incidents happen, wherever you land on the Dove-Hawk continuum. And you <u>must</u> stick to them. No family member can undermine by slipping the person some cash or hiding their sleeping bag in the garden shed so they can sleep there, if you've agreed that those things can't happen. Trust among family members is destroyed when members break agreements. And you've got to stand firm as a unit against Grandma or the neighbor or anyone else who criticizes or undermines your family decisions.

B. <u>Find support groups for family members</u>: Maybe it's Al-Anon, Ala-Teen, Families Anonymous, SMART Recovery, or others. It doesn't really matter whether different family members go to the same groups or different groups, but each family member needs to find a group where he or she can normalize, vent, listen, cry, learn, and feel accepted.

C. <u>Go out and have some fun together</u>: You've got to get away from the obsession with the addicted person, wondering what they may be doing at any given moment, who they're with, how unsafe they are, and whether you're doing the right thing for them. Just choose some activity that has bonded you in the past, from going to a movie, skiing, watching a race or running in one, having dinner in a favorite restaurant, or anything else that works for your family. And agree not to talk about addiction during this outing.

13. Most important – NEVER disconnect completely!!

No matter your child's age (he or she can be twelve or fifty), let them know that you will *always* be available if and when they want to make positive choices and take positive steps. You can set boundaries, such as, "you can't come to dinner if you're high," but you can bring them a sandwich (not every day) and say, "I love you and I'm ready to help when you are." *Never* say, "I've had it with you. Go away until you've fixed this thing yourself." They may not be able to fix it and you may never see them again.

SOLUTIONS FOR SCHOOL PERSONNEL:

1. Develop and implement curricula about drugs.

   It's absolutely essential to have broad, comprehensive education about drugs, their effects, and consequences, as well as the brain science of addiction. Don't be afraid of brain science – it can be presented in terms easy to understand at age-appropriate levels. Certainly, don't relegate drug education into a tiny, dry unit in health class. Drugs are such a national problem in terms of cost, crime, safety and hygiene in communities, homelessness and the invasion of parks and other public spaces by the homeless, and broken families that we <u>have</u> to talk and educate about these issues. It isn't a choice anymore.

2. Use evidence-based prevention programs.

   Prevention has come a long way, and there is now an entire discipline called Prevention Science. Old programs that are based on a fear model are not only ineffective, but they can incite curiosity about drugs and make them seem mysterious and alluring to some students. Many new programs have been developed and they involve community, family, peer, and school participation. Teachers and school counselors work with student leaders to hold seminars, make videos, hold lockbox giveaways, bring in speakers, and host gala events with a serious purpose.

It's all about bringing the topics of drugs and addiction out into the open and weaving them into other events that students enjoy.

3. Bring in people in recovery as speakers.

Many schools are afraid to bring in people in recovery from addiction to speak at school assemblies or in classes because they think hearing these people will put ideas into students' heads. Believe me, students already know about drugs in their communities, where to find them, and probably some exaggerated tales of how they make people feel. But having people in recovery speak about the other side of drugs – the defeat, sickness, losses (financial and many others), regrets, hopelessness and depression, and the doors that closed – is powerful and necessary. These speakers provide an antidote that everyone invested in education and prevention hopes for. Bring them into the schools often and without apology. Push back against administrators who say no. These speakers will change students' minds and provide them visible, memorable reasons to think twice about trying drugs.

4. Have recovery clubs in high schools and colleges.

There are people in recovery from addiction as young as twelve years old! Schools and colleges have to recognize recovery clubs and student recovery support groups just as they would math clubs or football. They need to have meeting spaces at school, access to faculty sponsors, be allowed to hold events just as any other club, and receive financial support that other clubs receive. (Example: https://www.facebook.com/cougsforrecovery). Such clubs not only benefit the students involved, but they normalize the condition of addiction as something people can talk about, relate to, and see as a part of our world.

5. Advocate for recovery high schools and recovery dormitories in colleges.

Recovery high schools are a wonderful idea if a community is large enough, as students in recovery draw support from each other and need to feel that they're not different. Recovery dormitories on college campuses are essential. Now that alcohol is allowed on many or most college campuses, students in recovery need to have safe, alcohol-free places to live.

SOLUTIONS FOR EMPLOYERS

1. Recognize that the workplace is full of drugs.

There isn't an office, store, job site, or company you can name that doesn't have people using and hiding drugs or alcohol at work. Sometimes people are functional most of the time, but they also cause accidents, lost productivity, and low morale among the co-workers who know what's going on. Realize that the presence of addicted or using people in your workplace is a fact of life and any other assumption is naïve. Since you can't afford to be naïve, make plans to address the issue.

2. Institute programs to talk about drugs.

It's helpful to have lunch-and-learn meetings, safety assemblies, training sessions, retreats, and other seminars at work that include the topics of drugs, addiction, and alcoholism just as you would include other topics such as highway safety, hotel safety, safe use of tools, heart health, stop smoking programs, and many other topics. Since addiction and/or alcoholism affects approximately one in every thirteen Americans, there is no sensible reason not to include this subject as part of ongoing employee education. These programs should not be the same old "drugs are bad" lectures all of us have heard. They should be realistic, open, interactive, and use evidence-based prevention principles.

3. Test for drugs and alcohol on a regular basis.

   It just makes common sense to screen for these substances, because untreated substance abuse can bring havoc and safety issues into your company. Make sure everyone is tested at some regular interval, with random selections and without warning. Don't confine testing just to sensitive groups such as doctors, nurses, truck drivers, and crane operators. Making the testing mandatory and across the board for everyone inspires a sense of fairness in all your employees.

4. Have employee assistance programs and policies with open doors.

   In your company, have programs and designated people to whom employees with drug or alcohol problems can go and ask for help, without fear of reprisal. Most insurance policies now cover drug and alcohol treatment as part of behavioral health, but if your company lacks this insurance coverage, get it. Make sure your employees know they can come in and admit their struggles and the company will provide treatment, at least two or three times, and reinstate them in their jobs when they complete treatment. Reasons for their absence when they go to treatment can be kept confidential, but most people will figure it out anyway through the grapevine. It shouldn't be any more shameful than having to take time off for cancer surgery.

5. Make sure company insurance policies cover non-opiate therapy for pain.

   Non-opiate therapies for pain include physical therapy, yoga, meditation, ultra-sound muscle stimulation, and other methods.

Often, these can be more expensive and time-consuming than simply prescribing pain pills, and they require trial and error to determine which therapies will work for which persons. However, in the long run, they are less expensive than paying for the absenteeism, low productivity, and safety risks of an employee who becomes addicted to pain pills. Make sure your company insurance covers these alternative therapies.

6. Give second chances.

Hire people in recovery based on their qualifications, just as you would hire anyone else. Don't make people check boxes on their employment applications admitting to having had drug or alcohol problems, unless you have check boxes for every other disease a person possibly could have. If an applicant tells you he or she is in recovery, congratulate them and say you're glad they're doing well.

7. Be sensitive to employees in recovery when planning company events.

If all your company-sponsored events are pub crawls or wine tastings, you've just excluded some employees or their spouses and made them feel different. Serve alcohol at company events only rarely and always have lots of soft drinks, water, coffee, and tea available. Limit alcohol at such events to a system such as "two-drink tickets per person," to send the message that some social drinking is fine for some people, but drunkenness is not. Don't raffle bottles of wine, liquor, or beer as door prizes at company events. Better yet, if possible, have your company gala events be breakfasts or lunches, with no alcohol.

8. Allow time and space for AA or NA meetings in the workplace.

Employees who need these meetings may not have the time or transportation to make offsite evening meetings or meetings before the workday begins. Make time and space at work for these meetings at the workplace, while still requiring a full day's work. Break periods can be consolidated to make time, or the meetings can be held during lunchtime. And don't make the meetings a secret. People will figure out through grapevines anyway who is going into such meetings, so let the meetings be posted on work message boards just like messages about bowling leagues and company softball teams.

SOLUTIONS FOR FAITH LEADERS

1. Do many of the same things at Educators and Employers must do:

   - Recognize that people in recovery and people in active addiction are already part of your church family.
   - Be open to the topic of addiction and incorporate it into "regular" discussions in sermons, messages, small groups, and learning topics. Don't bury it in whispers, and let congregation members know they can talk to you about it.
   - Bring in speakers who are in recovery.
   - Be sensitive when planning events. Serve mostly (or exclusively) soft drinks and coffee, keeping alcoholic beverages to a minimum (or not serving them at all).
   - Educate yourself about treatment and recovery programs in your area, so when people ask for help you can direct them.
   - Give second chances when people come back from treatment, Incorporate them into church life and groups, and give them some tasks to do so they feel they can "give back."
   - Allow AA, NA, Celebrate Recovery and other mutual-help groups to meet in your church.

2. However, you can do more than other professions and groups can do. You can pray for and with people suffering from addiction, harnessing the power of Jesus Christ in their fight against the darkness.

3. Recognize that addiction is the work of Satan, and call it out as the evil it is (while always being careful not to label those suffering from addiction as evil).

4. Educate your congregation by bringing in treatment providers and other experts in addiction to speak, and to dispel old myths that addiction is a moral flaw.

5. Be sure that church committees who visit the sick and bring meals extend those courtesies and services to families dealing with addiction.

SOLUTIONS FOR PUBLIC OFFICIALS, POLICY MAKERS, POLICE AND SHERIFFS, AND COMMUNITIES

1. Educate yourselves and advocate.

Being a good public servant starts with education. People with the diseases of alcoholism and addiction aren't necessarily bad people (although, as in all groups, some can be very bad). However, these diseases often produce obnoxious and troublesome behavior that must be stopped. It's really easy to get tired of repeat shoplifters, loiterers, panhandlers, and other petty criminals who are obviously intoxicated or high, especially if they "mouth off" when being arrested or told to move along. However, remember that short-term arrests only produce a revolving door. You're in a good position to advocate for instituting drug courts, programs for detox and treatment in jail, no-penalty voluntary substance confiscation programs, and policies that mandate treatment as an alternative to incarceration. People will tend to listen to you because you've been there on the front lines, so speak up.

2. Provide alternatives.

If your city or county has no treatment services or very inadequate ones, put this concern on the agenda of regular meetings or call special public meetings. Gather local facts and statistics about numbers of arrests, recidivism, costs per night in jail, costs in officer time to make and process arrests, costs to send out emergency medical services teams or fire trucks, number of treatment beds or clinics, distance to services in other areas, and other pertinent realities. Then ask the public what they would like to do. There are many hidden costs in doing nothing except continuing revolving door arrests and transports to hospital emergency departments. If you can show the voting public that costs actually will go down if you build a local treatment center, they'll probably authorize you to move ahead.

3. Insist on mandatory Prescription Monitoring Programs (PMPs).

While all fifty states have PMPs, almost none are mandatory, and prescribers can just say they are too busy, or the computer systems too cumbersome, or any number of other excuses for not entering their data. This allows drug-seeking patients to "doctor-shop" and get opiate prescriptions from multiple sources. Legislators need to make PMPs mandatory, and they need to share information across state lines.

4. Insist on prescribing limits.

We need maximum limits on how many opiate pills can be prescribed per patient and per medical visit, with obvious exceptions for surgical, cancer, and end-of-life pain. Medical personnel who treat persons with chronic pain should be required to thoroughly and frequently document the facts of the patients' conditions, with mandatory review by other professionals, to make sure excessive pain pills aren't being prescribed. Yes, chronic pain is a real condition, but scams are so easy to perpetrate that extra safeguards are needed.

5. Insist on mandatory education about opiates for all prescribers.

We all hear stories from doctors, dentists, and nurses who prescribed and administered pain pills in the past with almost no thought to the addiction potential. We also hear that opiate addiction essentially was not covered in their medical, dental, and nursing schools. These trusting and uninformed practices have contributed to nearly a million American deaths from opiate addiction in the last twenty-five years. Robust and straightforward education about opiates and addiction must be mandated for medical personnel – both those in practice and those still in school.

6. Mandate insurance companies to cover alternative pain therapies.

Physical therapy, meditation, yoga, acupuncture, massage therapy, ultrasonic muscle stimulation, and other methods are very effective for pain in some patients. Yet, many insurance programs don't cover these therapies because it's quicker and cheaper to cover an opiate pill prescription. Legislatures who license insurance companies to operate in their states can insist on non-opioid therapies as a condition of licensure.

7. Fund education programs for substance use disorder peers and professionals.

Virtually all local community colleges should have certification programs for Substance Use Disorder Professionals (SUDPs – a two-year degree), and all states and counties should have certification programs for SUD Peers (people with at least one year in recovery, with no college degree needed). These programs should be widely available and have generous scholarship programs to allow motivated people to fill the many roles that will be needed to turn around the raging addiction epidemic. These programs are good investments.

8. Make it easier for professional social workers and counselors to obtain licenses after obtaining their Master's degrees.

   Many states require long practicum or "associate" periods of 3,000-4,000 hours after completing Master's degrees. Usually, people must work for lower pay during these periods, and can have difficulty finding a licensed professional who has time to supervise them. These long practicum periods are driving many potential counselors and social workers from the field, thus exacerbating a national shortage of behavioral health professionals. State legislatures can correct this problem as they write the requirements for their states.

9. Offer follow-up care for all overdoses.

   Many overdoses never come to the attention of emergency personnel, doctors, or even families, because addicted people and their friends use naloxone to revive people who have overdosed and want to hide their drug use. This situation is very unfortunate, because crisis opportunities are missed. For those overdoses that do come to hospital emergency rooms or are treated by city or county Emergency Medical Services (EMS) personnel or police, follow-up is essential. Simply waking up people and sending them on their way is cruel. It reinforces shame and hopelessness. True, some overdose victims may not welcome follow-up, but it should at least be offered. And simply handing out a sheet of paper with a list of AA meetings isn't good enough. Personal care, with real alternatives (i.e., treatment, counseling in real time, and other interventions) should be made available in an easy, non-judgmental manner. If we do that, we'll change at least some lives.

10. Investigate drug deaths just as other deaths are investigated.

Gather evidence carefully, even if the cause of death is obvious. Doing so can make it possible to prosecute the people who supplied the drugs for manslaughter or even murder. Then make sure they get long prison sentences. Thus, a community can start to shut down small-time dealers and suppliers one-by-one, and also send a message to other small drug runners that your community is not where they can operate freely.

11. Don't punish over and over again after people recover.

If you're a prosecutor, judge, or arresting officer, make sure you give credit to people in recovery, especially those who've achieved years of sobriety, earned degrees, gotten jobs, and fulfilled all conditions of their previous sentences. Rebuilding lives after addiction is incredibly difficult, and many people don't make it. For those who do, give them some grace. If they make a small mistake such as a traffic infraction or inadvertently leave a store without paying for a small item because they're distracted, don't punish harshly and assume they are back to using drugs.

12. Crack down on underage sales of alcohol to kids.

Police and sheriffs know where the local trouble spots are, the all-night stores, and where kids are gathering nearby or in parking lots. Do frequent checks and even sting operations to catch stores selling illegally and make sure they get stiff fines or a few days with their doors locked.

13. Punish and incarcerate larger drug dealers and smugglers as strongly as possible.

    These people are predators in our midst, as surely as if they were alligators or rattlesnakes. Pursue them and put them away for as long as you possibly can!

REFERENCES

1 Maclean, Norman, <u>A River Runs Through It</u>, University of Chicago Press, 1976.

2 From "I'm Free," author unknown.

3 Sesame Street is a trademarked property of the Public Broadcasting Network.

4 Peanuts is a cartoon character created by Charles Shultz, with a copyright now owned by Iconix Brand Group of New York.

5 Chutes and Ladders is a trademarked product of Hasbro Corp., of Pawtucket, Rhode Island.

6 Legos is now a trademarked product of Lego A/S of Denmark.

7 Lincoln Logs is now a trademarked product of K'NEX Limited Partnership of Delaware.

8 Bill W., <u>Twelve Steps and Twelve Traditions</u>, *AA World Service Organization* (Originally *AA Publishing*) (New York), first printing 1952, p. 5.

9 Care-A-Lot Kids was a product of the Care Bears, trademarked products of American Greetings Corp. of Cleveland, OH.

10 *Woman's Day* is owned by the Hearst Corporation of New York.

11 These are some of the same traits observed by teachers in Janis Joplin, the notoriously rebellious rocker who was addicted to drugs and died of a heroin overdose at age 27. See George-Warren, Holly, <u>Janis: Her Life and Music</u>, Simon and Schuster (New York), 2019, p. 17.

12 Proverbs 3:5, Trust in the LORD with all your heart and lean not on your own understanding; in all your ways submit to him, and he will make your paths straight (New International Version [NIV]).

13 The Muppets originally were trademarked products of Disney Studios of Burbank, CA, and later of Jim Henson Productions of Hollywood, CA.

14 Monopoly is a trademarked product of Hasbro Corp., of Pawtucket, Rhode Island.

15 Sorry is a trademarked product of Hasbro Corp., of Pawtucket, Rhode Island.

16 Go Fish is a trademarked product of Hoyle Gaming Co., which is a subsidiary of U.S. Playing Card Co. of Erlanger, KY.

17 *Nevermind* and its songs are owned by Geffen Records, a subsidiary of Universal Music Group of Santa Monica, CA.

18 Attribution unknown.

19 Jane's Addiction band was marketed by Warner Brothers Records of Burbank, CA.

20 The Doors band was marketed by Elektra Records of New York City.

21 Huxley, Aldous, <u>Doors of Perception</u>, Chatto and Windus (London, United Kingdom), 1954.

22 Acid refers to lysergic acid diethylamide (LSD)

23 Moyers, William Cope, with Ketcham, Katherine, <u>Broken: My Story of Addiction and Redemption</u>, Viking (Penguin Publishers), (New York), 2006, pp. 71, 73.

24 Alcoholics Anonymous (AA), The <u>Big Book</u>, AA World Services Inc. (General Service Office, New York), 4th Edition, 2001.

25 Moyers, <u>Broken</u>, p. 133.

26 Chilton Manuals are products of Haynes North America of Newbury Park, CA.

27 Klebold, Sue, <u>A Mother's Reckoning</u>: <u>Living in the Aftermath of Tragedy</u>, Crown Publishers (NY), 2016 p. 197.

28 U.S. Centers for Disease Control (CDC), "Drug Overdose Deaths," CDC. May 26, 2022, at https://www.cdc.gov/nchs/nvss/drug-overdose-deaths.htm

29 U.S. CDC, "Drugs, Death and Data," CDC, May 6, 2022, at https://www.cdc.gov/surveillance/blogs-stories/drugs-death-data.html; U.S. CDC, "Transcript for CDC Telebriefing; EIS Conference, " CDC, April 25, 2017, at Transcript for CDC Telebriefing: EIS Conference | CDC Online Newsroom | CDC (https://www.cdc.gov/media/releases/2017/t0425-eis-conference.html)

30 OxyContin was a trademarked product of Purdue Pharma of Stamford, Connecticut.

31 Meier, Barry, <u>Pain Killer: A "Wonder" Drug's Trail of Addiction and Death</u>, Rodale (Emmaus, Pennsylvania), 2003, p. 12.

32 Macy, Beth, <u>Dopesick: Dealers, Doctors and Drug Companies that Addicted America</u>, Little Brown & Co. Hachette Books (New York), 2018, p. 32.

33 U.S. CDC, "Prescribing Data," U.S. CDC, December 20, 2016 at https://www.cdc.gov/drugoverdose/data/prescribing.html

34 Johnson & Johnson sold Tasmanian Alkaloids and Noramco in 2016, amidst lawsuits for its role in the opioid epidemic.

35 Fisher, Erik, <u>The Urge: Our History of Addiction</u>, Penguin Press (New York), 2022, pp. 28-29.

36 Meier, <u>Pain Killer</u>, p. 76.

37 Ibid., pp. 98, 257.

38 Quinones, Sam, <u>The Least of Us: True Tales of America and Hope in the Time of Fentanyl and Meth</u>, Bloomsbury Publishing (New York), 2021, p. 65.

39 Quinones, Sam, <u>Dreamland: The True Tale of America's Opiate Epidemic</u>, Bloomsbury Press (New York), 2015, pp. 95-96.

40 Meier, <u>Pain Killer</u>, p. 292.

41 Solomon, Andrew, <u>The Noonday Demon, An Atlas of Depression</u>, Scribners (New York), 2001, pp. 222-223.

42 Grisel, Judith, <u>Never Enough: The Neuroscience and Experience of Addiction</u>, Doubleday Publishers (New York), 2019, p. 62.

43 Martins, Sylvia S., Segura, Luis, E., Santaela-Tenorio, Julian, Permutter, Alexander, Fenton, Miriam C., Cerda, Magdalena, Keyes, Katherine M., Ghandour, Lillian A., Storr, Carla L., And Hasin, Deborah S., "Prescription Opioid Use Disorder and Heroin Use Among 12-34 Year-Olds in the United States from 2002-1014," in *Addictive Behaviors*, October 2016.

44 *Every Breath You Take* was the property of Emi Music Publishing, Ltd. of London, England.

45 *Billie Jean* was the property of Epic Records of New York.

46 *Flashdance* was the property of Casablanca Records, a division of Universal Music Group of Santa Monica, CA.

47 Meier, <u>Pain Killer</u>, p. 161.

48 Ibid., pp. 224-225.

49 Ibid., *Pain Killer,* p. 245.

50 Government Accountability Office (GAO), "OxyContin Abuse and Diversion and Efforts to Address the Problem," GAO-04-110, GAO (Washington, DC), January 22, 2004.

51 Frisbee is a trademarked product of Wham-O, Inc., of Carson, California.

52 Franklin, G.M., Mai, J., Wickizer, T., Turner, J.A., Fulton-Kehoe, D., and Grant, L. "Opioid Dosing Trends and Mortality in Washington State Workers' Compensation, 1996-2002," *American Journal of Industrial Medicine*, Vol.48 (2), August 2005, pp. 91-99.

53 Kennedy, Patrick, <u>A Common Struggle</u>, Blue Rider Press (Penguin/Random House: New York), 2015, p. 209.

54 Herzanek, Joe, <u>Why Don't They Just Quit?</u>, Changing Lives Foundation (Loveland, CO), 2009 & 2012, p. 223.

55 Woodruff, Lee and Woodruff, Bob, <u>In an Instant: A Family's Journey of Love and Healing</u>, Random House (New York), 2007, p. 270.

56 Suboxone was a trademarked product of Reckitt Benckiser Pharmaceuticals (Slough, Berkshire, United Kingdom) and is now a trademarked product of Invidior Pharmaceuticals (Slough, Berkshire, United Kingdom).

57 Quinones, <u>The Least of Us</u>, p. 41.

58 Office of the Attorney General, "Washington to Receive Share of $19.5 Million Settlement with OxyContin Maker," News Release, Olympia, WA, May 8, 2007 at http://www.atg.wa.gov/news/news-releases/washington-receive-share-195-million-settlement-oxycontin-maker

59 Moyers, <u>Broken</u>, p. 167

60 U.S. Centers for Disease Control (CDC), "Trends in Drug Poisoning Deaths Involving Opiod Analgesics: United States, 1999-2012," CDC (Atlanta, GA),

2015, at <u>Products - Health E Stats - Trends in Drug-poisoning Deaths: United States, 1999–2012 (cdc.gov)</u>

61 Transformers are trademarked products of Hasbro Corp., Pawtucket, Rhode Island.

62 NIDA, "Heroin: How is Heroin Linked to Prescription Drug Abuse," NIDA (Washington, DC), November 2014 at https://www.drugabuse.gov/publications/research-reports/heroin/how-heroin-linked-to-prescription-drug-abuse; CDC, "Today's Heroin Epidemic," CDC (Atlanta, GA), July 7, 2015 at <u>Today's Heroin Epidemic | VitalSigns | CDC</u>

63 Quinones, <u>Dreamland</u>, pp. 36, 55, 39.

64 Grisel, <u>Never Enough</u>, p. 63.

65 Szalavitz, Maia, <u>Unbroken Brain: A Revolutionary New Way of Understanding Addiction</u>, St. Martin's Press (New York), 2016, p. 142.

66 Moyers, <u>Broken</u>, p. 295.

67 Herzanek, <u>Why Don't They Just Quit?</u>, p. 163.

68 Moyers, <u>Broken</u>, pp. 112-113

69 Bill W., <u>The Twelve Steps and Twelve Traditions</u>, p. 46

70 Kennedy, <u>A Common Struggle</u>, p. 234.

71 Moyers, <u>Broken</u>, p. 145.

72 Kennedy, <u>A Common Struggle</u>, p. 185.

73 Szalavitz, <u>Unbroken Brain</u>, p. 160.

74 Kennedy, <u>A Common Struggle</u>, pp. 147, 154-155.

75 Bill W., <u>Twelve Steps and Twelve Traditions</u>, p. 21.

76 Henley, William E., in <u>The Oxford Book of English Verse, 1250–1900</u>, 1st edition, Clarendon Press (Oxford, England), 1939. Copyright expired.

77 *A Hard Rain's Gonna Fall* originally was a trademarked product of Warner Brothers Inc. of Burbank, CA, but in 1991 the copyright was renewed by Special Rider Music of New York.

78 *Dignity* was released by Columbia Music, a division of Sony Music Corp (New York), 1994.

79 *Things Have Changed* was released by Columbia Music, a division of Sony Music Corp (New York), 1999.

80 *Not Dark Yet* was released by Columbia Music, a division of Sony Music (New York), 1997.

81 *Hunger Strike* was released by A&M Records (Hollywood, CA), 1991.

82 Henley, <u>Oxford Book.</u> Copyright expired.

83 Neibuhr, Reinhold, *The Serenity Prayer,* as cited in Zaleski, Philp and Carol <u>Prayer: A History</u> Houghton Mifflin (New York), 2005, p. 127.

84 Moyers, <u>Broken</u>, p. 113.

85 2 Corinthians 11:14, And no wonder, for Satan himself masquerades as an angel of light. (NIV)

86 Herzanek, <u>Why Don't They Just Quit?</u>, Introduction, pp. 2-3.

87 Quinones, <u>Dreamland</u>, p. 306.

88 Lustig, Robert, <u>The Hacking of the American Mind</u>, Penguin Random House (New York), 2017, p. 64.

89 Neurontin is a trademarked product of Pfizer Pharmaceuticals of New York.

90 Szalavitz, <u>Unbroken Brain</u>, p. 160.

91 Moyers, <u>Broken</u>, p. 74.

92 Grisel, <u>Never Enough</u>, p. 2.

93 CDC, "Drug Poisoning Deaths Involving Opioid Analgesics: United States, 1999-2011," CDC (Atlanta, GA), 2014, at <u>Products - Data Briefs - Number 166 - September 2014 (cdc.gov)</u>

94 Herzanek, <u>Why Don't They Just Quit?</u>, p. 71.

95 1 Peter 5:8, Be alert and of sober mind. Your enemy the devil prowls around like a roaring lion looking for someone to devour. (NIV)

96 Moyers, <u>Broken</u>, p. 278.

97 Vivitrol is a registered trademarked product of Alkermes, Inc. of Dublin, Ireland.

98 Naltrexone is a product of Pfizer Pharmaceuticals of New York.

99 Bill W., <u>AA Big Book</u>.

100 Woodruff and Woodruff, <u>In An Instant</u>, p. 136.

101 Ritalin originally was a trademarked product of Novartis Corp. of Basel, Switzerland, but now is marketed as a generic drug to treat hyperactivity and narcolepsy. It is an energizer and slight mood elevator.

102 Robaxin is a trademarked product of Endo Pharmaceuticals of Dublin, Ireland.

103 Kennedy, <u>A Common Struggle</u>, p. 99

104 Revelation 12:9, The great dragon was hurled down—that ancient serpent called the devil, or Satan, who leads the whole world astray. He was hurled to the earth, and his angels with him. (NIV)

105 Adderall is a trademarked product of Shire Pharmaceuticals of Lexington, MA.

106 Chilton car repair manuals are trademarked products of Cengage Learning, Inc., of Boston, MA.

107 Bill W., <u>Twelve Steps and Twelve Traditions</u>, p. 65.

108 Dayquil is a trademarked cold medicine in the Vicks family of products, owned by Proctor and Gamble Corp. of Cincinnati, OH.

109 PowerPoint* is a registered trademark of Microsoft Corporation, One Microsoft Way, Redmond, Washington 98052.

110 Banta-Green, Caleb, "Opioid Trends Across Washington State," Alcohol and Drug Abuse Institute, University of Washington (Seattle), April 2015, at http://adai.uw.edu/pubs/infobreifs/ADAI-IB-2015-01.pdf

111 <i>Bright Grey</i> was released by Anchorite Productions in September 2012.

112 1 Corinthians 13:13, And now these three remain: faith, hope and love. But the greatest of these is love. (NIV)

113 Luke 17:3-4 So watch yourselves. "If your brother or sister sins against you, rebuke them; and if they repent, forgive them. Even if they sin against you seven times in a day and seven times come back to you saying 'I repent,' you must forgive them." (NIV)

114 Volkow, Nora, "To End the Drug Crisis, Bring Addiction Out of the Shadows," National Institute on Drug Abuse (NIDA), (Bethesda, MD), November 8, 2021, at To End the Drug Crisis, Bring Addiction Out of the Shadows | National Institute on Drug Abuse (NIDA) (nih.gov)

115 Grisel, Never Enough, p. 22

116 Szalavitz, Unbroken Brain, p. 109.

117 Lustig, The Hacking of the American Mind, pp. 48, 13.

118 Ibid., pp. 69-70.

119 Quinones, Sam, Dreamland, p. 39.

120 Grisel, Never Enough, pp. 33, 77.

121 Kessler, David, Unraveling the Mystery of Mental Suffering, Harper Collins (New York), 2016, pp. 43, 25-26, 85.

122 Quinones, The Least of Us, p. 153.

123 American Society of Addiction Medicine (ASAM), "Definition of Addiction," ASAM (Rockville, MD), 2022, at What is the Definition of Addiction? (asam.org)

124 Grisel, Never Enough, pp. 187-190.

125 Ibid., p. 192.

126 Substance Abuse and Mental Health Services Administration (SAMHSA), "Treatment Improvement Protocol 32: Treatment of Adolescents with Substance Use Disorders," SAMHSA (Rockville, MD), 1999, Executive Summary p. 4.

127 Herzanek, Why Don't They Just Quit?, p. 251.

128 Lustig, The Hacking of the American Mind, p. 65.

129 Williams, James, and Hagger-Johnson, Gareth, "Childhood Academic Ability in Relation to Cigarette, Alcohol and Cannabis Use from Adolescence into Early Adulthood," in BMJ Open, (British Medical Journal), Volume 7, #2, February 2017.

130 Volkow, "To End the Drug Crisis…"

131 NIDA, "Scientists Closer to Finding Inherited Traits in Addiction," NIDA News Release, January 14, 2019, at Scientists closer to finding inherited traits in addiction | National Institute on Drug Abuse (NIDA) (nih.gov)

132 Grisel, Never Enough, p. 4.

133 NIDA, "Scientists Closer to Finding Inherited Traits…".

134 Grisel, Never Enough, p. 195

135 John 8:44, You belong to your father, the devil, and you want to carry out your father's desires. He was a murderer from the beginning, not holding to the truth,

for there is no truth in him. When he lies, he speaks his native language, for he is a liar and the father of lies. (NIV)

136 Job 4:7-8, "Consider now: Who, being innocent, has ever perished? Where were the upright ever destroyed? As I have observed, those who plow evil and those who sow trouble reap it. (NIV)

137 Volkow, "To End the Drug Crisis…"

138 Volkow, Nora, "Addressing the Stigma That Surrounds Addiction," NIDA (Bethesda, MD), April 22, 2020, at <u>Addressing the Stigma that Surrounds Addiction | National Institute on Drug Abuse (NIDA) (nih.gov)</u>

139 Volkow, Nora, "Suicide Deaths Are a Major Component of the Opioid Crisis that Must be Addressed," NIDA (Bethesda, MD), September 19, 2019, at <u>Suicide Deaths Are a Major Component of the Opioid Crisis that Must Be Addressed | National Institute on Drug Abuse (NIDA) (nih.gov)</u>

140 Solomon, <u>The Noonday Demon</u>, pp. 252-254. See also Jamison, <u>Night Falls Fast</u>, pp. 184-192.

141 Case, Anne, and Deaton, Angus, <u>Deaths of Despair,</u> Princeton University Press, (Princeton, NJ), 2020, pp. 95-96.

142 Joiner, Thomas, <u>Why People Die by Suicide</u>, Harvard University Press (Cambridge, MA), 2005, pp. 180-202.

143 Hoos, Michele, "Rethinking Suicide: A New Approach by Dr. Victoria Arango," Columbia University Medical Center Newsroom (New York), November 2, 2012 at <u>www.cuimc.columbia.edu/news/rethinking-suicide-a-new-approach-by-dr-victoria-arango</u>

144 Solomon, <u>The Noonday Demon</u>, p. 59; Stockmeier, Craig, and Rajkowska, Grazyna, "Cellular Abnormalities in Depression: Evidence from Postmortem Brain Tissue," *Dialogues in Clinical Neuroscience*, Vol. 8, Issue 2, June 2004, pp. 185-197; Jamison, <u>Night Falls Fast</u>, p. 193. There are many other studies.

145 Jamison, <u>Night Falls Fast</u>, p. 236, 184.

146 Idid., p. 292.

147 Klebold, <u>A Mother's Reckoning</u>, p. 272.

148 Quinnett, Paul, <u>Suicide: The Forever Decision</u>, QPR Institute (Spokane, WA), 1992, pp. 74-75.

149 Jamison, <u>Night Falls, Fast</u>, pp. 103-104.

150 Quinnett, <u>Suicide: The Forever Decision</u>, pp. 75-76.

151 Jamison, <u>Night Falls Fast</u>, p. 93, 5.

152 Klebold, <u>A Mother's Reckoning,</u> p. 157.

153 SAMHSA, "Treatment Improvement Protocol 42: Substance Abuse Treatment for Persons with Co-Occurring Disorders," SAMHSA (Rockville, MD), 2005, p. 327.

154 Quinnett. <u>Suicide: The Forever Decision</u>, p. 27.

155 Jamison, <u>Night Falls Fast</u>, p. 67.

156 Arango, cited in Hoos, "Rethinking Suicide."

157 NIDA, "NIH Analysis of Reddit Forum Suggests Experience on Non-Suicidal Self-harm Shares Characteristics with Addiction," NIDA News Release (Bethesda, MD), March 21, 2022, at NIH analysis of Reddit forum suggests experience of non-suicidal self-harm shares characteristics with addiction | National Institute on Drug Abuse (NIDA)

158 Case and Deaton, Deaths of Despair, p. 99.

159 Jamison, Night Falls Fast, p. 92.

160 Ibid., pp. 190-192, 198.

161 Ibid., pp. 292-295, 24.

162 Quinnett, Suicide: The Forever Decision, p. 125.

163 Vanderbilt, Gloria, A Mother's Story, pp. 119, 121.

164 Jamison, Night Falls Fast, pp. 73-74.

165 Vanderbilt, A Mother's Story, p. 138.

166 Klebold, A Mother's Reckoning, p. 249.

167 Seiden and Lukas, Silent Grief, pp. 150-155.

168 Woodruff and Woodruff, In an Instant, p. 140.

169 Lardner, George Jr., The Stalking of Kristin: A Father Investigates the Murder of His Daughter, Atlantic Monthly Press (New York), 1995, p. 5.

170 Douglas, John, and Olshaker, Mark, Law and Disorder, Kensington Books (New York), 2013, p. 102.

171 Vanderbilt, A Mother's Story, pp. 4, 118.

172 1 Samuel 16:7, But the Lord said to Samuel, "Do not consider his appearance or his height, for I have rejected him. The Lord does not look at the things people look at. People look at the outward appearance, but the Lord looks at the heart." (NIV)

173 Proverbs 4:23, Above all else, guard your heart, for everything you do flows from it. (NIV)

174 Geisel, Theodore Suess, How the Grinch Stole Christmas, Random House (New York), 1957.

175 Niebuhr, "Serenity Prayer".

176 Book of Wisdom, 3: 1-3.

177 Wolterstorff, Nicholas, Lament for a Son, William B. Eerdmans Publishing (Grand Rapids, MI and Cambridge, MA), 1987, p. 15.

178 John 16:33, "I have told you these things, so that in me you may have peace. In this world you will have trouble. But take heart! I have overcome the world." (NIV)

179 Philippians 4:7, And the peace of God, which transcends all understanding, will guard your hearts and your minds in Christ Jesus. (NIV)

180 John 11:25-26, Jesus said to her, "I am the resurrection and the life. The one who believes in me will live, even though they die; and whoever lives by believing in me will never die. Do you believe this?" (NIV)

181 1 Corinthians 13:12, For now we see only a reflection as in a mirror; then we shall see face to face. Now I know in part; then I shall know fully, even as I am fully known. (NIV)

182 Vanderbilt, A Mother's Story, pp. 138-139.

183 Psalm 46:10, He says, "Be still, and know that I am God; I will be exalted among the nations, I will be exalted in the earth." (NIV)

184 Romans 8:31, What, then, shall we say in response to these things? If God is for us, who can be against us? (NIV)

185 Copyright expired.

186 Quinones, The Least of Us, p. 282.

187 Goodman, Joshua, and Mustian, Jim, "Drug Distributor License Revoked Over Opioid Crisis Failures, May 26, 2023, at After yearslong delay, DEA revokes license of drug distributor over opioid crisis failures - ABC News (go.com)

188 CDC, "CDC Guidelines for Prescribing Opioids for Chronic Pain — United States, 2016," U.S. CDC (Washington, DC), March 2016 at https://www.cdc.gov/media/modules/dpk/2016/dpk-pod/rr6501e1er-ebook.pdf

189 DaVita, Vincent, and DaVita-Raeburn, Elizabeth, The Death of Cancer, Sarah Crichton Books (Farrar, Strauss and Giroux: New York), 2015, pp. 4-8.

190 James 1:1-3, James, a servant of God and of the Lord Jesus Christ, to the twelve tribes scattered among the nations: Greetings. Consider it pure joy, my brothers and sisters, whenever you face trials of many kinds, because you know that the testing of your faith produces perseverance. (NIV)

191 Romans 5:3-4, Not only so, but we also glory in our sufferings, because we know that suffering produces perseverance; 4 perseverance, character; and character, hope. (NIV)

192 Bill W., Twelve Steps and Twelve Traditions, pp. 113-114.

193 Personal Communication, to remain Anonymous.

194 Donne, John, Holy Sonnet 10.

195 Hugo, Victor, AZQuotes, at http://www.azquotes.com/quote/1303915

196 1 Corinthian 15:52-55, in a flash, in the twinkling of an eye, at the last trumpet. For the trumpet will sound, the dead will be raised imperishable, and we will be changed. For the perishable must clothe itself with the imperishable, and the mortal with immortality. When the perishable has been clothed with the imperishable, and the mortal with immortality, then the saying that is written will come true: "Death has been swallowed up in victory." "Where, O death, is your victory? Where, O death, is your sting?" (NIV)

197 Isaiah 43:2-3a, When you pass through the waters, I will be with you; and when you pass through the rivers, they will not sweep over you. When you walk

through the fire, you will not be burned; the flames will not set you ablaze. For I am the Lord your God, the Holy One of Israel, your Savior; (NIV)

198 John 8:12, When Jesus spoke again to the people, he said, "I am the light of the world. Whoever follows me will never walk in darkness, but will have the light of life." (NIV)

199 Matthew 5:4, Blessed are those who mourn, for they will be comforted. (NIV)

200 Luke 6:21, Blessed are you who hunger now, for you will be satisfied. Blessed are you who weep now, for you will laugh. (NIV)

ABOUT THE AUTHOR

Michele Gerber, PhD, a researcher, writer, and presenter, won multiple awards and honors, and wrote a bestselling book on American nuclear history. When her son died of addiction, she founded a grassroots, all-volunteer Recovery Coalition, the largest such organization in Washington State. She's researched and studied the disease of addiction; advocated for recovery programs to local, state, and federal officials; testified at the Washington State legislature; organized classes for families of addicted persons; and more. She is helping to build a large Recovery Center for addiction and mental illness in eastern Washington State.